Responses to the 'Arabellions'

This book studies the reactions by external actors, including the European Union, to the events unfolding in the Arab world beginning in December 2010. In particular, contributors look at external actors' attempts to balance their desire for stability with their normative principles toward human rights and democracy. The book compares the action (and inaction) of the EU with other international and regional players, including the United States, Russia, Turkey and Israel, and assesses the response of these actors to the 'Arabellions' events, analysing changes in their approaches to the Arab region.

The contributions to this book answer three questions: (1) How have external actors assessed the 'Arabellions' and what role did they see for themselves in this context? (2) Which goals and instruments did external actors pursue toward the MENA region? In particular, how did they deal with conflicting goals, such as support for human rights and democracy, on the one hand, and concerns about security and stability, on the other? (3) How can we explain the varying responses of external actors to the 'Arabellions'?

This book was published as a special issue of the *Journal of European Integration*.

Tanja A. Börzel is Professor of Political Science and holds the Chair for European Integration at the Otto-Suhr-Institute for Political Science, Freie Universität Berlin, Germany. She is co-coordinator of the Research College 'The Transformative Power of Europe', and directs the Jean Monnet Center of Excellence 'Europe and its Citizens'.

Assem Dandashly is a Lecturer in European Public Policy in the Department of Political Science at Maastricht University, The Netherlands. Prior to that, he was a Research Fellow at the Kolleg-Forschergruppe 'The Transformative Power of Europe', Freie Universität Berlin, Germany. He holds a PhD in Political Science (2012) from the University of Victoria, British Columbia, Canada.

Thomas Risse is Professor of International Politics at the Otto-Suhr-Institute for Political Science, Freie Universität Berlin, Germany, where he is co-coordinator of the Research College 'The Transformative Power of Europe', and coordinator of the Collaborative Research Center 'Governance in Areas of Limited Statehood'.

Journal of European Integration Special Issues

Series editors:
Thomas Christiansen, Maastricht University, The Netherlands
Simon Duke, European Institute of Public Administration, The Netherlands

The *Journal of European Integration* book series is designed to make our Special Issues accessible to a wider audience. All of the themes covered by our Special Issues and the series are carefully selected with regard to the topicality of the questions addressed in the individual volumes, as well as to the quality of the contributions. The result is a series of books that are sufficiently short to appeal to the curious reader, but that also offer ample depth of analysis to appeal to the more specialist reader, with contributions from leading academics.

Responses to the 'Arabellions'
The EU in comparative perspective
Edited by Tanja Börzel, Assem Dandashly and Thomas Risse

Representation and Democracy in the EU
Does one come at the expense of the other?
Edited by Richard Bellamy and Sandra Kröger

Coping with Crisis: Europe's Challenges and Strategies
Edited by Jale Tosun, Anne Wetzel and Galina Zapyanova

Globalization and EU Competition Policy
Edited by Umut Aydin and Kenneth Thomas

Redefining European Economic Governance
Edited by Michele Chang, Georg Menz and Mitchell P. Smith

PREVIOUSLY PUBLISHED BOOKS FROM THE JOURNAL

The Maastricht Treaty: Second Thoughts after 20 Years
Edited by Thomas Christiansen and Simon Duke

Europe after Enlargement
Edited by Yannis Stivachtis and Mark Webber

Euroscepticism within the EU Institutions
Diverging Views of Europe
Edited by Nathalie Brack and Olivier Costa

The Performance of the EU in International Institutions
Edited by Thomas Oberthür, Knud Erik Jørgensen and Jamal Shahin

Functional and Territorial Interest Representation in the EU
Edited by Michèle Knodt, Christine Quittkat and Justin Greenwood

European Neighbourhood through Civil Society Networks?
Policies, Practices and Perceptions
Edited by James Wesley Scott and Ilkka Likanen

European Parliament Elections after Eastern Enlargement
Edited by Hermann Schmidt

The Common Agricultural Policy
Policy Dynamics in a Changing Context
Edited by Grace Skogstad and Amy Verdun

The External Dimension of Justice and Home Affairs
A Different Security Agenda for the European Union?
Edited by Sarah Wolff, Nicole Wichmann and Gregory Mounier

Policy Coherence and EU Development Policy
Edited by Maurizio Carbonne

The Future of European Foreign Policy
Edited by Erik Jones and Saskia van Genugten

The EU as a Global Player
The Politics of Interregionalism
Edited by Fredrick Soderbaum and Luk Van Langenhove

Responses to the 'Arabellions'

The EU in comparative perspective

Edited by
Tanja A. Börzel, Assem Dandashly and
Thomas Risse

LONDON AND NEW YORK

First published 2016
by Routledge
2 Park Square, Milton Park, Abingdon, Oxon, OX14 4RN, UK

and by Routledge
711 Third Avenue, New York, NY 10017, USA

Routledge is an imprint of the Taylor & Francis Group, an informa business

© 2016 Taylor & Francis

All rights reserved. No part of this book may be reprinted or reproduced
or utilised in any form or by any electronic, mechanical, or other means,
now known or hereafter invented, including photocopying and recording,
or in any information storage or retrieval system, without permission in
writing from the publishers.

Trademark notice: Product or corporate names may be trademarks or
registered trademarks, and are used only for identification and
explanation without intent to infringe.

British Library Cataloguing in Publication Data
A catalogue record for this book is available from the British Library

ISBN 13: 978-1-138-93357-6

Typeset in Sabon
by RefineCatch Limited, Bungay, Suffolk

Publisher's Note
The publisher accepts responsibility for any inconsistencies that may have
arisen during the conversion of this book from journal articles to book chapters,
namely the possible inclusion of journal terminology.

Disclaimer
Every effort has been made to contact copyright holders for their permission to
reprint material in this book. The publishers would be grateful to hear from any
copyright holder who is not here acknowledged and will undertake to rectify
any errors or omissions in future editions of this book.

Contents

Citation Information	ix
Notes on Contributors	xi

1. Responses to the 'Arabellions': The EU in Comparative Perspective — Introduction
Tanja A. Börzel, Assem Dandashly & Thomas Risse — 1

2. Institutional Governance of European Neighbourhood Policy in the Wake of the Arab Spring
Gergana Noutcheva — 19

3. The EU Response to Regime Change in the Wake of the Arab Revolt: Differential Implementation
Assem Dandashly — 37

4. A Pragmatic Actor — The US Response to the Arab Uprisings
Daniela Huber — 57

5. Russia and the Arab Spring: Supporting the Counter-Revolution
Roland Dannreuther — 77

6. Turkish Foreign Policy in a Changing Arab World: Rise and Fall of a Regional Actor?
Bilgin Ayata — 95

7. Comparative Assessment of Israel's Foreign Policy Response to the 'Arab Spring'
Amichai Magen — 113

8. The EU, External Actors, and the Arabellions: Much Ado About (Almost) Nothing — Conclusion
Tanja A. Börzel, Thomas Risse & Assem Dandashly — 135

Index — 155

Citation Information

The chapters in this book were originally published in the *Journal of European Integration*, volume 37, issue 1 (January 2015). When citing this material, please use the original page numbering for each article, as follows:

Chapter 1
Introduction: Responses to the 'Arabellions': The EU in Comparative Perspective — Introduction
Tanja A. Börzel, Assem Dandashly & Thomas Risse
Journal of European Integration, volume 37, issue 1 (January 2015) pp. 1–17

Chapter 2
Institutional Governance of European Neighbourhood Policy in the Wake of the Arab Spring
Gergana Noutcheva
Journal of European Integration, volume 37, issue 1 (January 2015) pp. 19–36

Chapter 3
The EU Response to Regime Change in the Wake of the Arab Revolt: Differential Implementation
Assem Dandashly
Journal of European Integration, volume 37, issue 1 (January 2015) pp. 37–56

Chapter 4
A Pragmatic Actor — The US Response to the Arab Uprisings
Daniela Huber
Journal of European Integration, volume 37, issue 1 (January 2015) pp. 57–75

Chapter 5
Russia and the Arab Spring: Supporting the Counter-Revolution
Roland Dannreuther
Journal of European Integration, volume 37, issue 1 (January 2015) pp. 77–94

Chapter 6
Turkish Foreign Policy in a Changing Arab World: Rise and Fall of a Regional Actor?
Bilgin Ayata
Journal of European Integration, volume 37, issue 1 (January 2015) pp. 95–112

CITATION INFORMATION

Chapter 7

Comparative Assessment of Israel's Foreign Policy Response to the 'Arab Spring'
Amichai Magen
Journal of European Integration, volume 37, issue 1 (January 2015)
pp. 113–133

Chapter 8

Conclusion: The EU, External Actors, and the Arabellions: Much Ado About (Almost) Nothing
Tanja A. Börzel, Thomas Risse & Assem Dandashly
Journal of European Integration, volume 37, issue 1 (January 2015
pp. 135–153

For any permission-related enquiries please visit:
http://www.tandfonline.com/page/help/permissions

Notes on Contributors

Bilgin Ayata is Assistant Professor at Universität Basel, Switzerland.

Tanja A. Börzel is Professor of Political Science and holds the Chair for European Integration at the Otto-Suhr-Institute for Political Science, Freie Universität Berlin, Germany. She is co-coordinator of the Research College 'The Transformative Power of Europe', and directs the Jean Monnet Center of Excellence 'Europe and its Citizens'.

Assem Dandashly is a Lecturer in European Public Policy in the Department of Political Science at Maastricht University, The Netherlands. Prior to that, he was a Research Fellow at the Kolleg-Forschergruppe 'The Transformative Power of Europe', Freie Universität Berlin, Germany. He holds a PhD in Political Science (2012) from the University of Victoria, British Columbia, Canada.

Roland Dannreuther is based in the Faculty of Social Sciences and Humanities at the University of Westminster, London, UK.

Daniela Huber is based in the Middle East and Mediterranean Department in the Instituto Affari Internazionali, Rome, Italy.

Amichai Magen is based in the Lauder School of Government, Diplomacy and Strategy, and the Governance and Political Violence Programme, at IDC, Herzliya, Israel.

Gergana Noutcheva is based in the Political Science Department at Maastricht University, The Netherlands.

Thomas Risse is Professor of International Politics at the Otto-Suhr-Institute for Political Science, Freie Universität Berlin, Germany, where he is co-coordinator of the Research College 'The Transformative Power of Europe', and coordinator of the Collaborative Research Center 'Governance in Areas of Limited Statehood'.

Responses to the 'Arabellions': The EU in Comparative Perspective — Introduction

TANJA A. BÖRZEL, ASSEM DANDASHLY & THOMAS RISSE

Otto-Suhr-Institute for Political Science, Freie Universität Berlin, Berlin, Germany; Department of Political Science, Maastricht University, Maastricht, The Netherlands

ABSTRACT   This article introduces the themes of this special issue which is devoted to the reactions by external actors including the EU to the events unfolding in the Arab world beginning in December 2010. In particular, we look at the balancing act by external actors between their desire for stability, on the one hand, and their normative principles toward human rights and democracy, on the other. We compare the action (and inaction) of the European Union (EU) with other international and regional players, including the United States, Russia, Turkey and Israel. The contributions assess the response of these actors to the Arabellions events and analyse changes in their approaches to the Arab region. We ask three questions: (1) How have external actors assessed the 'Arabellions' and what role did they see for themselves in this context? (2) Which goals and instruments did external actors pursue toward the MENA region? In particular, how did they deal with conflicting goals, such as support for human rights and democracy, on the one hand, and concerns about security and stability, on the other? (3) How can we explain the varying responses of external actors to the Arabellions?

The Tunisian protests triggered by Mohamed Bouazizi's self-immolation on 17 December 2010, led to a spiral of revolutions and rebellions across North Africa, the Middle East and the Gulf.[1] For a short period of time, there was hope that the peoples were finally empowered to get rid of their autocratic rulers who had prevented political and economic progress in the

Arab world for a long period of time. A few years later, these hopes had somehow been shattered. Tunisia is still in the midst of a difficult transition process. Egypt is now ruled by President Abdel Fattah el-Sisi who was elected following a military coup against the Muslim Brotherhood who governed the country for a short time. Libya has turned into a failing state whereby large parts of the territory are outside the control of the central government and the country suffers from insecurity and instability. The Syrian civil war is still ongoing, but the rebels have lost significant ground to the Assad regime. In Bahrain, the monarchy has reasserted itself.

The 'Arabellions'[2] have presented quite a few challenges to external actors. While it took everybody by surprise, particularly Western actors quickly realized that they had to walk a fine line between their principled support for human rights and democracy, on the one hand, and their quest for security and stability in the region, on the other. Moreover, their experiences in Libya and, to a greater extent, Iraq, have had many Western powers (the US, in particular) question their abilities to adequately adapt to and intervene in a region that is rapidly changing. 'The ebbing of "western" political and economic influence places great strain on the military and security dimensions of relationships that have for so long underpinned the structure and balance of regional power' (Held and Ulrichsen 2014).

This special issue examines the balancing act by external actors between their desire for stability, on the one hand, and their normative principles toward human rights and democracy, on the other. In particular, we compare the action (and inaction) of the European Union (EU) with other international and regional players, including the United States, Russia, Turkey and Israel. The contributions assess the response of these actors to the Arabellions events and analyse changes in their approaches to the Arab region.

The changes taking place in the Middle East and North Africa (MENA) provide an excellent testing ground for the role of external actors who seek to promote democracy, security and stability, ensure access to natural resources or develop strong trade ties. By 'external', we mean states and regional organizations, which are not themselves subject to protests and opposition during the Arabellions. We focus on three actors outside the region (the US, EU and Russia) and one regional actor (Israel), with Turkey being a case in between. The five actors differ in their regime type and actorness, which allows us to explore how important these two variables are in accounting for what goals the actors pursue, which instruments they employ and how consistent and coherent their foreign policies are.

The special issue tries to accomplish two tasks. The first task is empirical stocktaking: How have the EU and other international as well as regional players reacted to the Arabellions? In this context, we address two sub-questions:

- How have external actors assessed the Arabellions and what role did they see for themselves in this context?
- Which goals and instruments did external actors pursue toward the MENA region? In particular, how did they deal with conflicting goals, such as support for human rights and democracy, on the one hand, and concerns about security and stability, on the other?

The results of the empirical analyses are rather straightforward: Only the US and the EU perceived the events in the MENA region as opportunities for democratic change, at least initially, seeing themselves as active shapers or more passive facilitators (see Dandashly 2014; Huber 2014; Noutcheva 2014). Turkey, under the Islamic Justice and Development Party (AKP), viewed the Arabellions as an opportunity to spread its model of democracy and vision for a new regional order. The more events unfolded, however, the more the two Western powers joined with other external actors who had initially prioritized security and stability, including preventive measures, should Islamic extremism sweep over the remaining MENA countries. The contrast between Turkey and Israel is particularly relevant in this context (see articles by Ayata 2014; Magen 2014): While Turkey, under Prime Minister Erdogan, saw itself as a transformative power for the region, Israel — the only stable democracy in the region — tried to insulate itself as a somewhat 'active by-stander' from the perceived security risks emanating from the Arabellions.

All external actors 'struggled to find a consistent response and a long-term strategy to events, which are changing by the day and sometimes by the hour' since any action will affect them, not only regarding their role in the region, but also domestically (Malmvig and Tassinari 2011, 94). Therefore, Western actors based their actions heavily on what was happening on the ground. In most cases, the EU and US policies have been mainly reactive. This 'wait-and-see approach' might have been, if not a brave and visionary policy, at least a prudent option. Both the EU member states and the US 'eventually managed to get from the new Arab governments — even in the case that they included representatives from Islamist parties — the same basic assurances as to their main regional interests they got from their predecessors' (Alcaro 2012, 18). Their policies towards MENA countries might have simply looked for assurances that their regional interests would be protected under the rule of these new governments. Neither the EU nor the US 'seems convinced that existing policies towards North Africa and the Middle East are in need of a radical review, based on a long-term perspective of how the region can reasonably look like in the next years' (Alcaro 2012, 17).

The second task of the special issue is theoretical: How can we explain the varying responses of external actors to the Arabellions? In this context, we utilize a diverse set of theoretical approaches drawn from the field of foreign policy analysis. The individual contributions look at three explanatory factors as drivers of the external actors' responses:

(1) Geostrategic interests as theorized by realism and its variants;
(2) self-understandings of actors including their collective identities as suggested by social constructivist approaches;
(3) domestic as well as bureaucratic politics as privileged by liberal approaches.

Once again, the findings are rather clear: In each and every case, geostrategic — both security and economic — considerations did play a role, but not in a deterministic sense. Rather, these geostrategic 'interests' have been filtered by collective self-understandings and identities, on the one hand, and by domestic as well as bureaucratic politics, on the other. The two latter factors account, for example, for the variation in responses to the Arabellions by three rather different actors, namely the EU, the US and Russia (Dannreuther 2014; Huber 2014; Noutcheva 2014). Actors' properties, by contrast, including actorness and regime type, cannot explain their responses. It is largely irrelevant whether the external actor is a state or a regional organization. Nor does it make much of a difference whether external actors are democratic, semi-democratic or authoritarian. We come back to this point in the conclusions.

The rest of the introduction lays out the analytical framework for the special issue. In the next section, we briefly provide a background on the Arabellions. We then discuss the dependent variable of the special issue, namely, the responses by external actors to the events in the MENA region. The third section discusses the three explanatory variables that form the common criteria for comparison among the various articles. Section four highlights the reasoning for our case selection. Finally, we provide an overview of the papers in this special issue.

The Arabellions

For decades, MENA countries have lived under oppressive and highly corrupt regimes that afforded them very little political freedoms and civil rights. In fact, the MENA region has been and continues to be one of the most autocratic regions in the world, in which Israel remains the only stable democracy. The lack of democracy in the region did not prevent the EU, the US and other Western powers from cooperating with its regimes — as long as stability and security were guaranteed. Yet, the security and stability that had prevailed on the EU's southern borders for decades could not withstand the unexpected protests that broke out in Tunisia and spilled over into Egypt, Libya, Syria and other Arab countries. While each country has had a unique experience, rising unemployment rates (especially youth unemployment),[3] high inflation, low growth, along with political oppression, resulted in a widespread call for change, particularly when the repercussions of the global financial crisis of 2008 and the European sovereign debt crisis worsened the economic situation.

The political developments that have unfolded since the Arabellions have been mixed, ranging from reassertion of authoritarian rule (Bahrain) to incremental democratic transition (Tunisia). Since January 2011, *Tunisia* has engaged in a steady process of institution building, including the first open and fair elections of a Constituent Assembly on 23 October 2011 and, most importantly, the first steps towards constitution building. However, the political parties that participated in the revolution have had difficulties to form a stable government. The current coalition, which had formed after the fall of Hamadi Jebali's government in February 2013, has been facing repeated protests sparked by the assassination of one of the opposition leaders, Mohammad Brahimi, on 25 July 2013.

In *Egypt*, the uprising was bloody and more deadly when compared to the similar experience of Tunisia. After several failed attempts of reforms to buy the silence of the people, President Mohammad Husni Moubarak had to step down and relinquish power to the Supreme Council of the Armed Forces. The army assured the protesters that free and fair elections would take place and that all regional and international obligations and agreements would be respected — a step that was welcomed by Israeli leaders. Elections took place thereafter and resulted in Islamists winning not only the majority of the parliament's seats, but also the Muslim Brotherhood's candidate Mohammed Morsi winning the presidential election. After a year of the Muslim Brotherhood's rule, millions of protesters returned to the streets calling for the removal of President Morsi. The new protests led to chaos and high numbers of casualties. The new violence caused the army to interfere; under the leadership of General Abdel Fattah el-Sisi, a military coup toppled Morsi from power. The military suspended the Egyptian constitution and arrested many of the Muslim Brotherhood leaders, including Morsi himself. Following these events, a new constitution was written, followed by new presidential elections that resulted in a victory for el-Sisi.

Bahrain's history of popular opposition to the rule of the al-Khalifa royal family dates back to the 1920s due to 'unequal and selective development' (Ulrichsen 2012, 28) — on sectarian basis between Sunnis and Shiites. The events in Tunisia and Egypt triggered protests in Bahrain in February 2011. Although the protestors were mainly youth from Sunnis and Shiites, shortly afterwards, the Shiite parties took over and were supported by secular leftist and liberal groups (*al-Jazeera* 30 August 2011). The protests escalated, quickly demanding the King to step down (Ulrichsen 2012, 29). In response to the opposition, the regime sponsored counter-demonstrations. The fact that the majority of the population is Shiite Muslims (about 70 per cent) ruled by a Sunni minority made it easy to blame Iran for the escalation of the violent protests. In March 2011, the Gulf Cooperation Council (GCC) — under Saudi leadership — sent forces through its Peninsula Shield Force to help the Bahraini regime maintain its grip over the situation. With the help of this force, the Bahraini military detained thousands of the protesters and oppressed the opposition.

Prior to the outbreak of the conflict in Syria, *Libya* experienced the most violent rebellion, highlighted by the toppling and killing of Mouammar al-Gaddafi. In a country lacking basic infrastructure and dominated by tribal structures, a civil war broke out between Gaddafi's regime and his allies and the opposition in that rich oil and gas country with a population of around 6.4 million. Concerned for its oil and gas deposits, Western countries rushed to interfere and ultimately helped bringing down Gaddafi's regime. The United Nations Security Council adopted several resolutions including the establishment and enforcement of a no-fly zone and authorized the use of force to protect Libyan civilians from Gaddafi's military attacks. Despite the fact that Gaddafi's regime fell after a bloody civil war, the divisions among the various tribal groups continue to block the country's progress toward democracy. Libya is currently a failing state which suffers from a severe lack of domestic security and stability.

The Western involvement in Libya and its eagerness to end Gaddafi's rule did not spillover to *Syria*. Rather, the experiences of Libya and the aftermath of the fall of the Gaddafi regime contributed to the decision not to intervene militarily in Syria. Shortly after the uprising in Libya, peaceful protests that called for the abdication of the Assad regime began in Syria. After these demonstrations were violently oppressed by the regime, a civil war broke out. More than 100,000 people have been killed thus far in Syria, making it the bloodiest instance of the Arabellions. In addition, the Assad regime used chemical weapons against the uprising triggering an international response which led to the chemical disarmament of Syria and its accession to the Chemical Weapons Convention. However, while Western powers asked Assad to step down, the UN Security Council has been blocked from implementing any meaningful action by vetoes of Russia and China (see article by Dannreuther 2014). The Syrian opposition has been split early on between various factions with Islamic fundamentalists — including local Al Qaeda forces — increasingly taking control. Moreover, the Syrian opposition has not been able to topple Assad and has been losing ground to Assad's army supported by Hizbullah, Iran and other groups. The Syrian crisis created more pressure on the Syrian neighbours (mainly Lebanon, Jordan and Turkey) and the EU. In 2013 alone, a quarter of the total detected illegal refugees came from Syria (25,500; according to Frontex 2014, 7).

This brief discussion of the Arabellions demonstrates that the road to reform and democracy is long and bumpy, to say the very least. Syria is still in the midst of a war. Libya is struggling to maintain security and stability in a failing state. While protests in Bahrain have been violently suppressed, Egypt is currently under military rule. Tunisia appears to be the only country in the region with any meaningful chance at democratic consolidation. Irrespective of their final outcomes, the Arab uprisings have significantly changed the situation on the ground for external actors and their foreign policies towards the MENA region.

The Dependent Variable: Responses to the Arabellions by External Actors

The various contributions to the special issue allow us to assess and compare the responses of various actors to the unfolding events of the Arabellions. Do the EU's external actions substantially differ from those of other international organizations and states with a stake in the region? Do we see similarities in the goals and the instruments used to pursue them? The comparison of the EU with the US, Israel, Turkey and Russia focuses on three key issues of the dependent variable: (1) assessments of the Arabellions and self-perception; (2) objectives and goals; (3) instruments and tools:

Assessments of the Arabellions and Self-perception

How have the EU and the other external actors perceived events in the MENA region? Have they seen them in terms of opportunities or rather as risks? What role have the EU and other external actors seen for themselves in relation to the Arabellions?

With regard to the assessment, external actors can either see the Arabellions as an opportunity for promoting their own model of 'good governance' or extending their sphere of influence in the region. Alternatively, external actors may fear the risks of regime change resulting in political instability, civil war and migration flows and threatening access to natural resources or the security of borders. Irrespective of their dominant perception, external actors can aspire to be active shapers trying to influence the developments in the region according to their own interests. Or they are passive bystanders being reluctant to rock the boat and trigger events that are beyond their control.

Goals

Does the EU's focus differ from the priorities of other international actors? Do we find a division of labour between (or rather a competition among) the various actors? And how did the goals change over time?

Most external actors pursue security or economic goals in the MENA region. The EU and the US explicitly seek to promote the respect for human rights, the rule of law and democracy, which they see as long-term strategies to ensure peace and prosperity. Yet, not all good things go together (Grimm and Leininger 2012). Promoting democratic change requires a transition of power that entails political uncertainty about the outcome and often involves violent conflict. This 'democratization-stability dilemma' (Gillespie and Youngs 2002; Jünemann 2003, 7), which is particularly virulent when states are fragile, requires external actors to prioritize their goals e.g. by putting security first. The goals external actors pursue may not only conflict with each other; they can also clash with the goals of other external actors seeking to secure their influence in the region. At the same time, they may also reinforce or complement each other by seeking to strengthen different parts of democracy or to foster socio-economic development rather than only providing military security.

Instruments

Does the EU prioritize different instruments than other international actors in pursuing its goals? Is the EU relying on trade and aid while others engage more heavily in diplomacy and political dialogue? What role does military action play?

We distinguish five different instruments external actors can deploy to realize their goals (cf. Magen and Morlino 2008; Magen, Risse, and McFaul 2009). Next to the use of military force (1), they may invoke positive conditionality rewarding progress (2) or impose sanctions punishing the lack thereof (3). Persuasion through diplomacy (4) aims at convincing the incumbent regimes to engage in changes external actors like to see. Financial and technical assistance (5) seeks to build or strengthen the capacities of MENA countries to introduce changes that are in line with the goals external actors pursue. While the various instruments are often combined, they are not equally available to all external actors. Moreover, external actors may differ in their inclination to make use of certain instruments, particularly when it comes to the deployment of military force. The contributions to this special issue analyse the assessments, self-perceptions, goals and instruments of the various external actors, explore the degree to which they changed over time as the events proceeded and discuss how far the explanatory factors, which we introduce in the next section, account for their findings. The concluding chapter by the editors provides a comparative assessment.

Explanations: Geostrategic Interests, Collective Identities, and Domestic Politics

The special issue explores three sets of explanatory factors that account for the various responses by external actors to the Arabellions. These explanations are derived from standard theories of international relations and from foreign policy analysis (see e.g. Carlsnaes 2013). We concentrate on geostrategic (economic and security) interests; on self-understandings and collective identity; and on domestic as well as bureaucratic politics.

Geostrategic Interests

The theoretical approach of relevance here is realism and its varieties (see e.g. Mearsheimer 2001; Morgenthau 1948; Waltz 1979). While not a theory of foreign policy per se, realism does suggest that an actor's foreign policy is primarily driven by the constraints and opportunities of its external environment. At the same time, the capacity to act is first and foremost a function of an actor's power measured in terms of mostly military and economic capabilities. For realism, a country's primary goal in the international environment is its survival as a result of which security interests take precedence over any other foreign policy goal a country might have. Economic interests come second, such as access to resources (oil!), but realism is rather sceptical with regard to the promotion of economic interdependence via trade and investments. A realist foreign policy, therefore, should prioritize a country's autonomy from outside interference or — if this is not an option because of a weak power status — should maximize influence over outcomes and events in its external environment (see Baumann, Rittberger, and Wagner 2001).

If we apply these considerations to the case of our external actors and their responses to the events in the Middle East, a number of pitfalls need to be avoided. First and strictly speaking, realism does not apply to the foreign policy of international or regional organizations such as the EU, since realism does not take IOs seriously as actors in their own right. As we argue below, however, our case selection does include the EU as one regional organization and we ascribe at least some 'actorness' to it which is not simply derivative of the interests of their member states. Nevertheless, we have to relax some realist core assumptions at this point.

Second and more important, one should not read off a realist foreign policy from the proclaimed goals of the various governments or the regional organization. In our cases, for example, nearly all external actors claimed at one point or another that events in the MENA region affected their security interests. From a realist standpoint, these proclaimed goals are irrelevant for the analysis which must take 'objective' security interests into account. To give a few examples: In the case of Israel, a realist would probably agree that the Arabellions immediately affect the survival interests of the state given the hostility of the Arab world toward Israel.[4] It is much harder to argue for the same effect of the Arabellions on the survival interests of the United States (or of Russia, for that matter), while Turkey and the EU are cases in between. For the latter, instability in the Arab world indeed affects some security interests with regard to transnational terrorism, on the one hand, and refugee flows, on the other.

In sum, 'geostrategic interests', in a realist sense, refers to 'objective' threats and opportunities emanating from an actor's external environment defined by the distribution of power. It does not include issues such as democracy or human rights which are irrelevant from a realist perspective. As to perceived security interests, they have to be weighed against the 'objective' security environment in which an actor — be it a state or a regional organization — finds itself.

Collective Identity and Self-understandings

Social constructivism is not a theory of international relations or foreign policy. It is an ontology and — as at least some proponents would argue — an epistemology that provides a particular lens on world politics, including foreign policy (see e.g. Adler 2013; Klotz and Lynch 2007; Wendt 1999). For example, there are no 'objective' interests from this perspective, but such 'national interests' are social constructions which help actors to be able to act in the world. From a social constructivist viewpoint, the self-understandings of actors — their collective identity — assume centre stage in any analysis of foreign policy. While collective identities are unlikely to affect behaviour directly, they should define the realm of the 'possible' in foreign policy, of that what is deemed appropriate behaviour with regard to the outside world (March and Olsen 1998). In other words, self-understandings and collective identities influence how actors define and perceive their interests and how they prioritize their goals. Who we are affects what we want. With regard to foreign policy, actors — states and regional organizations — are likely to develop their own foreign policy identity which then defines the realm of appropriate goals and instruments to enact this identity.

Applied to the responses by external actors to the Arabellions, such a social constructivist approach would first describe the foreign policy identity of the actor in question and then analyse how this identity fits into the Middle Eastern context. For example, the US has developed a foreign policy identity of both a liberal democracy and of a (military) superpower. It would, therefore, view the events in the MENA region as an opportunity for democracy promotion. At the same time and as a superpower, it should consider the whole range of foreign policy instruments — including military intervention — as appropriate tools to further its interests as defined by the US identity. In contrast, while the EU shares the American identity of a democratic power, its foreign policy identity privileges 'civilian' as well as 'soft' power and is rather reluctant to employ military means (see the debate about the EU's identity as a 'civilian' or 'normative' power e.g. Börzel and Risse 2009; Manners 2002; Sjursen 2006; on European identity in general see Risse 2010).

To conclude, a social constructivist approach privileges the self-understandings of actors as defining what they see in their interests, how they prioritize their interests and what instruments and tools they use to pursue these interests. There is nothing given about 'security interests', but they emerge out of discursive interactions and are constantly constructed and re-constructed, as the Copenhagen school of securitization reminds us (Buzan, Waever, and de Wilde 1998; Waever 1995, 1996).

Domestic and Bureaucratic Politics

Liberal approaches to international relations and to foreign policy privilege what is going on inside the state (or the regional organization, for that matter). Foreign policy behaviour is explained by domestic politics — the interplay of political and societal actors such as parties, interest groups or civil society organizations, as well as by domestic political institutions and the constraints they put on actors (see e.g. Czempiel 1981; Freund and Rittberger 2001; Moravcsik 1997; Putnam 1988). The latter includes regime type and has led to the 'democratic peace' argument according to which democratic states are peaceful and more cooperative when dealing with each other (Risse-Kappen 1995; Russett and Oneal 2001). A specific liberal approach to foreign policy focuses on bureaucratic politics and the inter-organizational bargaining struggles among the various agencies of state and other executives e.g. between foreign affairs departments and defence ministries (Allison 1972; Allison and Halperin 1989).

Applied to our actors and the Middle East, liberal approaches to foreign policy would explain the responses to the Arabellions in terms of the configuration of forces inside the state or the regional organization. Are there special — e.g. economic or security — interest groups holding intensive preferences with regard to the Middle East? How are the political forces inside a country or a regional organization aligned; and which foreign policy goals do they pursue? How do the bureaucratic alignments inside the government or the executive of the regional organization look like with regard to the Middle East? For example, bureaucratic infighting in the US administration between the National Security Council, the Pentagon and the State Department is legendary when it comes to the Middle East (see e.g. Woodward 2002 on the Iraq case). With regard to the EU, one might look at rivalries and conflicts between the various directorates of the Commission, the European External Action Service (EEAS), as well as at the interaction between the Commission, the EEAS and the Council bureaucracy(see article by Noutcheva). Moreover, one must also look at the configuration of forces within and between various member states. To explain Turkish behaviour, a liberal approach would focus on the Justice and Development Party under Prime Minister Erdogan and its attempt to establish moderate Islamism inside and outside the country (see article by Ayata 2014). In the case of Russia, it would emphasize the then prime minister and now President Putin's efforts to maintain and expand his domestic power base (see article by Dannreuther 2014).

To conclude, a liberal approach focuses on domestic politics and domestic institutions to explain the actors' responses to the Arabellions. This might include the self-understandings and collective identities of domestic actors. To this extent, liberal foreign policy analysis can accommodate social constructivism as long as the state (or the regional organization) is not treated as a unitary actor. Realism and liberalism, however, are mutually exclusive, since one cannot explain foreign policy simultaneously through 'objective' security interests *and* through domestic politics, despite various attempts to do so (see Legro and Moravcsik 1999, on this point). But this consideration does not exclude that external events are refracted and filtered through a state's or regional organization's domestic environment. Yet, by privileging the domestic over the international, we firmly remain in the realm of domestic politics and liberal foreign policy analysis.

Case Selection

At first glance, this special issue might appear to compare apples and oranges. The EU is a regional organization, while the US, Russia, Turkey and Israel are sovereign states. How can we compare these rather different players with regard to the same dependent variables and explanatory factors? We argue that what these entities have in common is their principal 'actorness' defined as the *ability and willingness to act*. While actorness has rarely been contested with regard to the foreign policy of sovereign states, a long debate has been looming concerning the actorness of regional organizations, particularly the EU (see e.g. Bretherton and Vogler 2006; Conceição-Heldt and Meunier 2014; Hettne, Söderbaum and Stålgren 2008; Jupille and Caporaso 1998). According to Jupille and Caporaso, four criteria have to be met in this context: authority, recognition, autonomy and cohesion (Jupille and Caporaso 1998). We agree with the first three, but not with the fourth, cohesion, which we replace with *capability*.

Authority refers to the legal competence of an actor to pursue a foreign policy vis-á-vis the MENA region. This authority is not questionable with regard to the four states analysed in this special issue, but it also applies to the EU. Since the Treaty of Maastricht, the EU has acquired comprehensive legal competences to develop and implement its own foreign policies.

Recognition refers to the acceptance of this authority by other actors. Once again, this recognition is given with regard to the states and the EU considered in this special issue. Note that 'recognition' should not be confused with legitimacy: US foreign policy toward the Middle East is considered illegitimate by a whole variety of other actors, even though the US has the authority to act.

Autonomy concerns the distinctiveness and independence of an actor vis-à-vis other actors. Once again, this criterion is usually met by sovereign states which do not face interferences with their 'Westphalian' sovereignty regarding foreign policy (on this term, see Krasner 1999). However, the autonomy requirement is harder to meet by regional organizations whose actions are firmly controlled by their principals, the member states. Yet, even in a principal–agent relationship, the agent — the regional organization in this case — usually has some slack i.e. some degree of autonomy. This certainly applies to the EU.

In contrast to Jupille and Caporaso, we do not consider *cohesion* as necessary ingredient for actorness. Whether an actor pursues an inconsistent and incoherent foreign policy is an empirical question, not a definitional criterion. As we argue in the conclusions, the US pursued one of the most incoherent foreign policies with regard to the Arabellions as compared to all other actors — including the EU — considered in this special issue.

Instead, we would like to add one criterion to the Jupille/Caporaso list, namely *capabilities*. An actor, which does not have the resources at its disposal to put goals into action, has little actorness in our view. Actorness requires that actors have significant resources and the institutions necessary to deploy them. These capabilities are, hence, directly linked to the instruments of external actors we defined in the previous section and can be divided into three broad categories: political (persuasion through diplomacy), economic (positive conditionality/sanctions) or military means. They include resources (financial and otherwise), knowledge and organizational capacities (March and Olsen 1995, 92–95). Among the actors considered in this special issue, the capabilities vary considerably. But each and every state analysed here has at least some at its disposal to pursue its goals. So does the EU.

In sum, all actors examined in this special have actorness. As we will argue in the conclusion, the distinction between states and the EU, which is more than an international organization and less than a state (Wallace 1983) is not particularly useful when it comes to analysing the responses to the Arabellions. The EU's foreign policy, for example, has been a lot more cohesive and consistent than US or Turkish foreign policy.

While all actors considered in this special issues share actorness, they have been selected according to their relevance for the MENA region and with regard to the strategic importance of the Middle East to their foreign policy. This is self-evident with regard to Israel as part of the MENA region. It is also obvious concerning the EU and Turkey bordering the region. The US is a global power which has considered the Middle East of utmost significance to its strategic interests for a long time. Finally, Russia might not have as strong economic and security interests in the MENA region as the other players, but has emerged as a major counter-weight to Western attempts to influence outcomes (see article by Dannreuther 2014).

Finally, our five actors differ with regard to their regime type. The US and the EU are democratic regimes that have inscribed the promotion of human rights, democracy and the rule of law into their foreign policies (Magen, Risse, and McFaul 2009). Israel is the only stable democracy in the region which refrains, however, from projecting its internal values onto its neighbours (see Magen 2014). Turkey has lost some of its democratic credentials in recent years because of Erdogan's increasingly authoritarian government style encroaching on the political freedoms of the domestic opposition (see Ayata 2014). At the same time, the AKP likes to portray Turkey as a model of a moderate, democratically embedded political Islam. Putin's Russia, finally is a semi-authoritarian state, which seeks to promote a non-Western form of 'sovereign democracy' based on a strong, unified nation (see Dannreuther 2014). This variation allows us to explore whether democracies have responded differently to the Arabellions than less or non-democratic regimes. While the contributions to this special issue do not focus on domestic impact, we will be able to draw some preliminary conclusions as regards the debate about whether non-democracies spoil the efforts of democracies at promoting democratic change.

Of course, there are actors which are not included in this special issue, but could have been, since they meet the criteria laid out above. Saudi Arabia and Iran come to mind as well as the Gulf Cooperation Council and the League of Arab States. While they are discussed and mentioned in various articles (see e.g. articles by Dandashly 2014; Huber 2014; Magen 2014), they are not part of the special issue for pragmatic reasons.

Overview of the Articles

The first set of articles deal with the responses of several regional organizations to the Arabellions. The special issue begins with two articles on the *European Union*.

Gergana Noutcheva analyses the goals and instruments of the European Neighbourhood Policy (ENP) before and after the Arabellions. She tries to understand 'why there has been little substantive change in the EU's approach to its Southern neighbourhood' despite the early enthusiasm regarding democracy promotion. In order to understand how and why the EU has responded to changes in its neighbourhood, Noutcheva focuses on the 'ENP's institutional set-up and the power relationships that exist between the different layers of governance involved in setting ENP goals and implementing policy'. The lack of substantive change in the ENP is mainly explained by bureaucratic and domestic politics: 'the freedom of action of EU institutions, and the (dis)unity of the EU member states in the main ENP policy areas'.

While Noutcheva focuses on the EU institutions, *Assem Dandashly* compares the EU's response on the ground to the Arabellions. With the beginning of the events, the EU had high hopes that the Arabellions would finally open the door for democratization processes after decades of stagnation. However, this early enthusiasm quickly withered away. The EU's response to unfolding events has been neither coherent nor consistent. Focusing on Tunisia, Libya and Egypt, Dandashly argues that EU goals remain security and stability driven, while the instruments used vary across time and targeted countries depending on their degree of domestic stability and security.

Daniela Huber analyses how the *United States* reacted to the Arabellions and how we can understand its 'dual role as an anchor of security and modest advocate of democracy'. Similar to the EU, the US had initially assessed the Arabellions as an opportunity for democratic transition. However, this view quickly started to give way to a perception of the unfolding events as risks rather than opportunities. With respect to goals and instruments, the US did not pursue a consistent approach. Rather, it 'switched from a default to an ad hoc modus in its foreign policy in the region', which is best explained by bureaucratic infighting, on the one hand, and growing domestic opposition against an interventionist foreign policy, on the other.

Roland Dannreuther's article explores *Russia's* reaction to the Arabellions. It seeks to detect the main 'factors explaining the evolution of Russia's stance towards' the MENA region and the conflicts in Libya and Syria. Similar to the EU and the US, Russia perceived the Arabellions as major transformations. However, the Putin government did not share their view of the events as an anchor for democratic changes. 'While initially welcoming the popular demands for political reform' in Tunisia and Egypt, 'the Russian reaction rapidly became more critical' as developments in the region resulted in Western military intervention, on the one hand, and the spread of Islamist extremism, on the other. Trying to understand the role played by Russia in several Arabellion countries, Dannreuther argues that geopolitical factors are important to understand Russia's general stance, but falls short to explain the Russian reaction on its own. Therefore, Dannreuther emphasizes the importance of ideational factors in accounting for Russian foreign policy as a counter-position to what it sees as the Western imposition of liberal democratic systems. Moreover, the domestic situation in Russia, characterized by political unrest and opposition to the results of the presidential and parliamentary elections, also played an important role in shaping the Russian reaction to the Arabellions.

Bilgin Ayata examines the *Turkish* reactions to the 'Arabellions'. Turkey's rise as an emergent regional power received a new dimension after the outbreak of protests in the Arab region in 2011. Turkey viewed the events as a window of opportunity to expand its influence in the region and promote its model of a democratically embedded, moderate Islam for emerging Muslim democracies. Turkey implemented a number of soft instruments to support regime change. However, what appeared as a golden opportunity for Turkey's aspirations to increase its regional power started to turn into a curse when the effects of the Arab regime changes and upheavals hit home and the developments in Egypt and Syria went against Turkey's interests in security and stability. Ayata argues that ideational and domestic explanations fare best in understanding Turkey's differential foreign policy to the region.

In his contribution, *Amichai Magen* demonstrates that in contrast to the EU and the US, *Israel* as the only stable democracy in the region did not interpret the advent of the Arabellions as the possible beginning of a wave of democratization, or an opportunity for pro-democratic engagement. The dominant Israeli reading of the Arabellions was overwhelmingly security-oriented, risk-averse and generally negative. Magen assesses the Israeli active/passive reaction according to the various stages that it went through. He shows that Israel was narrowly focused on defending its national security, preserving existing diplomatic and security assets and insulating its population and economy from the tumult around it. Magen argues that realist thinking is useful in understanding Israeli foreign policy. At the same time, the choices made by Israeli policy-makers in exercising 'strategic silence' and abstaining from portraying itself as a democratic role model and providing democratic aid to the Arabellion countries, reflected the Israeli self-image regarding the ideational differences with the Arab countries, lack of trust and the awareness of its inability to promote positive change.

The *conclusions* by the editors summarize the main findings of the contributions. We tease out the implications of our findings for the discussion on the EU's actorness and the theoretical debate on whether comparing the EU to other international actors amounts to comparing apples and oranges. We then concentrate on explaining the similarities and differences in the responses by the various external actors to the Arabellions. Finally, the conclusion highlights the lessons learnt and their long-term implications. A comparative perspective reveals that the EU does not suffer from problems of actorness any more than (democratic) states. Nor is it unique in prioritizing stability and security over democracy. While the EU is certainly not an effective normative or transformative power, strengthening its capability to speak with one voice will not necessarily do the trick.

Notes

1. This special issue was designed and made possible in the context of the Research College (*Kolleg-Forschergruppe*) 'Transformative Power of Europe?' at the Freie Universität Berlin, funded by the DFG German Research Foundation (Grant No. BO 1831/7-1/2) and codirected by Tanja A. Börzel and Thomas Risse. We thank the DFG for its generous support over the years. Draft papers were discussed at two workshops, held in Berlin on 8–9 June 2012 and 25–26 October 2013. We thank all the participants for their lively contributions and criticisms, in particular, Federica Bicchi, Sally Khalifa Isaac and Vera van Hüllen. We are also very grateful for the anonymous reviews of the special issue and for the continuous support by the editors of the Journal of European Integration.
2. There are various terms used in the literature for what happened in the Arab world beginning in 2011. Terms used are 'Arab spring', 'Arab revolutions', 'Arabellion' and others. Each of these terms is essentially contested. As a result, we use 'Arabellion', which we consider the least problematic, since 'rebellion' covers a very wide range of social protest activities.
3. Youth unemployment in the MENA region is among the highest in the world accounting for 23.2 per cent while the world average is only 13.9 per cent (see International Labour Organization 2012).
4. We ignore for the moment the varied causes of the conflict between Israel and the Arab world.

References

Adler, E. 2013. Constructivism in international relations: sources, contributions and debates. In *Handbook of international relations, 2nd ed*, eds. W. Carlsnaes, T. Risse and B. Simmons, 112–45. London: Sage.

Alcaro, R. 2012. Introduction. Bouazizi's inextinguishable fire. In *Re-thinking western policies in light of the Arab Uprisings*, eds. R. Alcaro and M. Haubrich-Seco, 11–9. Rome: InstitutoAffariInternazionali.

RESPONSES TO THE 'ARABELLIONS'

Al-Jazeera. 30 August 2011. Bahrain's contribution to the 'Arab spring'. http://www.aljazeera.com/indepth/opinion/2011/08/20118301473301296.html (accessed 12 December 2013).

Allison, G. 1972. *Essence of decision. Explaining the cuban missile crisis*. Boston: Little, Brown.

Allison, G.T., and M.H. Halperin. 1989. Bureaucratic politics: a paradigm and some policy implications. In *American foreign policy: theoretical essays*, eds. G. John Ikenberry, 378–409. Glenview, IL: Scott Foresman.

Ayata, B. 2014. Turkish foreign policy in a changing Arab world: rise and fall of a regional actor? *Journal of European Integration* 37, no. 1: 95–112.

Baumann, R., V. Rittberger, and W. Wagner. 2001. Neorealist foreign policy theory. In *German foreign policy since unification. Theories and case studies*, eds. V. Rittberger, 37–67. Manchester, NH: Manchester University Press.

Börzel, T.A., and T. Risse. 2009. Venus approaching mars? The European Union's approaches to democracy promotion in comparative perspective. In *Democracy promotion in the US and the EU compared*, eds. A. Magen, M. McFaul, and T. Risse, 34–60. Houndmills: Palgrave Macmillan.

Bretherton, C., and J. Vogler. 2006. *The European Union as a global actor*, 2nd ed. London: Routledge.

Buzan, B., O. Waever, and J. de Wilde. 1998. *Security. A new framework for analysis*. Boulder, CO: Lynne Rienner.

Carlsnaes, W. 2013. Foreign policy. In *Handbook of international relations*, 2nd ed, eds. W. Carlsnaes, T. Risse, and B. Simmons, 298–325. London: Sage.

da Conceição-Heldt, E., and S. Meunier. 2014. Speaking with a single voice: internal cohesiveness and external effectiveness of the EU in global governance. *Journal of European Public Policy* 21, no. 7: 961–79.

Czempiel, E.-O. 1981. *Internationale Politik: Ein Konfliktmodell* [International politics: a conflicted model]. Paderborn: Schöningh.

Dandashly, A. 2014. The EU response to regime change in the wake of the Arab revolt: differential Implementation. *Journal of European Integration* 37, no. 1: 37–56.

Dannreuther, R. 2014. Russia and the Arab Spring: supporting the counter-revolution. *Journal of European Integration* 37, no. 1: 77–94.

Freund, C., and V. Rittberger. 2001. Utilitarian-liberal foreign policy theory. In *German foreign policy since unification. Theories and case studies*, ed. V. Rittberger, 68–104. Manchester, NH: Manchester University Press.

Frontex. 2014. *Annual risk analysis 2014*. Warsaw: Frontex.

Gillespie, R., and R. Youngs. 2002. Themes in European democracy promotion. *Democratization* 9, no. 1: 1–16.

Grimm, S., and J. Leininger. 2012. Not all good things go together: conflicting objectives in democracy promotion. *Democratization* 19, no. 3: 391–414.

Held, D., and K.C. Ulrichsen. 2014. The Arab Spring and the changing balance of global power. *Open Democracy*. 26 February. http://www.opendemocracy.net/arab-awakening/david-held-kristian-coates-ulrichsen/arab-spring-and-changing-balance-of-global-power (accessed 20 June 2014).

Hettne, B., F. Söderbaum, and P. Stålgren. 2008. *The EU as a global actor in the south*. Swedish Institute for European Policy Studies (SIEPS), No. 8.

Huber, D. 2014. A pragmatic actor — the US response to the Arab uprisings. *Journal of European Integration* 37, no. 1: 57–75.

International Labour Organization. 2012. *Rethinking Economic growth: towards productive and inclusive Arab societies*. Geneva: Switzerland.

Jünemann, A. 2003. Security building in the Mediterranean after September 11. In *Euro-Mediterranean relations after September 11. International, regional and domestic dynamics*, ed. A. Jünemann, 1–20. London: Frank Cass.

Jupille, J., and J.A. Caporaso. 1998. States, agency, and rules: the European Union in global environmental politics. In *The European Union in the World community*, eds. C. Rhodes, 213–22. Boulder, CO: Lynne Rienner.

Klotz, A., and C. Lynch. 2007. *Strategies for research in constructivist international relations*. Armonk, NY: M.E. Sharpe.

Krasner, S.D. 1999. *Sovereignty. Organized hypocrisy*. Princeton, NJ: Princeton University Press.

Legro, J.W., and A. Moravcsik. 1999. Is anybody still a realist? *International Security* 24, no. 2: 5–55.

Magen, A. 2014. Comparative assessment of Israel's foreign policy response to the 'Arab Spring'. *Journal of European Integration* 37, no. 1: 113–33.

Magen, A., and L. Morlino eds. 2008. *Anchoring democracy: external influence on domestic rule of law development*. London: Routledge.

Magen, A., T. Risse, and M. McFaul eds. 2009. *Democracy promotion in the EU and the US compared*. Houndmills: Palgrave Macmillan.

Malmvig, H., and F. Tassinari. 2011. The "Arab Spring" and the external actor's role within the Euro-Mediterranean region. *Euromed Survey* 3: 94–9.

Manners, I. 2002. Normative power Europe: A contradiction in terms? *Journal of Common Market Studies* 40, no. 2: 235–48.

March, J.G., and J.P. Olsen. 1995. *Democratic governance*. New York, NY: Free Press.

March, J.G., and J.P. Olsen. 1998. The institutional dynamics of international political orders. *International Organization* 52, no. 4: 943–69.

Mearsheimer, J. 2001. *The tragedy of great power politics*. New York, NY: W. W. Norton.

Moravcsik, A. 1997. Taking preferences seriously: a liberal theory of international politics. *International Organization* 51, no. 4: 513–53.

Morgenthau, H.J. 1948. *Politics among nations*. New York, NY: McGraw Hill.

Noutcheva, G. 2014. Institutional governance of European neighbourhood policy in the wake of the Arab Spring. *Journal of European Integration* 37, no. 1: 19–36.

Putnam, R.D. 1988. Diplomacy and domestic politics: the logic of two-level games. *International Organization* 42, no. 3: 427–60.

Risse, T. 2010. *A community of Europeans? Transnational identities and public spheres*. Itahaca, NY: Cornell University Press.

Risse-Kappen, T. 1995. *Cooperation among democracies. The European influence on US foreign policy*. Princeton, NJ: Princeton University Press.

Russett, B., and J.R. Oneal. 2001. *Triangulating peace. Democracy, interdependence, and international organizations*. New York, NY: W. W. Norton.

Sjursen, H. 2006. The EU as a 'normative' power: How can this be? *Public Policy* 13, no. 2: 235–51.

Ulrichsen, K.C. 2012. After the Arab Spring: power shift in the Middle East? Bahrain's Aborted Revolution. IDEAS reports — special reports. In *SR011. LSE IDEAS* ed. K. Nicholas, 28–32. London: London School of Economics and Political Science.

Waever, O. 1995. Securitization and desecuritization. In *On security*, ed. R.D. Lipschutz, 46–86. New York, NY: Columbia University Press.

Waever, O. 1996. European security identities. *Journal of Common Market Studies* 34, no. 1: 103–32.

Wallace, W. 1983. Less than a federation, more than a regime: the community as a political system. In *Policy-making in the European community*, eds. H. Wallace, W. Wallace, and C. Webb, 403–36. Chichester: John Willey.

Waltz, K. 1979. *Theory of international politics*. Reading: Addison-Wesley.

Wendt, A. 1999. *Social theory of international politics*. Cambridge: Cambridge University Press.

Woodward, B. 2002. *Bush at war*. New York, NY: Simon & Schuster.

Institutional Governance of European Neighbourhood Policy in the Wake of the Arab Spring

GERGANA NOUTCHEVA

Political Science Department, Maastricht University, Maastricht, The Netherlands

ABSTRACT This paper analyses the goals and instruments of the European Neighbourhood Policy (ENP) before and after the Arab Spring, and enquires why there has been little substantive change in the European Union's (EU's) approach to the neighbourhood, notwithstanding the acknowledged opportunity for democratic change and the EU's stated willingness to contribute to it. It argues that the institutional governance of the ENP has largely conditioned the EU's response to the historic changes in the neighbourhood. The EU's actorness has been tamed by the underlying differences among EU member states and this has particularly played out in policy areas where the EU institutions have less freedom to act on behalf of the Union. Overall, the EU has asserted itself as neither a strategic actor nor a normative power, but rather as a bystander, trapped in its internal institutional process and passively reacting to crisis events by proposing long-term solutions with little short-term impact.

Introduction

The European Union (EU) was among those caught unawares by the societal awakening in the Arab world in 2011. To the European audience, the Arab revolts were a massive outcry against authoritarianism, while the protesters' slogans calling for human dignity, equal opportunities and equality before the law sounded like a classical call for liberal democracy. The fall of the Berlin Wall was the historical comparison through which the Arab

Spring events were most commonly interpreted (Deutsche Welle 2011; Ulrichsen, Held, and Brahimi 2011). And while the EU and the European governments were slow to recognise the momentous change in the region, a feeling of déjà vu dominated political commentary across Europe at the time when the Arab uprisings were unfolding (Saleh and Khalaf 2011; Whitaker 2011). Although no one expected a speedy transition to democracy as in Central and Eastern Europe two decades earlier, the 'Arab Spring' raised hopes for democratic change in the Arab world previously seen as immune to democratic governance.

The EU and its member states' governments were more lukewarm about the prospects for democracy in the Arab world and were confronted with the formidable difficulty posed by their previous support for authoritarian leaders in the region (Pace 2014). Not only were the policies of the past discredited in the eyes of the Arab street, but they also created a difficult climate for relations with the newly emerging political formations in the region that enjoyed popular legitimacy. The EU was not spared the embarrassment of previous wrongdoing and was quick to denounce the short-termism of its security preoccupations and lack of genuine support for democracy in the past (Füle 2011).

As instability gained momentum in the region, the EU was alarmed to find its southern border flooded by migrants trying to escape the turmoil and the violence in North Africa. The migration control deals struck with previous dictators were in tatters and no longer delivering border security to the EU. The Mediterranean member states faced an increasing number of migrants and highly mediatised instances of lost human life in the Mediterranean Sea as migrants sought safe haven. The number of refugees and migrants arriving in Italy, Greece, Spain and Malta via the Mediterranean has risen exponentially from 22,500 arrivals in 2012 to 60,000 in 2013 and 75,000 in just the first half of 2014 (UNHCR 2014). This upward trend has been accompanied by a rising number of lives lost at sea with 500 deaths in 2012, 600 in 2013 and some 800 in the first half of 2014 (UNHCR 2014). This migration influx activated the member states' instinct to seek the cooperation of the new authorities in the Arab countries to help curb the flow.

Beyond the initial reactions, the EU's strategic response to the momentous changes in the southern neighbourhood came with the launch of the Partnership for Democracy and Shared Prosperity with the Southern Mediterranean in March 2011 (European Commission 2011a) followed by a strategic review of the European Neighbourhood Policy (ENP) released in May 2011 (European Commission 2011b). This paper analyses the ENP's goals and instruments before and after the Arab Spring and enquires why there has been little substantive change in the EU's approach to the neighbourhood, notwithstanding the acknowledged opportunity for democratic change and the EU's stated willingness to contribute to it.

Understanding the EU's goals and instruments in the neighbourhood is inherently linked to the main motives of action or inaction in foreign policy (Tocci 2008). Some have described the very distinctness of the EU's international actorness as normative in nature (Manners 2002). Others have viewed the EU as a traditional actor seeking to advance its security in international politics just like any other state in the system (Hyde-Price 2006). Still others have conceived of the EU as an actor implicitly pursuing a liberal strategy through cooperation with other nations as the best approach to serving its interests (Smith 2011).

This scholarly debate has largely assumed the EU's unity of action and internal cohesion and disregarded the institutional pluralism of EU foreign policy-making. The reality of constructing and implementing the ENP shows that power within the EU over setting policy goals and taking action to achieve them is fragmented among various EU institutional bodies and the EU member states. To understand how and why the EU has acted in the neighbourhood, serious attention needs to be paid to the ENP's institutional set-up and the power relationships that exist between the different layers of governance involved in setting ENP goals and implementing policy. This paper argues that the institutional relations within the EU, both within the Brussels bureaucracy and between the EU institutions and the member states, explain how it is that the ENP has remained a bureaucratic framework, missing out on the opportunity to make a more decisive impact on the neighbourhood in the wake of the Arab Spring.

The paper begins by laying the conceptual foundations for the analysis. It then examines consecutively the continuity and change in ENP goals and instruments before and after the Arab Spring in the areas of democracy, mobility and migration, conflict management and economic development. It finally analyses the reasons for the lack of substantive ENP change, claiming a primary explanatory role for two institutional factors: the freedom of action of EU institutions and the (dis)unity of purpose of the EU member states in the main ENP policy areas.

EU Actorness in the Neighbourhood

The EU's foreign policy has often been reduced to a simple juxtaposition between 'values vs. security' or between identity-based and interest-based motivations for foreign policy action (Noutcheva, Pomorska, and Bosse 2013). The EU's endorsement of the peaceful societal protests and demands for democratic change in the Arab world can be seen through the prism of the EU's own self-perception as a beacon of liberal democracy and human rights. The EU interpreted the Arab nations' aspirations for pluralistic and accountable polities as a welcome confirmation of the attractiveness of its own democratic values and European soft power more generally, even though the Arab street had a different perception of what it fought for and why (Pace 2014). Undoubtedly, identity considerations were a factor in launching various new programmes aiming at democracy support post Arab Spring. Considering its failures in supporting democracy in the past, the EU was under pressure to put its democratic values at the core of a new framework of relations with its southern neighbours. Identity reasons, however, cannot explain the EU's response to the migration influx in the months following the Arab Spring and the renewed security focus of exchanges with the new governments in the Arab region (see Dandashly 2014).

It would be naïve to think that the EU has no interests to pursue in the neighbourhood. The European Security Strategy (2003) acknowledges the EU's interest in a well-governed neighbourhood: '[n]eighbours who are engaged in violent conflict, weak states where organised crime flourishes, dysfunctional societies or exploding population growth on its borders all pose problems for Europe'. The existing literature has demonstrated that prior to the Arab Spring, the EU supported authoritarian rulers in exchange for their cooperation on migration, counterterrorism and other security matters (Bicchi 2009; Burnell and Schlumberger 2010; Pace 2009; Seeberg 2009; Van Hüllen 2012; Youngs 2010). In the post-Arab Spring period, the violent break-up of the Libyan regime and the weak public order in its aftermath have predetermined the EU's prioritisation of security in that country. The ongoing civil war in Syria has exposed the EU's vulnerability to the instability and humanitarian crisis in the whole region. Above all, the migration issue and its consequences for the EU's internal order have reinvigorated the EU's preoccupation with border security and control. The EU's overall reaction to the Arab uprisings, however, cannot be solely explained by a narrow focus on the security threats coming from the region. Alongside their security concerns, the Europeans have genuinely welcomed the democratic opening in the Arab world and the possibility to help the region democratise.

The emphasis on either values or security interests in explaining EU foreign policy assumes a unitary actor and overlooks the complex institutional set-up, in which EU policies are made and implemented. Scholars have long discussed the EU's actorness, reflecting on EU's institutional complexities and attempting to conceptualise the unusual nature of the EU's international role (Bretherton and Vogler 2006; Jupille and Caporaso 1998; Sjöstedt 1977). At the centre of the actorness debate is the EU's unique institutional establishment and how it affects the EU's external representation, effectiveness and recognition by other players (Gehring, Oberthür, and Mühleck 2013; Ginsberg 2001; Groenleer and Van Schaik 2007; Jupille and Caporaso 1998). By focusing on the multifaceted influence of EU institutional structure on its foreign policy, the actorness criteria put forward by scholars are useful not only in describing whether the EU can act, but also, and more importantly, in accounting for why the EU acts or does not act.

The actorness debate, while zooming in on EU institutional relationships in the area of foreign policy, overlooks the substantial variation in the EU's recognition, authority, autonomy and capability (see Börzel, Dandashly, and Risse 2014) in the various foreign policy domains. This variation is very visible in the case of the ENP. As a composite policy with multiple objectives (security, economic prosperity and democracy), the ENP cuts across various functional areas governed by different institutional arrangements. The freedom of action of the Brussels establishment differs in areas such as external trade, visa policy, conflict management or democracy support. In principle, the EU bureaucracy would not object to seeing its power expand in various foreign policy areas by being proactive in the neighbour-hood on behalf of the Union, but it does not have control over all EU instruments and as such, a strong institutional mandate for its actions in all foreign policy areas.

The EU member states' agreement on concrete policies vis-à-vis the neighbours in various functional domains, in turn, is a moving target. Institutional channels to iron out differences on ENP matters do exist, as member states' representatives meet regularly in Brussels in the framework of the Maghreb–Mashreq working party (the so-called MAMA) and the Eastern Europe and Central Asia working party (the COEST). Chaired by the European External Action Service (EEAS) since the Lisbon Treaty, these permanent bodies aim at consensus building and preference convergence through regularised intense discussions among the EU member states, sometimes on a daily basis.[1] Yet, agreement is not always possible. In prin-ciple, a high degree of unity of purpose among the EU member states with regard to both concrete ENP objectives and instruments will serve as a strong mandate for EU action on certain goals and through certain means. The absence of such unity may indicate ambiguity of goals and/or indecisive EU action.

ENP Goals: Continuity or Change?

The EU's official discourse has aimed at democracy, security and economic prosperity in the neighbourhood as mutually reinforcing and complemen-tary objectives in both pre- and post-Arab Spring periods. In this sense, there has been more continuity than change in the ENP goals. At the level of implementation, however, the priorities have always dictated a higher concern for security than for democracy and economic development (see Dandashly 2014).

Democracy

The democracy rhetoric has always been present in the EU's official dis-course. Prior to the Arab Spring, the EU insisted on 'shared values' as the basis for developing relations with neighbours (European Commission 2004, 2006, 2007). As stated in an ENP strategy paper,

> [t]he privileged relationship with neighbours will build on mutual commitment to common values principally within the fields of the rule of law, good governance, the respect for human rights, including minority rights, the promotion of good neighbourly relations, and the principles of market economy and sustainable development. (European Commission 2004)

In practice, the EU's support for democracy was either absent, as in North Africa prior to 2011 (Youngs 2011) or inadequate, as in the former Soviet republics that went through 'colour revolutions' in the 2000s (Stewart 2009).

After the Arab Spring, the EU has placed the normative component at the core of its policy vis-à-vis its neighbours (European Commission 2011a, 2011b). Not only did the EU admit its past mistakes in supporting seemingly stable regimes that lacked democratic legitimacy (Füle 2011), it also announced its intention to reverse this trend and boost its efforts and resources for democracy support. In particular, it launched two new instruments for support of the civil society and emerging political actors in the neighbourhood: the Civil Society Neighbourhood Facility and the European Endowment for Democracy (European Commission 2011b). This marks a clear departure from previous policies focused on dealings with governments only, at the expense of engaging societal actors and fledgling opposition forces. Furthermore, the EU pledged to reinforce its conditionality policy vis-à-vis neighbouring governments and tie its financial assistance more firmly to reforms, the so-called 'more for more' policy (Ashton 2011), promising to bridge talk and action.

The ultimate goal with regard to political governance the EU describes as 'deep and comprehensive democracy', a concept it proposed as the cornerstone of its relations with neighbours in the aftermath of the Arab Spring. While the EU has avoided defining the term, there is an implicit understanding that it means Western-style liberal democracy, implying free and fair elections, institutional checks and balances, rule of law guaranteeing social justice and human rights and fundamental freedoms (Kurki 2011; Wetzel and Orbie 2011a). The EU proclaimed the universality of these values, a notable shift from the 'shared values' rhetoric that characterised earlier ENP policy documents. There has, however, been no substantive change to the EU's conception of democracy, despite the discursive modifications (Pace 2014; Teti 2012). In theory, no EU member state will ever oppose 'deep and comprehensive democracy' as an aspiration and goal for the neighbourhood. In practice, they may do little to advance it, as the past has shown.

Mobility and Migration

The EU has been concerned about managing migration flows from the neighbourhood, both before and after 2011. The Arab Spring did not bring about a fundamental change in how the EU views and treats migration via the Mediterranean Sea routes. The EU's immediate response to the post-Arab Spring migration influx has put an emphasis on surveillance and border checks through the involvement of the EU border agency Frontex; pressure on the new governments in North Africa to contain illegal immigration at the source; and humanitarian assistance to resolve the refugee crisis in the region itself (Carrera, den Hertog, and Parkin 2012; see also Dandashly 2014).

The EU's strategic response to the migration issue consisted in launching a Dialogue on Migration, Mobility and Security with the Southern Mediterranean partners intended to build up capacity within these countries to manage irregular immigration against the promise to the EU member states of enhanced mobility for their citizens (European Commission 2011c, 7–8).

Mobility Partnerships, the primary EU instrument for achieving these objectives, have been offered to a first group of countries led by Morocco, Tunisia and Jordan. First estimations of these partnerships reveal that they impose disproportionate obligations on the partner states such as strict control of their external borders, cooperation with Frontex and negotiation of readmission agreements with the EU, against visa facilitation for restricted categories of their citizens (students, researchers, business leaders) and vague opportunities for legal migration to interested EU member states (Carrera, den Hertog, and Parkin 2012). The Visa Liberalisation Action Plans offered simultaneously to the eastern neighbours with the incentive of visa-free travel commit the EU more concretely on human mobility for neighbouring citizens upon evidence of domestic reforms.

Conflicts

The EU has long pledged its interest in a stable and secure neighbourhood (European Commission 2007; European Security Strategy 2003). Above all, the EU's resolve to help settle the regional conflicts across the eastern and southern neighbourhoods has been emphasised time and again in ENP strategic papers and reviews (European Commission 2007, 6, 2011b, 5). The ENP review of May 2011 confirms this objective: to 'enhance the EU involvement in solving the protracted conflicts', counting on the new institutional structures in the area of foreign policy introduced by the Lisbon Treaty intended to make the EU 'a more effective actor' (European Commission 2011b, 5).

The reality has however proven quite different from the EU's proclaimed intentions, with the EU showing a varying appetite for foreign policy action aiming at the settlement of the ethnic disputes marring the security of the neighbourhood (Popescu 2011). It has progressively become more involved in the settlement of some of the protracted conflicts in its vicinity by participating in various negotiating formats and being present on the ground through CSDP missions, such as in Transnistria, Abkhazia/South Ossetia and the Israeli–Palestinian conflict (Tocci 2007), and most recently, in the Ukraine crisis. It has nevertheless remained inactive in other conflicts such as Nagorno–Karabakh or Western Sahara (Darbouche and Zoubir 2008; Popescu 2011).

The Arab awakening has resulted in new lines of conflict in the southern neighbourhood with the bloody collapse of the Gaddafi regime in Libya and the violent breakdown of the status quo in Syria, posing new challenges to EU foreign policy. The Libya case, widely cited as a successful example of swift international intervention, has shown again the EU's inaction, notwithstanding the 'right conditions' for initiating military intervention under the EU flag (Biscop 2012). In Syria, the EU has struggled to respond in a coherent and adequate way to the escalating civil war, ultimately adopting a comprehensive sanctions regime (Lehne 2012), but failing to take more decisive action to halt the bloodshed. The EU's record on conflict management in the neighbourhood is one of hesitation and indecisive action, putting into question member states' support for the EU's officially declared security objectives for both itself and its neighbours.

Economic Development

The economic objectives of the ENP are the most pronounced, given the predominantly economic nature of the incentives the EU can offer to its neighbours willing to reform. The core of the ENP's bargain is convergence of the neighbouring economies on the norms of the European single market, promising to create prosperity for both sides (European Commission 2006, 2007). The advantages of anchoring neighbours' economies on the European economic model are presented as a major vehicle for wealth generation and higher living standards in neighbouring nations. Through improved access to the EU market, better regulation and financial assistance from the EU, the neighbouring economies are expected to converge with the European economy, not only in terms of economic governance standards, but also, and more importantly, in terms of level of development. This has been an official objective both prior to and after the Arab Spring.

In the post-Arab Spring period, the EU has championed the concept of Deep and Comprehensive Free Trade Areas (DCFTAs) as a model for wealth generation in the southern neighbourhood, borrowing from its experience with the eastern neighbours. In principle, the EU is well positioned to support economic development through trade, as it is a key trade partner for the majority of ENP countries (Eurostat 2013). At the same time, the ENP countries are not important trade partners for the EU itself and the majority of EU member states 'exhibit extremely low import and export shares [to and from the ENP countries] in relation to their GDPs' (Petrakos *et al.* 2013, 12). The EU runs trade surpluses with all but the energy-exporting ENP countries (Algeria, Azerbaijan and Libya) (Eurostat 2013). In essence, consensus within the EU on a trade-liberalising agenda is not difficult to arrive at, even if the economic imperative to invest in such a project may not be strong.

What is more debatable with regard to the DCFTA formula is its potential to generate economic growth in the neighbourhood in the short run. First estimates of the DCFTAs suggest that they result in a very costly regulatory convergence for the neighbours in the short term, which the EU financial assistance and promise of institutional inclusion cannot compensate for (Messerlin *et al.* 2011; Dreyer 2012). The resulting perception is that adjustment costs for the neighbours are unjustifiably high and their economies, initially at a lower level of development, may take years to fully benefit from regulatory approximation with the EU (Dreyer 2012; Liargovas 2013). And while countries from the eastern neighbourhood may have an implicit incentive to adopt the EU *acquis* in the hope of acceding to the EU one day, the Mediterranean neighbours have no such prospect, not even in theory. The euro crisis has in the meantime shaken the image of the EU as an economic model worthy of emulation for the sake of its superior economic results.

Overall, there has been little substantive change in the EU's goals towards its southern neighbourhood in response to the Arab Spring (see Table 1).

ENP Instruments: Continuity or Change?

The ENP academic debate to date has disproportionately focused on the instruments the EU uses to influence domestic change in the neighbourhood. The tendency has been to compare the ENP toolbox with the EU enlargement policy and to recognise the substantial overlap in operational means the EU uses in both contexts, with one big exception: the lack of EU membership prospects for the neighbouring states (Weber, Smith, and Baun 2007; Whitman and Wolff 2010). In the aftermath of the Arab Spring, the EU launched a series of new operational instruments such as the SPRING programme (Support for Partnership, Reform and Inclusive Growth) with a budget of EUR 3.5 billion for the period 2011–2013, to provide additional funding to southern partners showing commitment to democratic reform in line with the 'more for more' principle (European Commission 2013a). It also extended a series of instruments that were already on offer to the eastern neighbours such as DCFTAs, Mobility Partnerships with a muted promise of visa liberalisation, civil society engagement schemes, etc. Do these novel operational means constitute a real change in the EU's approach to its southern neighbours?

Positive conditionality has been the EU's main instrument of channelling its influence (Börzel 2011; Sasse 2008). While always present at the rhetorical level, it had never been practised prior to the Arab Spring vis-à-vis the authoritarian regimes in North Africa. With the collapse of some of the dictators in the region, the EU pledged to reinforce the 'more for more' principle in its relations with neighbours, meaning rewarding reform while abstaining from punishing non-reform. Positive conditionality is now the

Table 1. ENP goals pre and post Arab Spring

ENP goals	Democracy	Mobility and migration	Conflict management	Economic development
Pre Arab Spring	Declaratory support for liberal democracy justified as 'shared values'	Border controls and fight against illegal migration at the expense of human mobility	Token support for conflict management	Economic development through trade liberalisation
Post Arab Spring	Declaratory support for liberal democracy described as 'deep and sustainable democracy' and justified as 'universal values'	No change	No change	No change

main mechanism in most of the policy areas included in the ENP, from democracy and trade to mobility and sectoral cooperation.

Sanctions have always been part of the EU foreign policy toolbox, but they had rarely been applied in the Southern Mediterranean prior to the Arab Spring. Although the EU had not shied away from imposing sanctions on the Lukashenko regime in Belarus in the east (Giumelli and Ivan 2013), the southern dictators had never experienced the bite of EU leverage. The violence triggered by the authoritarian regimes that fought back during the Arab awakening marked a turning point in the EU's use of sanctions in the region, the ultimate aim being containment of internal conflicts. The imposition of sanctions is nevertheless not a measure the EU is likely to employ in many instances of severe democratic transgression, as reactions to Egypt's *coup* in the summer of 2013 have shown (see Dandashly 2014).

Diplomacy has been used as a foreign policy tool in both pre- and post-Arab Spring periods. The EU's use of diplomatic means in the neighbourhood has had more to do with its own internal developments than with external events. The entry into force of the Lisbon Treaty in 2009 institutionalised the external representative power of the High Representative and the role of the External Action Services as the core of the EU diplomatic system. Catherine Ashton's mediating roles in Egypt, Iran and Kosovo during her term of office have to be understood as part of the overall strengthening of the EU's capabilities for diplomatic action, rather than a rethink of the suitability of the instrument for achieving objectives in the neighbourhood.

Financial assistance has been a major incentive offered to the ENP partner states, and between 2007 and 2013, the EU allocated around EUR 12 billion to the neighbourhood under the European Neighbourhood and Partnership Instrument (ENPI). The European Commission requested EUR 18 billion, a substantial increase (50%) in the ENPI budget, for the next financial framework 2014–2020 in line with the ENP policy ambitions and the EU's pledged support for the domestic transformation of the countries in both neighbourhoods (European Commission 2012). It secured just above EUR 15 billion (current prices), an amount comparable to the funding allocated for the previous financial period (European Commission 2013b). While there have been critical assessments of the way in which EU money has been spent in the past to achieve declared goals (European Parliament 2012), financial assistance has been and remains a substantial part of the EU's offer to its neighbours.

In sum, the paper finds only minor changes in the EU's instruments (see Table 2). They entail the use of positive conditionality with respect to democracy and the invoking of sanctions with respect to conflict management.

Explaining the EU's Response to the Changing Neighbourhood

How can we explain the lack of substantive change in the ENP's official goals and instruments, irrespective of the operational innovations and the launch of new initiatives? It is fair to say that the ENP discourse has been framed in Brussels, first by the European Commission between 2003 and

Table 2. ENP instruments pre and post Arab Spring

ENP instruments	Democracy	Mobility and migration	Conflict management	Economic development
Pre Arab Spring	Token conditionality; financial assistance	Conditionality; financial assistance	Diplomacy; selective deployment of CSDP missions	Conditionality; financial assistance
Post Arab Spring	Diplomacy; positive conditionality; financial assistance	No change	Diplomacy; selective deployment of CSDP missions; sanctions	No change

2009 and afterwards by the EEAS. Early research on the ENP has convincingly demonstrated that EU institutions have been in the driver's seat when defining EU ambitions in the neighbourhood, and EU staff have drafted all important policy documents with strong references to the EU enlargement experience (Kelley 2006; Magen 2006). Not sharing a consensual view over the *finalité* of the EU's relationship with its neighbours, the EU member states have delegated the management of the neighbourhood to the Brussels bureaucracy, which has crafted a slow but predictable response to unfolding events, offering the usual mix of incentives (money, mobility and market access) on the strength of vague expectations of reforms in partner countries.

The Brussels bureaucracy however does not possess all the means to deliver on the ambitious goals it has set for the Union and cannot commit the EU to using all the instruments at its disposal. It is empowered to achieve results in the economic sphere, but is constrained, to varying degrees, with regard to conflict management, democracy support and mobility of people. The EU member states hold the key to projecting a strong external image of the EU as a capable and consistent actor. When they see eye to eye with the EU institutions and with their peers on how to approach the neighbourhood, the EU is able to pursue a strong policy, as in the areas of trade liberalisation and migration. When there are profound divisions among the EU member states on what means are to be employed towards what ends, as in the areas of democracy promotion and conflict management, EU inaction or inadequate action follows, often contradicting the officially declared objectives.

Freedom of Action of EU institutions

The *democracy* dimension is most difficult to pin down with regard to decision-making responsibility because it does not involve concrete legal competences located at various levels of governance. The principal mechanism of EU democracy promotion — conditionality — is embodied in various instruments for which the EU institutions and the member states have sole or shared responsibility. Democracy support through the European Instrument for Democracy and Human Rights is the sole responsibility of DG Development of the European Commission. The imposition of sanctions in the case of political repression and gross human rights violations — such as asset freezes, travel and visa bans, arms embargos, etc. — is in the hands of the EU member states, which act by unanimity in the framework of CFSP. The ENP Action Plans and Progress Reports where democracy conditions are set and appraised are a product of the EEAS. The Foreign Affairs Council Conclusions encode the reactions of the EU member states to current affairs linked to democracy questions. This cacophony of voices has not always produced consistent messages in the past and there is no reason to expect that this will change in the future.

With regard to *mobility of people*, a key incentive offered to the neighbours but fundamentally a question of security for the EU itself, the EU institutions are partially empowered. In particular, DG Home of the European Commission has an important role in managing the external dimension of EU migration policy. It possesses key levers of power in EU decision-making with regard to short-term visa policy and is the leading EU actor in exchanges with third countries on mobility partnerships, visa facilitation, readmission agreements and visa liberalisation action plans. It sets the conditions, monitors the countries' performance and evaluates the readiness of neighbouring states to proceed to a new phase of relations with the EU in the framework of these instruments.[2] The EU member states nevertheless closely scrutinise the work of the Commission on these dossiers and have in-built mechanisms to control every step of the process.[3] For example, DG Home can negotiate visa facilitation and readmission agreements with the neighbours on behalf of the EU, but needs a negotiating mandate from the EU member states. It has an important managing and monitoring role in the Visa Liberalisation Action Plans, but the decision to open the instrument to specific countries and ultimately to offer visa facilitation or liberalisation to specific neighbours is political in nature and for the EU member states to make. And while the Commission enjoys a wide margin to manoeuvre in externally representing the EU on these matters, it is not empowered to negotiate on legal migration routes to the EU, a *domaine reservée* of the member states (Cassarino and Lavenex 2012). These institutional mechanisms have in essence re-enforced the security rationale behind DG Home's approach to mobility in the neighbourhood and largely explain the lack of real change in EU migration policies in the post-Arab Spring period.

When it comes to *managing the protracted conflicts* in the neighbourhood, the EU institutions are most constrained. In order to have a more pronounced impact on conflict settlement and transformation, the EU has to rely on a combination of CFSP and ENP instruments, with deployment of the former relying heavily on consensus among member states. In general, the conflict management instruments in the hands of the EU institutions are geared towards long-term change, but have often remained disconnected from the short-term crisis management measures that member states can initiate through CFSP channels. In rhetoric, the need to build bridges between the CFSP and the ENP has been recognised (European Commission 2011b, 5), but in practice, the synergies between the two have not been fully explored. The High Representative and the EEAS can play a more active role in conflict mediation, as demonstrated in 2013 by their successes in facilitating negotiations between Serbs and Kosovars, between Iran and the international community and among the various political factions in Egypt before the military *coup*. The success of these diplomatic initiatives is in fact largely attributable to the lack of interference by member states in the work of the EU institutions (Glenny 2013). The EEAS is however greatly constrained in cases when the member states disagree, a limitation openly admitted in its own review: '... in the absence of collective political will and agreement between Member States, this is a limiting factor on decision-making' (EEAS 2013). Given the institutional realities, it is unsurprising that the post-Arab Spring EU line on conflicts in the neighbourhood repeats previously made general commitments to peace and security without a clear plan on what the EU is willing to do in practice.

When it comes to *economic development*, the EU institutions are better equipped to define policy direction. The negotiation of DCFTAs is an exclusive competence of the European Commission. While not completely free of member state influence, the trade component of the ENP is one of strong EU autonomy, especially in comparative terms. The same can be said about the allocation and disbursement of financial aid to the neighbours, with regard to both development and macro-financial assistance. DG Trade, DG Development and DG Economic and Financial Affairs of the European Commission hold important levers of power in the EU's relations with its neighbours, especially when it comes to two of the ENP's main incentives: money and markets. It is for this institutional reason that the new initiatives launched by the EU post Arab Spring promise more financial assistance and more market opening.

(Dis)unity of purpose among EU member states

While fragmentation of decision-making power is not a problem for EU actorness per se, the EU can be seriously restricted when internal disunity prevents collective external action. The *democracy* dimension is less consensual, notwithstanding the general agreement on democracy as a core European value and a basis for developing relations with neighbours. The authoritarian temptation is strong in both southern and eastern neighbourhoods, with regimes ranging from consolidated and semi-consolidated autocracies to hybrid regimes (Freedom House 2014). The EU does not possess a blueprint for policies targeting different regime types and does not go beyond the usual assertion of the principle of differentiation as a basis for relations with neighbours (European Commission 2011a, 2011b). This vagueness conceals a divergence of views on what to do about promoting democracy, which led to failure to reach agreement on the formal adoption of a 'European Consensus on Democracy' (Wetzel and Orbie 2011b). The member states' views on how to deal with authoritarian regimes are particularly relevant when it comes to taking punitive action, either in the form of sanctions or strong condemnations in the case of crisis events. Not in control of these more political instruments and avoiding instances of public exposure of internal disagreement, the EU institutions have so far confined themselves to practising positive conditionality in the context of the ENP Action Plans and Progress Reports. The language of 'more for more' is illustrative of the Brussels institutions' instinct to speak about inducements and act through offering rewards, putting aside the negative aspect of conditionality: the 'less for less' side. In practice, this has meant that democratic transgression in the neighbourhood has often remained unpunished, while discussions among EU member states have not always resulted in strong collective action against authoritarian practices (Del Sarto and Schumacher 2011).

Promoting *mobility* for neighbouring citizens is a sensitive issue for the EU member states. Disagreements among the states on how to manage illegal migration to the EU are not new and were vividly demonstrated by the French–Italian spat in April 2011, when France temporarily imposed border checks with Italy after the latter issued residency documents to newly arrived migrants from North Africa, allowing them to move freely in the Schengen area (Brady 2012). While the issue was swiftly resolved, it opened a wider debate about reform of the Schengen rules (Brady 2012). The EU member states have differences about how to ensure an efficient and fair system of burden sharing in this area, but the security approach tends to prevail over a more sociopolitical view of offering more opportunities for legal migration to third-country nationals and better guarantees for the human rights of illegal migrants. In fact, some scholars have asserted that the main bone of contention in the management of EU migration lies between the security-obsessed interior ministry staff and the more politically sensitive foreign policy establishments across EU member states and within EU institutions (Carrera, den Hertog, and Parkin 2012). The weakness of the EEAS and the primacy of the DG Home of the European Commission in directing the Brussels policy response on migration issues after the Arab Spring have contributed to reinforcing the security rationale of the EU approach (Carrera, den Hertog, and Parkin 2012).

Among the reasons for the EU's weak performance in *conflict management* are the diverging perceptions among member states regarding security threats and priorities, and different attitudes to risk-taking in international politics more generally. There is no shared understanding about which conflicts constitute a priority for the EU and require more attention and resources (Biscop 2013). The necessity to come up with swift collective responses to crisis situations exposes the structural weaknesses of running a single foreign policy sanctioned by 28 capitals. Libya is illustrative of the continued relevance of member states' action outside the EU framework, when agreement to act collectively cannot be quickly found. Syria is an example of both the impotence of EU diplomacy at a global level and the internal difficulties of arriving at a unanimous decision to lift the embargo, at the insistence of Britain and France, on arming rebel groups in the conflict (ECFR 2014). Sanctions were considered but never agreed to in the case of Egypt in the summer of 2013.

On the *economic side*, there is general consensus among the EU member states on trade liberalisation and regulatory convergence of neighbouring economies with EU legislation. Not only are the EU economic stakes not

Table 3. Variation in EU actorness in the neighbourhood

	Democracy	Mobility and migration	Conflict management	Economic development
Freedom of action of EU institutions	Medium	Medium	Low	High
Unity of purpose among the EU member states	Medium to low	High	Low	High

that high, the adjustment costs are externalised and do not apply to the member states themselves. Various sensitivities nevertheless arise with regard to market opening of specific sectors in negotiations with partner states (Dreyer 2012; Liargovas 2013). The tendency to shield sensitive industries and agricultural sectors from external competition is not new for the EU, and the trade asymmetry between the EU and neighbouring states has allowed it to protect those interests in the past (Petrakos *et al.* 2013). The member states' agreement on these issues reinforces the current policies of export of EU regulatory rules and selective market opening.

Considering the variation in the freedom of action of EU institutions and in unity of purpose among the EU member states in key ENP areas (see Table 3), the absence of substantive change in the ENP after the Arab Spring is not surprising. The areas of economic development and conflict management are most straightforward to interpret. The economic component of the ENP benefits from the strong support of EU member states as well as the high operational autonomy of EU institutions to pursue a trade liberalisation and regulatory convergence agenda, around which there is wide consensus within the EU. In contrast, the conflict management area is characterised by disagreements among member states and the weak operational mandate of EU institutions, hence its vagueness with regard to goals and its weakness with regard to performance. The migration area is more consensual than it appears, as the key institutional players in it — the EU interior ministries and DG Home of the European Commission — share the same approach to migration management. The democracy domain is one of medium EU institutional empowerment and medium-to-low member state consensus on collective action, which explains why Brussels has been able to raise hopes for a genuine democracy support policy but has been unable to deliver on implementation, earning the EU a dubious reputation as democracy promoter in the neighbourhood.

Conclusion

The paper has argued that the institutional governance of the ENP has largely conditioned the EU's response to the historic changes in the neighbourhood. The EU institutions although not cohesive actors in themselves have been in a unique position to frame the EU response to the Arab Spring, but they have done so in a predicable way, given the levers of power they possess in the various functional fields of external policy and the constraints on their autonomy in committing EU resources and instruments. As such they have been relatively forthcoming in promising more money and more market access for advances in democracy, but vague on mobility and conflicts. Consensus among EU member states has been a key determinant of strong EU action in the area of migration and trade policy, whereas disagreements among them have resulted in inadequate EU action or inaction on democracy and conflicts.

The EU's actorness has thus been tamed by the underlying differences among member states, and this has particularly played out in issue areas where the EU institutions have less freedom to act on behalf of the Union. Overall, the EU has asserted itself as neither a strategic actor nor a normative power, but rather as a bystander, trapped in its internal institutional process and content to passively react to crisis events by proposing longterm solutions that have little impact in the short run.

Notes

1. Interview, EEAS, Brussels, September 2013.
2. Interviews, DG Home, European Commission, October 2013.
3. Interviews, DG Home, European Commission, October 2013.

References

Ashton, C. 2011. *Remarks by EU high representative Catherine Ashton on arrival to the extraordinary european council.* A 102/11., Brussels, 11 March.
Bicchi, F. 2009. Democracy assistance in the Mediterranean: an overview. *Mediterranean Politics* 14, no. 1: 61–78.
Biscop, S. 2012. Mediterranean Mayhem: lessons for European crisis management. In *An Arab Springboard for EU Foreign Policy*, eds. S. Biscop, R. Balfour, and M. Emerson, 75–81. Egmont Paper 54, Brussels: Academia Press, January.
Biscop, S. 2013. Peace without money, war without Americans: challenges for European strategy. *International Affairs* 89, no. 5: 1125–42.
Börzel, T. 2011. When Europe hits … beyond its borders: Europeanization and the near abroad. *Comparative European Politics* 9, no. 4: 394–413.
Börzel, T.A., A. Dandashly, and T. Risse. 2014. Responses to the "Arabellions": the EU in comparative perspective – Introduction. *Journal of European Integration* 37, no. 1: 1–17.
Brady, H. 2012. *The Schengen crisis in the framework of the Arab Spring.* London: Centre for European Reform.
Bretherton, C., and J. Vogler. 2006. *The European Union as a global actor.* New York, NY: Routledge.
Burnell, P., and O. Schlumberger. 2010. Promoting democracy — promoting autocracy? International politics and national political regimes. *Contemporary Politics* 16, no. 1: 1–15.
Carrera, S., L. den Hertog, and J. Parkin. 2012. *EU migration policy in the wake of the Arab Spring: what prospects for EU-Southern Mediterranean relations?* MEDPRO Technical Report No. 15. Brussels: Centre for European Policy Studies.
Cassarino, J.P., and S. Lavenex. 2012. *EU Migration Governance in the Mediterranean Region: the promise of (a balanced) partnership?* 284–8. IEMed: IEMed Mediterranean Yearbook, Barcelona.
Darbouche, H., and Y.H. Zoubir. 2008. Conflicting international policies and the Western Sahara stalemate. *The International Spectator* 43, no. 1: 91–105.
Dandashly, A. 2014. The EU response to regime change in the wake of the Arab revolt: differential Implementation. *Journal of European Integration* 37, no. 1: 37–56.
Del Sarto, R.A., and T. Schumacher. 2011. From Brussels with love: leverage, benchmarking, and the action plans with Jordan and Tunisia in the EU's democratization policy. *Democratization* 18, no. 4: 932–55.
Deutsche Welle. 2011. *Peace researchers demand more german support for Arab Spring.* Berlin: Deutsche Welle, 25 May.

RESPONSES TO THE 'ARABELLIONS'

Dreyer, I. 2012. *Trade policy in the EU's neighbourhood: ways forward for the deep and comprehensive free trade agreements*. Paris: Notre Europe.

EEAS. 2013. *EEAS review*. Brussels: European External Action Service.

European Commission. 2004. *European neighbourhood policy: strategy Pape*, COM(2004)373.

European Commission. 2006. *On strengthening the European neighbourhood policy*. COM(2006)726.

European Commission. 2007. *A strong European neighbourhood policy*. COM(2007)774.

European Commission. 2011a. *A partnership for democracy and shared prosperity with the Southern Mediterranean*. COM(2011) 200 final. 8 March.

European Commission. 2011b. *A new response to a changing neighbourhood*. COM(2011) 303. 25 May.

European Commission. 2011c. *The EU's neighbouring economies: coping with new challenges*. Occasional Papers 86. November.

European Commission. 2012. *Multiannual financial framework 2014–2020: strengthening Europe's place in the world*. Brussels, http://ec.europa.eu/europeaid/how/finance/mff/financial_frame work_news_en.htm (accessed 16 January 2014).

European Commission. 2013a. *EU's response to the 'Arab Spring': the state-of-play after two years*. MEMO/13/81.

European Commission. 2013b. *The multiannual financial framework: the external action financing instruments*. MEMO/13/1134. 11 December.

European Council on Foreign Relations (ECFR). 2014. *European Foreign Policy Scorecard 2014*. London, January.

European Parliament. 2012. *Improving the EU's aid to its neighbours: lessons learned from the ENPI, recommendations for the ENI*. Briefing Paper DG EXPO/B/PolDep/FWC/2009-01/LOT 1/33. Brussels.

European Security Strategy. 2003. *A secure Europe in a better world*. Brussels, 12 December.

Eurostat. 2013. *European Neighbourhood policy countries: essential macro-economic indicators*. Luxembourg: European Commission.

Freedom House. 2014. *Freedom in the world 2014: an eighth year of decline in political rights and civil liberties*. Washington, DC: Freedom House.

Füle, S. 2011. *European commissioner for ENP. Speech on the Recent Events in North Africa, SPEECH/ 11/130, Committee on Foreign Affairs (AFET)*. Brussels: European Parliament, 28 February.

Gehring, T., S. Oberthür, and M. Mühleck. 2013. European Union actorness in international institutions: why the EU is recognized as an actor in some international institutions, but not in others. *Journal of Common Market Studies* 51, no. 5: 849–65.

Ginsberg, R.H. 2001. *The European Union in international politics: Baptism by fire*. Lanham, MD: Rowman and Littlefield.

Giumelli, F., and P. Ivan. 2013. The effectiveness of EU sanctions. An analysis of Iran, Belarus, Syria and Myanmar (Burma). *EPC Issue Paper N 76*. Brussels: European Policy Centre.

Glenny, M. 2013. Balkans deal confirms Europe's Clout. *Financial Times*, 22 April.

Groenleer, M., and Van Schaik L. 2007. United we stand: the European Union's international actorness in the cases of the international criminal court and the Kyoto Protocol. *Journal of Common Market Studies* 45, no. 5: 969–98.

Hyde-Price, A. 2006. Normative power Europe: a realist critique. *Journal of European Public Policy* 13, no. 2: 217–34.

Jupille, J., and J. Caporaso. 1998. States, agency, and rules: the European Union in global environmental politics. In *The European Union in the world community*, ed. C. Rhodes, 213–29. Boulder, CO: Lynne Rienner.

Kelley, J. 2006. New wine in old wineskins: Promoting political reforms through the new European neighbourhood policies. *Journal of Common Market Studies* 44, no. 1: 29–55.

Kurki, M. 2011. Governmentality and EU democracy promotion: the European instrument for democracy and human rights and the construction of democratic civil societies. *International Political Sociology* 5, no. 4: 349–66.

Lehne, S. 2012. *The role of sanctions in EU Foreign Policy, Carnegie Endowment for international peace*. Brussels, 14 December.

Liargovas, P. 2013. *EU trade policies towards neighbouring countries*. Working Paper WP2/01. University of Barcelona, Spain.

Magen, A. 2006. The shadow of enlargement: can the european neighbourhood policy achieve compliance? *The Columbia Journal of European Law* 12, no. 2: 384–427.

Manners, I. 2002. Normative power europe: a contradiction in terms? *Journal of Common Market Studies* 40, no. 2: 235–58.

Messerlin, P., M. Emerson, G. Jandieri, and A. Le Vernoy. 2011. *An appraisal of the EU's trade policy towards its eastern neighbours: the case of Georgia*. Groupe d'Economie Mondiale. Brussels: Science Po, Paris and Centre for European Policy Studies.

Noutcheva, G., K. Pomorska, and G. Bosse (eds.). 2013. *The EU and its neighbours: values versus security in European Foreign Policy*. Manchester, NH: Manchester University Press.

Pace, M. 2009. Paradoxes and contradictions in EU democracy promotion in the Mediterranean: the limits of EU normative power. *Democratization* 16, no. 1: 39–58.

Pace, M. 2014. The EU's interpretation of the 'Arab Uprisings': understanding the different visions about democratic change in EU-MENA relations. *Journal of Common Market Studies* 52, no. 5: 969–84.

Petrakos, G., D. Kallioras, P. Artelaris, and M. Tsiapa. 2013. Israel wary of transition in Egypt, concerned about regional stability. *The geography of trade relations between the EU and the ENP countries: emerging patterns and policy recommendations*. Discussion Paper Series 19(1). Greece: University of Thessaly Pedion Areos.

Popescu, N. 2011. *EU Foreign Policy and Post-Soviet conflicts: stealth intervention*. New York, NY: Routledge.

Saleh, H., and R. Khalaf. 2011. March to Arab democracy 'Unstoppable', *Financial Times*, London, 20 May.

Sasse, G. 2008. The European neighbourhood policy: conditionality revisited for the EU's eastern neighbours. *Europe-Asia-Studies* 60, no. 2: 295–316.

Seeberg, P. 2009. The EU as a realist actor in normative clothes: EU democracy promotion in Lebanon and the European neighbourhood policy. *Democratization* 16, no. 1: 81–99.

Sjöstedt, G. 1977. *The external role of the European community*. Farnborough: Saxon House.

Smith, M.E. 2011. A liberal grand strategy in a realist world? Power, purpose and the EU's changing global role. *Journal of European Public Policy* 18, no. 2: 144–63.

Stewart, S. 2009. Democracy promotion before and after the 'colour revolutions'. *Democratization* 16, no. 4: 645–60.

Teti, A. 2012. The EU's first response to the 'Arab Spring': a critical discourse analysis of the partnership for democracy and shared prosperity. *Mediterranean Politics* 17, no. 3: 266–84.

Tocci, N. 2007. *The EU and conflict resolution: promoting peace in the Backyard*. London: Routledge.

Tocci, N. 2008. *Who is a normative Foreign policy actor? The European Union and its global partners*. Brussels: Centre for European Policy Studies.

Ulrichsen, K.C., D. Held, and A. Brahimi. 2011. The Arab 1989? *OpenDemocracy*, 11 February.

United Nations High Commissioner for Refugees (UNHCR). 2014. *UNHCR calls for urgent European action to end refugee and migrant deaths at sea*. Geneva. 24 July, http://www.unhcr.org/53d0e2d26.html (accessed 25 July 2014).

Van Hüllen, V. 2012. Europeanisation through cooperation? EU democracy promotion in Morocco and Tunisia. *West European Politics* 35, no. 1: 117–34.

Weber, K., M.E. Smith, and M. Baun (eds.). 2007. *Governing Europe's neighbourhood: partners or periphery?* Manchester, NH: Manchester University Press.

Wetzel, A., and J. Orbie. 2011a. Promoting embedded democracy? Researching the substance of EU democracy promotion. *European Foreign Affairs Review* 16: 565–88.

Wetzel, A., and J. Orbie. 2011b. With map and compass on narrow paths and through shallow waters: discovering the substance of EU democracy promotion. *European Foreign Affairs Review* 16: 705–25.

Whitaker, B. 2011. The Arab Spring is brighter than ever. *The Guardian*, London, 14 March.

Whitman, R., and S. Wolff. 2010. *The European neighbourhood policy in perspective*. Basingstoke: Palgrave Macmillan.

Youngs, R. (ed.). 2010. *The EU and democracy promotion: a critical global assessment*. Baltimore, MD: Johns Hopkins University Press.

Youngs, R. 2011. What not to do in the Middle East and North Africa. Policy Brief N 70, *FRIDE*. Madrid, March.

The EU Response to Regime Change in the Wake of the Arab Revolt: Differential Implementation

ASSEM DANDASHLY

Political Science Department, Maastricht University, Maastricht, The Netherlands

ABSTRACT Following the Arab Spring, one might expect a paradigm shift in the EU's attitude towards the MENA — at least with respect to democracy promotion. However, the EU response has been neither consistent nor coherent. This paper seeks to answer the following questions: How did the EU react to the Arab Spring events in North Africa? Is there evidence of any change in the goals and instruments pursued by the EU after the Arab Spring? And, do these goals and instruments change coherently across countries? The paper argues, first, that EU goals remain security and stability driven. While the EU viewed the Arab Spring as a window of opportunity for democracy, as events developed the EU prioritized security concerns as a response to the threat of instability in the MENA. And second, the utilization of instruments varied across time and cases due to the domestic politics of the targeted countries.

Introduction

The European Union (EU) has been evolving as an international and regional actor, venturing into various new domains such as conflict management, economic development and democracy promotion in different parts of the world. The EU's role in international and regional affairs has increased significantly following the 1992 Maastricht Treaty by developing its relations with its eastern and Mediterranean neighbours. These relations were heavily shaped by the EU's security and stability concerns on its borders — mainly Middle East and North African (MENA) countries.

MENA regimes have cooperated with the EU on fighting illegal migration and maintaining stability on the EU southern borders for decades. The EU in return provided economic incentives and turned a blind eye to violations of democracy, human rights and civil liberties. The main goal of the EU and its member states in the MENA countries has been maintaining security and stability, fighting illegal migration and combating terrorism. Among the main aims of the EU action plans with ENP countries is border management. The cooperation of ENP countries is needed in that field, for security reasons.[1]

The Arab Spring events that were a surprise to the EU, its member states and the entire world have changed one of the challenges facing EU action beyond its borders: the unfavourable domestic politics for democratic reforms in some Arab Spring countries. The events that started in Tunisia and resulted in the overthrow of former Tunisian president Zein al-' Abedin Ben Ali spilled over to other countries such as Bahrain, Egypt, Jordan, Libya, Morocco and Syria. The only two countries, in addition to Tunisia, that witnessed a regime change are Egypt and Libya. With the outbreak of the protests, Libya and Egypt's leaders took a more aggressive attitude towards their people, which ultimately led to the toppling of their governments. The three cases witnessed a similar outcome, regime change; however, the changes manifested themselves in different ways, forcing the EU to prioritize different instruments according to the targeted country. The reason for the EU's pragmatic reaction to these issues ultimately stems from its recognition of each countries unique domestic political situation.

This paper seeks to answer the following questions: How did the EU react to the Arab Spring events in North Africa? Is there evidence of any change in the goals and instruments pursued by the EU after the Arab Spring? And, do these goals and instruments change coherently across countries? Answering these questions, the paper focuses on three Arab Spring North African countries (Tunisia, Libya and Egypt) and argues, first, that EU goals remain security and stability driven. While the EU viewed the Arab Spring as a window of opportunity for democracy, as events developed the EU prioritized security concerns as a response to the threat of instability in the MENA. And second, the utilization of instruments varied across time and cases due to the domestic politics of the targeted countries.

Following the introduction, section two highlights the stages of EU response to the Arab Spring events and the analytical framework. Section three analyses the EU goals in the MENA pre- and post-Arab Spring. Section four discusses the EU instruments used in Egypt, Libya and Tunisia, and demonstrates how the fine tuning of the instruments used is shaped by the domestic politics. Section five discusses the rationale behind the EU policies in the three countries. The final section concludes with the main findings.

EU Response to the Arab Spring Events

The Arab Spring incidents caught the EU by surprise and triggered an immediate review of the EU's policies vis-à-vis the MENA in order to address the new challenges (see Noutcheva 2014). The EU, like the US (see Huber 2014), fostered some hope that this could be a window of opportunity for democratic transition. The 2011 review of the ENP that followed the events highlighted the EU has not been successful in the area of democracy promotion, spelling out what measures needed to be taken to address these deficiencies 'to build and consolidate healthy democracies, pursue sustainable economic growth and manage cross-border links' (European Commission 2011a, 1). Significant research has been conducted on the topic since then assessing the EU response to the Arab Spring events (such as Echagüe, Michou, and Mikail 2011; Pace 2014; Pace and Cavatorta 2012; Schumacher 2011; Teti 2012; Teti, Thompson, and Noble 2013, etc.). Many scholars have been sceptical regarding the EU reforms and argued that the EU has not adopted any major change in its policies towards the MENA (see e.g. Balfour 2012; Behr 2012; Pace 2014; Teti 2012; Teti, Thompson, and Noble 2013). Pace and Cavatorta (2012, 134) draw the conclusion that 'there does not seem to be any serious reflections on lessons learnt from past mistakes of supporting authoritarian regimes in the name of stability at the expense of the protection of human rights and civil liberties'. In terms of democracy promotion, Teti, Thompson, and Noble (2013) analysed the EU documents pre- and post-Arab Spring and concluded that the difference between the two eras is insignificant.

This paper tries to understand the EU policy in the wake of the Arab Spring by focusing on the importance of the domestic politics of the targeted countries. The domestic political changes in North Africa pushed the EU to view the events as a window of opportunity for democratic transition. However, the initial belief that the Arab Spring events represented an opportunity to push for democratic reforms was quickly replaced by stability and security concerns. This shift in the reading of the Arab Spring events and the policies that will be taken in response are heavily based on the domestic changes on the ground — with the increased instability of the southern Mediterranean. With the post-Arab Spring chaos in Libya, Egypt, the Syrian civil war and the silencing of the revolution in Bahrain, stability and security goals were once again a priority for the EU. Its security concerns were sparked by a dramatic increase in illegal migration caused by instability in North Africa, 'worrying both EU officials fearing political consequences in [2014 European Parliamentary] elections and human rights advocates concerned about deaths at sea and other abuses of vulnerable migrants' (Daragahi and Spiegel 2013). The increase in illegal migration pushed the EU to reshift its focus to security concerns and combat it at the source by supporting the domestic authorities' measures to maintain stability in the North African countries — such as in Libya.

The changing domestic politics in the MENA countries meant that the EU had to utilize different instruments to deal with unique contextual issues. This paper argues that the variation in the EU's approach and instruments towards the MENA countries pre- and post-Arab Spring is heavily dependent on the domestic politics of the targeted countries. The main factors that have changed with the Arab Spring events in the three countries are the domestic politics and the domestic elites. Although some of the new elites (at least in Tunisia) have shown interest in democratic transition, the challenges they face go beyond democratic reforms to cover economic development, stability and security.

Börzel and Risse (2012, 11) highlighted the importance of domestic politics and considered 'that domestic institutional change responding to EU rules and regulations is unlikely to take place unless domestic actors in politics or society take them up and demand reforms themselves'. In case of domestic violence and lack of stability, the EU democratic instruments will not be used and the focus will be on restoring stability (Börzel and van Hüllen 2014; see also Börzel 2011; Grimm and Leininger 2012). In instances where the EU backed democratic reforms threaten domestic stability, it will abstain from progressing with these reforms, instead reverting to previous security concerns. Moreover, by looking at the domestic situation in the North African countries, they have major socio-economic problems that need to be addressed. Therefore, 'international actors face the challenge of balancing the fulfilment of humanitarian and social needs with democracy support. Although supporting efficient and effective governance to facilitate access to basic services and public goods has become a mainstay of international development cooperation, socioeconomic development is likely to outrank democracy support in these contexts' (Grimm and Leininger 2012, 403). In sum, the domestic politics in targeted countries influence the EU selection of instruments and policies.

EU Goals in North Africa Pre and Post Arab Spring — Priority for Stability?

Since the institutionalization of the EU-MENA relations through the Barcelona Process in 1995, maintaining security and curbing illegal migration have been the EU's key goals. One way this can be achieved is through developing economic conditions and creating more jobs in those countries.[2] Most of the EU documents discuss topics related to institution building, civil society support, civil liberties, human rights, democratic reforms, in addition to economic development and trade. However, when it comes to practice, the focus rests on security concerns and all other issues related to democracy promotion are deprioritized. Even the democracy partnership document included issues related to migration and border security. The review of the ENP did not really change this reality and the major issues remained — despite the fact that the new EU documents highlighted the need for democratic change in the MENA countries.

The 2008 report on the Implementation of the European Security Strategy highlighted threats to the EU from the southern neighbours. 'State failure affects our security through crime, illegal immigration and, most recently, piracy. Terrorism and organised crime have evolved with new menace, including within our own societies. The Iranian nuclear programme has significantly advanced, representing a danger for stability in the region and for the whole non-proliferation system' (Council of the European Union 2008, 1). These threats 'combined with rising radicalism, continues to sow instability' (Council of European Union 2008, 7). These various kinds of external security threats to the EU have led to internal security threats — especially when it comes to terrorism, organized crime and illegal migration.

Even prior to the Arab Spring events, the EU has made migration, the rise of fundamentalism and counter terrorism issues of central concern. All Arab dictators 'shared with the Union an interest in controlling the risk of terrorism locally' (Wouters and Duquet 2013, 15). In the wake of the Arab Spring events and the increased instability and security threats, restoring stability in the MENA region is now a priority for the EU. The region's instability and increase in the number of refugees, illegal migrants and asylum seekers have raised the potential for security concerns. Consequently, all EU member states have shown interest to address the security concerns emanating from the MENA countries. However, achieving a state of stability requires that instrument selection be based on the unique domestic politics possessed by the MENA countries.

EU Toolbox: Utilization of Instruments

Tunisia

The well-established political parties, strong unions and highly educated middle class created a favourable domestic political environment for democratic reforms following Ben Ali's fall. This situation enabled the first free and fair elections to take place on 23 October 2011, ultimately won by *En-Nahda Party*, who formed a coalition with the centre-left Congress for the Republic and the left party *Et-Takatol*. This does not mean that the new era was peaceful and did not experience political assassinations and strife between the newly established government and opposition. In fact, issues among the various political parties led to the fall of Hamadi Jebali's government in February 2013 and to protests against *En-Nahda* coalition government, inflamed by the assassination of one of the opposition leaders MP Mohammad Brahimi on 25 July 2013. However, continual political upheaval and violence in Egypt convinced both the opposition and *En-Nahda* coalition to discuss possible scenarios for solving their divisions.

The *Union Générale Tunisienne du Travail* (UGTT) (Trade Union Federation), along with members of the employers' organization *Union Tunisienne de l'Industrie, du Commerce et de l'Artisanat* (UTICA) (Tunisian Union for Industry and Handicrafts), the Tunisian League for Human Rights and the national order of lawyers served as mediators between *En Nahda and the opposition*. After tense negotiations, Tunisian elites managed to come to an agreement that resulted in approving a new constitution that adheres to the pillars of a democratic system and appointing a caretaker government tasked with running parliamentary and presidential elections in October and November 2014.[3]

The domestic politics in Tunisia have been favourable for democratic reforms and the Tunisians have taken significant initial steps towards democracy. This domestic environment and political bargaining has made it easier for the EU to implement its democracy support instruments in Tunisia. Despite the blunt support of the EU to Ben Ali's regime, the EU is still viewed positively in Tunisia and Tunisians consider the EU as a legitimate actor in the region.[4] The agreement between the EU and Tunisia on a Privileged Partnership and the signature of a new Action Plan on 19 November 2012 focused mainly on economic development and democratic transition.

Economy, Financial Aid and Trade

The EU has been supporting economic development in Tunisia and other countries for a long time. In fact, it is the most advanced aspect of EU–Tunisia relations. Following the revolution, Tunisia has sought more EU support to address socio-economic problems and its marginalized regions.[5] A significant percentage of illegal migrants come from those regions. The EU approach regarding economic support has led to some improvements in comparison with the Ben Ali era. The EU agreed to provide more funding to develop marginalized regions and deal with social and economic imbalances. For example, the EU allocated EUR 12 million to reform the health-care systems in the poorest regions (European Commission 2012a).

With the Privileged Partnership, the EU 'reiterated its offer to gradually integrate Tunisia into the European internal market, to re-launch negotiations on liberalising trade in agriculture, to make rapid progress in the aviation discussions and to improve the mobility of EU citizens and Tunisians through the conclusion of a mobility partnership' (Council of the European Union 2012). The Privileged Partnership promised to increase the financial and technical aid to Tunisia, in addition to opening Tunisian agricultural products to the single market, advancing industry and liberalizing the service sector. While the liberalization of the service sector will facilitate European companies' access to the Tunisian market, reciprocity in this context is absent. Tunisians do not enjoy free movement in Europe and Tunisian companies have difficulties in getting the necessary visas to access the EU (B'Chir 2012).

When it comes to trade, the EU is considered Tunisia's primary partner. Access to the market has increased over the years, leading to deeper integration. With the exception of the slowdown in 2009 due to the euro crisis, trade relations between the EU and Tunisia have increased since the 2003. The EU absorbs around 74.1% of Tunisia's exports, while 66.9% of the country's imports come from the EU (European Commission 2012b). In 2008, Tunisia was the first Mediterranean country to remove tariffs for industrial products, thus, entering into a free trade area with the EU. Tunisia has become the EU's 31st largest trading partner (European Commission 2010a). Furthermore, on 14 December 2011, the negotiations for creating Deep and Comprehensive Free Trade Agreements (DCFTAs) with Egypt, Jordan, Morocco and Tunisia were adopted by the Council (European Commission 2014a). The DCFTA 'could lead to a gradual integration of Tunisia's economy into the EU single market. The main objective of the DCFTA is to bring Tunisian legislation closer to EU legislation in trade-related areas' (European Commission 2014a).

Democracy Promotion

At the democratic level, the EU created an observatory mission to monitor Tunisia's first post-revolution elections held on 23 October 2011. The elections were deemed free and fair by EU observers and other civil society and NGOs' groups. Another area that witnessed increased support from the EU and its member states is the judiciary that had been rife with corruption since the independence of Tunisia in the mid-1950s. Tunisians have trust issues with the justice system and new reforms are in place to address these issues in the judiciary. The EU's attempts to support this domain were blocked by the previous regime. However, as part of the Support for Partnership, Reform and Inclusive Growth (SPRING) programme launched by the EU in 2011, the EU has agreed (in October 2012) to increase its financial support to 'political/governance reform and inclusive economic growth, notably targeting the reform of the justice sector, capacity building of civil society, support to the renovation of popular neighbourhoods and support to the implementation of the association agreement and to the democratic transition' (European Commission 2013a).

EU support for civil society has gained momentum as well after being blocked by the previous regime. In the current reform period, many civil society groups in the EU and its member states are helping develop their Tunisian counterparts. Poland, for example, has set up a programme to support Tunisian civil society and democratic transition within the framework of *Support for Democracy 2012 in the form of foreign aid and training*. For example, the following projects were implemented in 2012, aiming at not only developing the civil societies' work but also educating the participants on the important role of active citizens and their relation to the state in a functioning democracy: 'Project I: Training programme for Tunisian youth non-governmental organisations (in cooperation with the Embassy of the Republic of Poland in Tunis); Project II: Study visit to Poland for Tunisian local leaders' (Polska Fundacja Międzynarodowej Współpracy na Rzecz Rozwoju 'Wiedzieć Jak' 2012).

Migration, Mobility and Security

The EU has used financial and technical assistance and conditionality to help keep its borders secured and the flow of illegal migrants under control. Soon after the revolution, the number of illegal migrants and asylum seekers originating from Tunisia increased significantly. This forced the EU to take several measures to tackle the issue (see European Commission 2010b, 2011b, 2011c on the European Commission's response to the migratory flows from North Africa). Furthermore, the EU and the Southern Mediterranean countries launched the *Dialogue for Migration, Mobility and Security* to strengthen the cooperation in this area. Regarding Tunisia, the Seahorse programme was launched in 2013 to enhance the Tunisian authorities' capacity to deal with irregular migration and illicit trafficking (European Commission 2013b). Tunisia will be the first MENA country to benefit from this initiative.

On 3 March 2014, the EU and Tunisia formally established a Mobility Partnership that focuses on facilitating the movement of people between Tunisia and the EU, managing migration and simplifying visa process. The EU support will also target the Tunisian authorities' efforts 'in the field of asylum, with a view to establishing a system for protecting refugees and asylum-seekers. Through this Partnership, the EU and Tunisia will not only develop their bilateral relations in the fields of migration, mobility and security, but will cooperate together to better meet the challenges faced in the Mediterranean' , according to Cecilia Malmström (EU Commissioner for Home Affairs) (European Commission 2014b).

In sum, some changes to the level of economic support addressing the urgent needs of the Tunisian political and economic reforms can be observed. The EU has been more involved in supporting Tunisia's efforts to deal with issues related to migration and mobility, marginalized areas, unemployment, economic growth, healthcare, institutional and political reform and building active civil society. Maintaining economic support is crucial to the efforts of the Tunisian authorities not only regarding political reforms but also to maintain security and stability in this EU neighbour. By helping Tunisia economically and supporting its reform, the EU would be dealing with the security concerns at their source and enabling the elites to implement democratic reforms. For example, by addressing the socio-economic reasons leading to illegal migration, the EU would be addressing this problem and providing the infrastructure for Tunisians to stay in their country. In sum, the EU's instruments in Tunisia focus on financial and technical assistance, conditionality and strategic instruments such as signing the privileged Partnership.

Libya

While Tunisia's toppling of Ben Ali was purely domestic, Libya's revolution came about through NATO intervention. Since the toppling of Gaddafi, Libya's domestic politics' situation has suffered from many security problems, lack of stability and increased crime levels. Despite the July 2012 elections in which non-Islamists won a majority, the new government was unable to immediately form.[6] The main task of the government involves stabilizing the country and addressing security concerns brought on by the various militias, an issue underlined by the killing of the American Ambassador J. Christopher Stevens by a jihadist militia in Benghazi on 11 September 2012.

The domestic political situation has not been conducive to democratic, institutional or economic reforms. The Libyan government has tried to address the security issue by 'declaring the south of the country a closed military zone and formally shutting the southern borders'; integrating the militias that participated in toppling Gaddafi in the security forces and military — with limited success (European Commission 2013c, 2). Up until now, the consecutive Libyan governments have failed to control or disarm the militias, provide security for the people, reform the infrastructure and restore the economy to pre-revolution levels. With this situation, there is a risk that Libya will become a failed state on the EU borders. In addition to the security problems, Libya is more divided than at any other time and that increases the need for national reconciliation and opening dialogue between the various tribes and conflicting groups. This lack of stability and security ties the EU hands with respect to supporting economic development and democracy promotion. As a result the EU can only afford to focus on security concerns.

It is important to note that the EU's involvement in Libya is much less when compared to its neighbours (Tunisia for example). While member states are playing a more active role in the institutional transition, the EU role has been very limited 'in particular in the demobilisation and integration of members of revolutionary brigades, the reorganisation of the armed forces and assistance in controlling land and sea borders' (European Parliament 2012). EU allocated resources and energy has been marginal. The European Parliament 'considers it regrettable that the EU contribution in the security sector is slow to materialise, and that difficulties in planning and implementing this contribution are leaving the field open to bilateral initiatives of doubtful visibility and consistency' (European Parliament 2012).

Post Revolution Measures: Technical, Financial and Humanitarian Aid

Among the first actions taken by the Commission, following the revolution, was allocating EUR 30 million in humanitarian aid to address 'the most immediate humanitarian needs in Libya and of displaced persons at the Tunisian and Egyptian borders' (European Commission 2011d). By January 2012, the EU became the biggest donor to Libya in terms of humanitarian aid in which the humanitarian and civil protection funding reached EUR 158,733,523 (European Commission 2012c).

The EU contribution to Libya's reforms amounted to EUR 79 million focusing on security, migration, institutional reform, democratic transition, healthcare, civil society and educational and vocational systems' reform. The security sector alone received EUR 24.3 million allocated as follows: 10 million to the rule of law and security sector reform; 4.3 million is allocated for criminal investigations and crisis response; 5 million for physical security and stockpile management (PSSM) of conventional weapons and ammunition; and another 5 million to dispose of unused munitions and provide Libyans a safe living environment (European Commission 2013c, 4).

The EU supported other programme, which are mainly of an economic nature: technical vocational education and training (EUR 6.5 million), healthcare (EUR 8.5 million), public administration and democratic transition, migration (EUR 19 million prior to the revolution in addition to 10 million as of 2011) and protection of vulnerable groups (EUR 4 million). All these programme not only support the economy and the quest for security, but also help in combating illegal migration by creating a safe working environment. At the moment, the EU is addressing the same areas (reconciliation, public administration capacity, civil society and integrating women in public life, migration, healthcare and education) with a budget of EUR 30 million (EEAS 2013). However, due to the increased violence and the lack of stability and security, the focus has been diverted to those areas.

Migration, Mobility and Security

The increasing number of migrants, refugees and asylum seekers that use the central Mediterranean route to get to Europe (see Figure 1) has forced the EU to concentrate on security and migration concerns. The instability and fragmentation of political control in Libya have made it easier for migrants (main nationalities are Eritreans, Somalis, other sub-Saharan Africans and Syrian nationals) to cross the Mediterranean via Libyan borders. This situation has pushed the Greek prime minister, Antonis Samaras to say that Libya is 'an open door to the Mediterranean Sea' (Daragahi and Spiegel 2013).

Therefore, the main concern for the EU in Libya is the migration issue as Libya is 'both a destination country for economic migrants and a transit country for irregular migrants and people in need of international protection, heading towards the EU' (European Commission 2014c). Therefore, at the beginning of 2014, the EU announced a new programme to support human rights-based migration management and asylum system. The EU allocated EUR 10 million to the programme, financed through the European Neighbourhood and Partnership Instrument (ENPI). The aim of this programme is to strengthen the Libyan authorities' capacities in border management and control. It also aims at limiting the number of those migrants who arrive in Libya (for better economic opportunities or escaping from conflict zones) from trying to cross the Mediterranean. In order to limit this migration, EU and Libyan officials have focused 'onimproving living conditions for migrants in retention facilities by reviewing administrative procedures, improving services provided to migrants and facilitating their access to the local labour market' (European Commission 2014c).

Most of the EU's instruments are of financial and technical nature, meant to help stabilize the country, address the urgent issues and maintain the borders' control. On one hand, the EU involvement in Libya has lacked

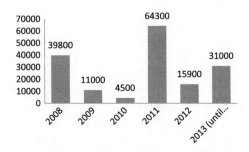

Figure 1. EU Illegal Border crossing via central Mediterranean
Source: see Frontex (online edition), 2014.

the necessary recourses to push for significant political reforms. On the other, the weak Libyan infrastructure and unfavourable domestic politics have created more challenges for both the Libyan authorities and the EU's active engagement. Despite the EU's support for democratic elections, Libya's current domestic politics and lack of stability have forced the EU to focus on stability and security, financial and technical assistance, training programme for security forces and border control. These threats pose great risk to EU security, forcing them to become its main focus.

Egypt

The violence that started during the last month of the Muslim Brotherhood rule continued even after the recent military coup and constitutional vote. Among the reasons for this is the polarization of the Muslim Brotherhood and those who oppose them. The military and the interim government, following the fall of Morsi, have taken several hostile measures including the persecution of most of the Muslim Brotherhood's senior leaders including the elected president Morsi. This instability had strained the economy, despite generous financial contributions from some GCC countries such as United Arab Emirates, Saudi Arabia and Kuwait. Under military rule, Egypt has seen limited stability, successfully electing a new President Abdel Fattah el-Sisi.

Instability in Egypt's domestic politics limits the EU's ability to push for more democratic reforms, as there is an urgent need to deal with more pressing stability and security concerns which continue to threaten Egypt's delicate economic situation. The persistent unrest in Egypt only heightens the EU's fear of illegal migration, especially in Greece and Italy. According to an EU diplomat, Egypt is 'a country of almost 90 million people on the EU's southern fringe. If things keep getting worse, where do you think that they will go?' (EUobserver 11 October 2013).

For many years, the EU has made minimal use of its democratic instruments, or has suspended their use in Egypt. The usage of positive conditionality, financial assistance and diplomacy to instil democracy did not work under the Mubarak regime and has since been ineffective after the revolution. The European Court of Auditors (ECA) documented the ineffectiveness of EU spending in various areas of governance before and after the January 2011 uprising. Karel Pinxten (ECA member responsible for the report) stated that the soft 'approach has not worked, and the time has come for a more focused approach which will produce meaningful results and guarantee better value for the European taxpayers' money' (ECA 2013). Following the outbreak of the revolution, the EU emphasized its support for 'the Egyptian population's legitimate request for their civil, political and socio-economic rights' (European Commission 2013d).

Democracy Promotion

Soon after Mubarak stepped down, there was hope among EU leaders that Egypt would finally move to civilian leadership after 60 years of military rule. The EU launched a package of EUR 20 million aimed at supporting civil society and approved programmes for 2011 in the amount of EUR 132 million that targeted Egypt's socio-economic problems (European Commission 2011e). The EU's offer to monitor the Egyptian parliamentary and presidential elections was declined by Egyptian authorities. Instead, the EUR 2 million (under the Instrument for Stability) was allocated to 'assist the High Electoral Commission in its work and provide support to civil society organisations' (European Commission 2011e). The EU showed readiness to start negotiations on Mobility Partnership and Deep and Comprehensive Free Trade Area (DCFTA), however, the Egyptians authorities did not move forward with this goal (European Commission 2011e).

The parliamentary and presidential elections increased the EU's support towards democratic and socio-economic reforms. Following former President Morsi's visit to Brussels in September 2012, the EU and Egypt agreed to establish an EU-Egypt Task Force that met in Cairo on 14 November, 2012. The EU pledged EUR 253 million (EUR 90 million euro from SPRING and EUR 163 million from Neighbourhood Investment Facility). In addition, the European Investment Bank and the European bank for reconstruction and Development each committed an annual EUR 1 billion for the period 2012–2013 (EU-Egypt Task Force: Co-chairs conclusions 13 November 2012). Štefan Füle emphasized that most of the financial package money was '(a) linked to continuing reforms and transformation; and (b) promised by financial institutions and linked to the existence of good projects' (*Ahramonline* 31 October 2013). However, no significant reforms and transformations were conducted since the fall of Mubarak. And since the end of Brotherhood rule, the priority has been to deal with instability. Even prior to the overthrowing of Morsi, the European parliament expressed concerns regarding democratic transition, freedom of expression, respect of human rights, rule of law and the increased social and sectarian clashes.

Diplomacy

The July 2013 military coup that resulted in the forceful removal of the democratically elected president Mohammed Morsihas increased the level of violence and social division. The ECA report and the political crisis in Egypt challenge the feasibility of using soft diplomacy in a polarized society plagued by political and social distrust. Though 'the EU achieved some success in building relations with new forces and mobilising economic support, it was unable to make any real mark on Egypt's turbulent political scene' (European Council on Foreign Relations 2013). The EU emphasis 'on incremental cooperation and sectoral reform seemed poorly aligned with the realities of Egyptian political life' (European Council on Foreign Relations 2013).

Catherine Ashton called upon all the parties to 'rapidly return to the democratic process, including the holding of free and fair presidential and parliamentary elections and the approval of a constitution, to be done in a fully inclusive manner' (ENPI 2013). This soft tone did not work during Mubarak's era and was criticized by the ECA report. It seems that 'Ashton's statement showed little evolution from the EU's attitude in the immediate wake of Mubarak's resignation where they called for a "transition towards democracy and for free and fair elections"' (West 2013). Ashton has been critical of the use of force and the attempt to isolate the Muslim Brotherhood. In her opinion, 'the repression of the Muslim Brotherhood will at best bring short-term stability while damaging further the prospects of building democracy' (Ashton in Dempsey 2013). The EU's diplomatic instrument was on display during Ashton's numerous visits to Egypt to mediate between the different political powers.

Threat of Sanctions

With the increase of violence in Egypt following the military coup, EU officials threatened to review not only its aid to Egypt but also its diplomatic ties.[7] Moreover, the European Parliament raised deep concerns regarding the escalation of violence in Egypt and the stalling of social, economic and political reforms. On 14 March 2013, the European parliament embraced a non-binding decision calling for an EU suspension of assistance in case 'no major progress is made regarding respect for human rights, and freedoms, democratic governance and the rule of law' (European Parliament 2013). However, no economic sanctions were imposed and aside from agreeing 'to suspend exports to Egypt of any equipment that can be used for internal repression and review any arms sales', EU leaders stopped 'short of explicitly agreeing to end such trade' (Pawlak and O'Donnell 2013). The decision not to impose economic sanctions 'reflects a concern that abruptly cutting aid could shut dialogue with Cairo's military rulers and damage Europe's ability to mediate in any future negotiations to end the worst internal strife in Egypt's modern history' (Pawlak and O'Donnell 2013).

In sum, the EU role has not been at full power in Egypt due to many domestic political issues. However, that does not mean that the EU cannot be more influential. The 'EU may not have the leverage of the annual aid that the United States gives ... but it enjoys something far more desirable at the moment — credibility' according to Yasser El-Shimy (International Crisis Group) (*Middle East Online* 30 July 2013). However, the EU has yet to utilize all its instruments and capitalize fully on its credibility in its relation with Egypt. Volker Perthes (German Institute for International and Security Affairs in Berlin) believes that the EU's financial assistance, and diplomacy and conditionality are not well utilized. The EU's 'package of money, markets and mobility (linked to human rights) for its southern and eastern neighbourhoods could be better used. Money is fine, but its uses are exaggerated, and markets can always be expanded' (Perthes in Dempsey 2013). Social and physical mobility are important, i.e. 'allowing people to travel, to live and study abroad in societies as open as those in Europe in order to see how they function and how political coalitions and compromises are made' (Dempsey 2013).

Moreover, in comparison to Tunisia and Libya, the EU is not the main player in Egypt: (1) the Egyptian military is closer to the American administration and (2) the influence of some GCC countries (mainly Saudi

Arabia, Kuwait and United Arab Emirates) who promised to support Egypt to the tune of USD 12 billion dollars right after the removal of the Muslim Brotherhood. This is in addition to other loans and funds that have since been awarded by the GCC countries.

Overall, the EU utilized different instruments according to the targeted country. Table 1 summarizes the main findings in the three cases:

Understanding the EU Response to the Arab Spring Events in North Africa

The EU involvement in Tunisia, Egypt and Libya has shown that unique domestic environments with varying levels of domestic political instability and social-economic uncertainty have influenced the prioritization of goals (stability in the MENA over democracy promotion) and the instruments used by the EU. As we can see, the most advanced relations have been with Tunisia followed by Egypt and Libya and this was the case as well even prior to the Arab Spring. Depending on the domestic politics of the targeted country, the EU customized the instruments it employed

Geostrategic Interests

EU foreign policy, towards the MENA region for example, can be better explained by a neorealist claim in which the normative attitude is secondary to other strategic materialistic interests (Hyde-Price 2006) (such as economic interests, security, fighting terrorism, illegal migration, etc.). Instability in the Arab World affects the security concerns of the EU with respect to migration and transnational terrorism. As we have seen earlier, at the beginning of the Arab Spring, the EU viewed the events as a window of opportunity for democracy, however, as the events developed, the security threat resulting from instability in the MENA pushed the EU to prioritize its security concerns.

In Tunisia, we see a focus on economic development, mobility and migration and to a lesser extent on democracy. This approach has been applied due to the more stable situation in Tunisia in comparison to the other two countries. Even though, when the events creating instability and some Tunisians migrated to southern Italy, the EU and its member states raised major concerns regarding that issue and how to tackle it if it escalated. Dealing with the reasons that led to the revolution in Tunisia (mainly socio-economic) became a priority, as it will help create stability and more jobs in Tunisia that will lower the percentage of illegal migrants. In the case of Libya, the escalating violence has made border security the issue of primary importance. As the paper showed, Libya is considered the point of departure for illegal migrants and asylum seekers for the central Mediterranean route. Egypt went through two stages: the Muslim Brotherhood era and the post-military coup. In both stages, the EU fear of chaos in its large southern neighbour created a fear of floods of migrants coming from there.

In sum, security concerns pushed the EU to address the threats at their point of origin. By helping the MENA countries maintain stability and address economic hardships, the EU would be maintaining its security in addition to protecting its interests and its borders.

RESPONSES TO THE 'ARABELLIONS'

Table 1. EU involvement in the MENA

EU	Goals	Instruments	Domestic situation in the targeted Country and cooperation of targeted countries' domestic elites
Egypt	• Security • Stability and Order	• Conditionality • Financial Assistance • Financial pledges for democratic reforms (prior to the military coup) • Technical Assistance and knowledge transfer • Diplomacy: Mediation among the conflicting parties • Suspension of some military exports	• Unstable domestic situation • Too many domestic hindrances for reforms • Have its own domestic agenda • Narrow margin for the EU to get involved • Weak compliance and cooperation from the post revolution elites • Strong military intervention in political life • Heavy involvement of other players: US and some GCC countries
Libya	• Borders' Security • Stability	• Minor Financial assistance • Technical instruments targeted at border's security issues • Humanitarian aid	• Unstable and chaotic domestic situation • Very weak infrastructure • Unfavourable for effective EU involvement
Tunisia	• With the toppling of Ben Ali: Democracy building. • Soon after that: Security and Stability • Maintaining its position as Tunisia's main economic partner	• Conditionality • Financial and technical assistance • Assistance for Democratic reforms • Strategic Instruments: Conclusion of Privileged partnership	• Favourable; EU is viewed as a strong ally and major player • Tunisian citizens and elites differentiate between some member states and the EU • Increased support for some member states such as Germany and Poland at the expense of France

Collective Identity and Self-Understandings

The EU has developed a foreign policy identity of a liberal democracy that privileges 'civilian' as well as 'soft' power. Therefore, with the beginning of the Arab Spring events, the EU viewed the events in the MENA region as an opportunity for democracy promotion. At the same time, the EU considered the whole range of its foreign policy instruments — including economy, trade, aid, security, diplomacy, etc. The EU issued few documents to deal with the new challenges (see Noutcheva 2014); however, when it comes to implementation, the main focus has been more on EU security concerns 'than a vibrant partnership between both shores of the Mediterranean' (Dias 2014, 54). Even the newly negotiated mobility partnerships aim at 'combating irregular migration and implement effective readmission and return policy' (Dias 2014, 54).

There is an agreement among all EU leaders that democracy promotion in the MENA is uncontested, however, in practice, it becomes harder to implement due to several difficulties such as domestic situation in the targeted country and lack of incentives. This leads to different scenarios in different countries. In Tunisia, we notice a variety of instruments implemented, including democratization instruments — such as support for civil society, reform of the judiciary and institutions. While in Egypt, the EU attempt to support democratic reforms was faced by: some resistance from Egyptian elites during the Muslim Brotherhood era; a military coup followed by chaos and instability; and involvement of other more attractive players (US and some GCC countries). In Libya, the EU focused on humanitarian and financial aid with special attention to stability and border control and security.

This utilization of a variety of instruments reflects the EU's self-understanding of what actions it views as crucial to its interests. This prioritization of the EU interests, and what instruments and tools to pursue these interests is based on the domestic politics of the targeted countries and is clearly reflected in the cases at hand. As for the European identity of a democratic power, its foreign policy is not supported in the EU reaction to the Arab Spring. At the beginning of the events, the EU viewed the events as a window of opportunity for democratic change without transforming these democratic aims into consistent empirical steps to be implemented in all the countries. Security remained a priority while democratic support did not witness much change in comparison to the pre-Arab Spring era.

Domestic and Bureaucratic Politics

When discussing the bureaucratic politics and the various actors involved at the EU level, we notice several complications and sometimes conflicting interests (see Noutcheva 2014). However, as this article focused on the implementation process and EU utilization of instruments, one can notice a few things: First, it is important to differentiate between what the EU does and what some member state do individually — which does not have to be contradictory. This issue was clear in Tunisia for example, with respect to civil society support and sharing the Polish experience with the Tunisian counterparts. In Libya, the limited EU role has pushed member states to play a more active role at various institutional and political levels. In Egypt, the division between the EU institutions and member states was apparent especially during the military coup and the aftermath violence.

When member states feel their interests are threatened (in Libya for example), they take initiatives themselves. In Libya, for example, the slow reaction following the fall of Gaddafi pushed some member states to take the initiative and support borders control and security. The bureaucratic/internal EU politics matter as Noutcheva discussed in her article when drafting the policies. Therefore, one might look at rivalries and conflicts between the various EU institutions involved in foreign policy such as the Commission, the European External Action Service (EEAS) as well as at the interaction between the Commission, the EEAS and the Council bureaucracy. However, these interactions do not necessarily impair the EU's utilization of instruments or its effectiveness on the ground as we have seen in the three cases.

Conclusion

The Arab Spring caught the EU by surprise. Even though the EU launched a critical review of the ENP focusing on how to reform it, a lot of work still remains. The EU's democratization efforts have not been successful in the region due to its focus on security and stability at the expense of democracy. The EU's response to the Arab Spring events has been selective. The EU is heavily involved in Tunisia, and to a lesser extent Libya and Egypt. Among the reasons for this selective approach is the domestic politics in the targeted countries. Nevertheless, the EU is viewed more positively than other players in some MENA countries due to its credibility (that is based on its soft power) and its historic relations with the region.

The EU goals in the MENA region have not moved away from its previous prioritization of security and stability. Democracy promotion as a goal became a priority with the outbreak of the Arab Spring events; however, with the deterioration of stability in MENA, security and stability concerns have once again emerged as the EU's primary concerns. As for the instruments, the EU has mainly relied on financial and technical assistance, positive conditionality and diplomacy. Yet, we see some variation depending on the targeted country's domestic politics. For example, in Tunisia, the focus has been on financial assistance, technical assistance, conditionality and increased support for democratic transition. In Egypt, the focus has been on financial and technical assistance and diplomacy. In Libya, the EU instruments were mainly minor financial assistance, humanitarian aid and technical instruments targeted at border's security issues.

What emerges from the case studies is that the variation in the degree of stability in the MENA countries determines the variation in instruments used. So the level of instability and insecurity in these countries is a key characteristic of the domestic politics variable, with Libya being the most unstable, Tunisia the most stable and Egypt in-between. The EU use of instruments is in line with the realist argument — which complies with one of the explanations put forth by the introduction of this special issue (Börzel, Dandashly, and Risse 2014).

Acknowledgements

The author would like to thank professors Tanja Börzel and Thomas Risse in addition to the participants at the two workshops, held in Berlin on 8–9 June 2012 and 25–26 October 2013, for their comments and feedback on earlier draft of this paper. Moreover, the author would like to thank the Centre for Global Studies (CFGS) at the University of Victoria (Victoria, Canada) for hosting him for few months in 2013 and giving him the opportunity to work on his research and present it. The comments and feedback from the CFGS staff have been very helpful.

Notes

1. The 'Action Plans should [...] include measures to improve the efficiency of border management, such as support for the creation and training of corps of professional non-military border guards and measures to make travel documents more secure. The goal should be to facilitate movement of persons, whilst maintaining or improving a high level of security' (European Commission 2004, 16–17).
2. Interview with a member of the Tunisian National Constituent Assembly, October 2013.
3. By the time of writing, the second free and fair parliamentary elections (post Ben Ali) took place on 26 October 2014 with 60% of the registered voters participating. The elections' official provisional results show a victory of *Nidaa Tounes* (a secular party that was formed after the fall of Ben Ali by Beji Caid el Sebsi – a former prime minister from 27 February 2011 to 24 December 2011), which won around 38% out of the total 217 seats, while *Ennahda* party came second with 31% (Turak 2014).
4. Interviews with various members of the Tunisian Constituent Assembly and government officials, October 2013.
5. Marginalized regions are mainly regions outside the major cities that have not been developed for a long time and suffer from lack of infrastructure, lower education and lack of job opportunities.
6. Following the July 2013 parliamentary election, Dr. Mustafa Abu-Shagour was elected to succeed Abdurrahim El-Keib as Prime Minister in 2012. Abu Shagour's appointment 'represented a critical opportunity for the true independents and local interest groups to form an executive protected from destructive party politics that dominated the GNC' (Megrisis 2013). However, Abu-Shagour failed to receive congressional approval for his cabinet's nominees due to his 'failing to properly respect the power of local political groups and mishandling the bitter reaction of Mahmoud Jibril, [the head of the National Forces Alliance, which is one of the largest political parties in Libya,] opponent in the race for prime minister, to defeat' (Megrisis 2013). This caused few months delay before Prime Minister Ali Zidan secured the approval of the General National Congress to his new government that included 'a mixture of liberal figures and Islamists as he tries to build a coalition acceptable to all parties' (*BBC* 31 October 2012).
7. The EU called for a meeting in order 'to discuss whether the 5 billion (£3.2 billion) in loans and grants it has set aside for Egypt will make it there now that Morsi [...] is no longer in charge' (Ramsey 2013).

References

Ahramonline. 2013. *Inclusive political dialogue key to EU support for Egypt: EU commissioner.* 31 October. http://english.ahram.org.eg/NewsContent/1/64/85139/Egypt/Politics-/Inclusive-political-dialogue-key-to-EU-support-for.aspx (accessed 12 January 2014).

B'Chir, N. 2012. Tunisie — UE: Partenaire privilégié … Ni partenaire ni privilégié? [EU-Tunisia privileged partnership … Neither partnership nor privileged?] *Business News-Tunisia*, 20 November.

Balfour, R. 2012. EU Conditionality after the Arab Spring. Papers IEMed 16: 1–33.

BBC. 2012. *Libyan parliament approves new government*, 31 October. http://www.bbc.com/news/world-africa-20152538 (accessed 28 February 2014).

Behr, T. 2012. The European Union's Mediterranean policies after the Arab Spring: can the Leopard change its spots? *Amsterdam Law Forum* 4, no. 2: 76–88.

RESPONSES TO THE 'ARABELLIONS'

Börzel, T.A. 2011. When Europe hits ... across its borders. Europeanization and the near abroad. *Comparative European Politics* 9, no. 4: 394–413.

Börzel, T.A., A. Dandashly, and T. Risse. 2014. Responses to the "Arabellions": the EU in comparative perspective – Introduction. *Journal of European Integration* 37, no. 1: 1–17.

Börzel, T.A., and T. Risse. 2012. From Europeanisation to diffusion: introduction. *West European Politics* 35, no. 1: 1–19.

Börzel, T.A., and V. van Hüllen. 2014. One voice, one message, but conflicting goals: cohesiveness and consistency in the European Neighbourhood Policy. *Journal of European Public Policy* 21, no. 7: 1033–49.

Council of the European Union. 2008. *Report on the implementation of the European security strategy — providing security in a changing world.* S407/08, 11 December.

Council of the European Union. 2012. *EU Tunisia Association Council.* PRESS/12/479. 19 November.

Daragahi, B., and Spiegel, P. 2013. Libya instability fuels EU migrant fears. *Financial Times*, 28 October.

Dempsey, J. 2013. Influencing Egypt with soft power. *The New York Times*, 2 September.

Dias, V.A. 2014. A critical analysis of the EU's response to the Arab spring and its implications for EU security. *Human Security Perspectives* 10, no. 1: 26–61.

Echagüe, A., H. Michou, and B. Mikail. 2011. Europe and the Arab Uprisings: EU vision versus member state action. *Mediterranean Politics* 16, no. 2: 329–35.

EEAS. 2013. *Libya*, http://eeas.europa.eu/libya/ (accessed 10 October 2013).

ENPI. 2013. *Ashton: EU wants to help Egypt find its way to democracy in an inclusive way.* 4 October. http://www.enpi-info.eu/medportal/news/latest/33773/Egypt:-Ashton-urges-all-sides-rapidly-to-return-to-democratic-process (accessed 14 October 2013).

EU-Egypt Task Force: Co-chairs conclusions. 13 November 2012. http://www.consilium.europa.eu/ue docs/cms_data/docs/pressdata/EN/foraff/133511.pdf (accessed 12 January 2014).

EUobserver. 2013. EU fears economic migrants from Egypt'. 11 October. http://euobserver.com/for eign/121757 (accessed 30 January 2014).

European Commission. 2004. *Communication from the Commission, European Neighbourhood Policy.* Strategy Paper{SEC(2004) 564, 565, 566, 567, 568, 569, 570}/*COM/2004/0373 final*/

European Commission. 2010a. *Trade: bilateral relations — Tunisia*, http://ec.europa.eu/trade/creating-opportunities/bilateralrelations/countries/tunisia/index_en.htm (accessed 28 March 2012).

European Commission. 2010b. *Commission proposes better management of migration to the EU.* IP/11/532. 4 May.

European Commission. 2011a. *A new response to a changing neighbourhood: a review of European neighbourhood policy.* Joint Communication by the High Representative of the Union For Foreign Affairs And Security Policy and the European Commission. COM(2011) 303, 25 May.

European Commission. 2011b. *Frequently asked questions: addressing the migratory crisis.* MEMO/11/273, 4 May.

European Commission. 2011c. *The European Commission's response to the migratory flows from North Africa.* MEMO/11/226. 8 April.

European Commission. 2011d. *Joint Communication to the European Council, The European Parliament, the Council, the European Economic and Social Committee and the Committee of the Regions. A Partnership for Democracy and Shared Prosperity with the Southern Mediterranean.* COM(2011) 200 final. 8 March.

European Commission. 2011e. *The EU's response to the 'Arab Spring'.* MEMO/11/918. 16 December.

European Commission. 2012a. *Tunisia: more EU support for judiciary and health care.* http://ec.europa.eu/commission_2010-2014/fule/headlines/news/2012/10/20121002_en.htm (accessed 12 January 2013).

European Commission. 2012b. *Memo — mission for growth: creating economic ties to benefit Tunisia and the EU.* Memo/12/920.

European Commission. 2012c. *Humanitarian aid and civil protection-Libyan Crisis.* http://ec.europa.eu/echo/files/aid/countries/factsheets/libya_en.pdf (accessed 12 August 2014).

European Commission. 2013a. *EU's response to the "Arab Spring": The state-of-play after two years.* MEMO/13/81. 8 February.

European Commission. 2013b. *EU action in the fields of migration and asylum.* MEMO/13/862. 9 October.

European Commission. 2013c. *ENP Package — Libya.* MEMO/13/250. 20 March.

European Commission. 2013d. *EU-Egypt relations.* MEMO/13/751. 21 August.

RESPONSES TO THE 'ARABELLIONS'

European Commission. 2014a. *Trade: Countries and Regions: Tunisia.* (last update 19 May 2014) http://ec.europa.eu/trade/policy/countries-and-regions/countries/tunisia/ (accessed 12 August 2014).

European Commission. 2014b. *EU and Tunisia establish their mobility partnership.* IP/14/208. 3 March.

European Commission. 2014c. *Supporting human rights-based migration management and asylum system in Libya.* MEMO/14/26. 20 January.

European Council on Foreign Relations. 2013. *Middle East and North Africa — Egypt,* http://www.ecfr.eu/scorecard/2013/mena/56 (accessed 15 October 2013).

European Court of Auditors (ECA). 2013. Press Releases, Court of Auditors — ECA/13/18 18/06/2013, http://europa.eu/rapid/press-release_ECA-13-18_en.htm (accessed 30 September 2013).

European Parliament. 2012. *European Parliament Report on the implementation of the Common Security and Defence Policy* (based on the Annual Report from the Council to the European Parliament on the Common Foreign and Security Policy). 12562/2011 — 2012/2138(INI)), October 31. http://www.europarl.europa.eu/sides/getDoc.do?type=TA&reference=P7-TA-2012-0455&language=HR (accessed 12 August 2014).

European Parliament. 2013. *European Parliament Resolution P7_TA(2013)0095 on the situation in Egypt.* http://www.europarl.europa.eu/sides/getDoc.do?type=TA&reference=P7-TA-2013-0095&language=EN (accessed 12 August 2014).

Frontex (online edition). 2014. Update on Central Mediterranean Route. http://frontex.europa.eu/news/update-on-central-mediterranean-route-5wQPyW (accessed 30 January 2014).

Grimm, S., and J. Leininger. 2012. Not all good things go together: conflicting objectives in democracy promotion. *Democratization* 19, no. 3: 391–414.

Huber, D. 2014. A pragmatic actor — the US response to the Arab uprisings. *Journal of European Integration* 37, no. 1: 57–75.

Megrisis, T. 2013. Libya's house of cards. *MUFTAH.* http://muftah.org/libyas-house-of-cards/ (accessed 28 February 2014).

Middle East Online. 2013. Europe takes over from the US to resolve Egypt's Crisis, 30 July. http://www.middle-east-online.com/english/?id=60455 (accessed 2 September 2013).

Noutcheva, G. 2014. Institutional governance of European neighbourhood policy in the wake of the Arab Spring. *Journal of European Integration* 37, no. 1: 19–36.

Pace, M. 2014. The EU's interpretation of the 'Arab Uprisings': understanding the different visions about democratic change in EU-MENA Relations. *Journal of Common Market Studies* 52, no. 5: 969–84.

Pace, M., and F. Cavatorta. 2012. The Arab uprisings in theoretical perspective — an introduction. *Mediterranean Politics* 17, no. 2: 125–38.

Pawlak, J., and J. O'Donnell. 2013. Europe shies away from cutting aid for Egypt'. *Reuters,* 21 August. http://www.reuters.com/article/2013/08/21/us-egypt-protests-eu-idUSBRE97K0WE20130821 (accessed 28 February 2014).

Ramsey, A. 2013. Egypt's Foreign Aid isn't going anywhere fast. *Vice,* 28 August. http://www.vice.com/en_uk/read/egypts-foreign-aid-isnt-dissapearing-anywhere-fast1 (accessed 28 February 2014).

Schumacher, T. 2011. The EU and the Arab spring: between spectatorship and actorness. *Insight Turkey* 13, no. 3: 107–19.

Teti, A. 2012. The EU's first response to the 'Arab Spring': a critical discourse analysis of the partnership for democracy and shared prosperity. *Mediterranean Politics* 17, no. 3: 266–84.

Teti, A., D. Thompson, and C. Noble. 2013. EU democracy assistance discourse in its new response to a changing neighbourhood. *Democracy and Security* 9, no. 1–2: 61–79.

Turak, N. 2014. Nidaa Tounes leads Ennahdha by strong margin. *Tunisialive,* http://www.tunisia-live.net/2014/10/27/nidaa-tounes-leads-ennahdha-by-strong-margin/ (accessed 28 October 2014).

West, T. 2013. EU ineffective in Egypt once again. European Foundation, http://www.europeanfoundation.org/tom-west-eu-ineffective-in-egypt-once-again/ (accessed 12 June 2014).

Wouters, J., and S. Duquet. 2013. *The Arab Uprisings and the European Union: in search of a comprehensive strategy.* Leuven Centre for Global Governance Studies, Working Paper No. 98, January.

A Pragmatic Actor — The US
Response to the Arab Uprisings

DANIELA HUBER

Middle East and Mediterranean Department, Istituto Affari Internazionali, Rome, Italy

ABSTRACT   After the US had initially assessed the Arab uprisings as an opportunity and displayed a dual role understanding as an anchor of security and modest advocate of democracy, the second role understanding faded the more the US perceived the uprisings as a risk rather than an opportunity. In respect to practice, the US response did not show clear patterns in terms of goals or instruments it pursued, which would correspond to the development of these role understandings or to predefined geostrategic interests. Indeed, it seems that the US has switched from default to ad hoc modus in its foreign policy in the region which challenges both, the rational actor, as well as the normative actor model. Instead, it might be more appropriate to speak of a pragmatic actor who had to navigate through an array of constraints, including new realities in the MENA region on one hand and domestic and bureaucratic politics in the US on the other.

Introduction

As the Arab uprisings spread throughout the Arab world and US friends and foes alike tumbled or fell, a surprised Obama administration seemed to muddle its way through rather than reacting with a clear strategic vision. Observers immediately explained this by the long-standing tension between 'pursuing American "values" (US foreign policy idealism) and protecting American "interests" (foreign policy realism)' (Atlas 2012). However, rather than posing values against interests, it is *two normative preferences* in the Middle East which are producing a tension in US foreign policy: a normative preference for a stable order which the US believes fosters the security of

Israel, the secured flow of energy to keep the global economy running, and the global fight against terrorism[1] — and a normative preference for a democratic order. While the US foreign policy establishment has shown a propensity to believe that both preferences coincide in the long term (Ish-Shalom 2006), they frequently clash in the short term (see the introduction of the special issue on the democratization–stabilization dilemma).

That the normative preference for a democratic order has entered US foreign policy in the Middle East is a relatively recent phenomenon. While the US had inserted human rights and democracy elements into its foreign policy toward South America and Eastern Europe already under the Carter and Reagan administrations, in the Middle East throughout the cold war and in its immediate aftermath, it sought to uphold a stable order which would guarantee its security and energy interests in the region, even if this came at the cost of bolstering autocracy. Indeed, it seems that the unprecedented moment of US dominance in the Middle East in the 1990s came at the cost of democracy in the whole region. Below graph with Freedom House data for the Middle East, the Gulf, and North Africa, while by no means showing causations, still indicates that it was during the US' unipolar moment in the region that it lived through its most autocratic period since the 1970s.[2]

While the end of the cold war had thus not been a real turning point in US relations with the Arab world in terms of fostering democracy, this moment came with 9/11. Facing a highly uncertain world, the Bush administration began to see the lack of democracy in the Arab world as the breeding ground for 'the ideologies of murder' (Bush 2003) and developed its Freedom Agenda which made democracy promotion a US mission toward 'every nation and culture' (Bush 2005), even though its focus was on the Middle East. It justified the Iraq war with its democracy agenda which did not only bring about deep contradictions to the US' democracy agenda (Carothers 2006), but damaged the whole Western democracy agenda (Carothers 2009; Whitehead 2009). The Bush administration established the US–Middle East Partnership Initiative (MEPI), a democracy assistance program for the Middle East which — similar to the EU's EIDHR — focuses on bottom-up civil society assistance. It also sharpened its tone toward Egypt. While the US still felt dependent on the Egyptian regime in terms of guaranteeing Israel's security, overflight rights for the Afghanistan and Iraq wars, and cooperation against Al-Qaeda, it was also increasingly worried about the succession question of the ailing Egyptian president. Attempting to 'allow sustainable pro-US alternatives, other than Mubarak's heir apparent and the religiously conservative Muslim Brotherhood' (Brownlee 2012, 70), the US started to pressure for an opening of the political system. It did not only express its dismay on the imprisonment of AymanNour — the liberal opposition candidate for the presidency — but also advocated freer parliamentary elections in 2005. In that year Secretary of State Condoleezza Rice stated in Cairo 'that it is time to abandon the excuses that are made to avoid the hard work of democracy' (in Kessler 2005). This led to some degree of opening in Egypt, and in the region. Local analysts such as Dina Shehata acknowledged that the strong attention that the Freedom Agenda generated in the Middle East provided 'some kind of protection. All eyes were on Egypt, and it was hard for the regime to be too heavy-handed' (in Brownlee 2012, 88). The Bush administration celebrated the opening periods in several Middle Eastern countries (see Graph 1) as a 'Baghdad Spring' and 'Arab Spring.'

This democracy euphoria, however, was soon cushioned when electoral gains of political Islam kicked in relatively free elections in Iraq, Egypt, and Lebanon in the 2005/2006 period. Crowned by the electoral victory of Hamas in the 2006 parliamentary elections in Palestine, this represented a foreign policy disaster for an administration that had been entirely driven by its Freedom Agenda in pushing the Palestinian Authority to hold free elections and that consequentially was being caught off guard by Hamas' electoral victory according to then Secretary of State Condoleezza Rice herself (Weisman 2006). The dilemma between the two normative preferences for a stable and a democratic order in the Middle East appeared in full verge: while democratisation is likely to lead to peace and stability in a region in the long term as suggested by the democratic peace theory,[3] in the short term, it might not only increase the likelihood of war (Mansfield and Snyder 1995, 2002) — as in the case of Palestine where a fratricidal war between Fatah and Hamas started, fuelled by the US (Asseburg 2007, 3); but it might also bring forces to power which challenge both, the US preference for a democratic, as well as a stable order. As a result, the Bush administration backtracked on its Freedom Agenda and what emerged 'was a policy caught between free trade liberalisation, as the positive route to eventual democratization, and domination, to the extent that it increasingly favoured regional stability, the continuation of long-term security interests and the undermining of regimes that challenged its hegemony over the region' (Hassan 2012, 127).

Barack Obama's rise to presidency imbued people in the region with hopes for a 'new beginning' (Obama 2009) in US–Arab relations. Facing not only a world but also a home public increasingly doubtful of democracy promotion, the Obama administration at first de-emphasized the issue (Carothers 2012) and qualified it by highlighting the necessity of being a good example at home as in its 2010 National Security Strategy (Obama

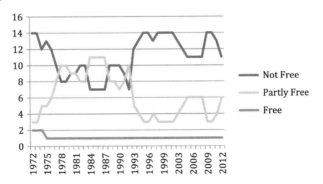

Graph 1. Freedom House data by country for the Middle East, Gulf, and North Africa 1972–2012
Source: Freedom House (2013).

2010) or when Obama distanced himself from the coercive imposition of democracy and gave more emphasis to universal human rights as in his Cairo speech (Obama 2009). Despite these differences in rhetoric, in practice the Obama administration largely continued democracy promotion in the Middle East where Bush had left it, namely through a low-risk gradual approach which did not endanger regional stability (Carothers 2012; Gerges 2011; Hassan 2012). Increasingly, the US focused on some key interests in the region only, while shifting its attention to South Asia and the Asia-Pacific region, and to issues such as the global economy and nonproliferation. But as the US was withdrawing from Iraq, protests in the Arab world peaked, turning into a wave of protests that swept across North Africa, the Middle East, and the Gulf. The uprisings forced the US not only back into the region, but also to the issue of democracy promotion. How has it reacted to the uprisings?

This article is divided in three parts. The first section observes how the US perceived the uprisings and its own role in them on the rhetorical level over time. It shows that the US initially saw the uprisings as an opportunity for the spread of democracy and voiced a dual role perception as an anchor of regional security as well as a modest advocate of democratic change. When the US increasingly saw the developments in the region as risky, its role understanding as a modest advocate of democratic change was voiced less frequently. The article then turns from rhetoric to practice and analyzes US goals and instruments in its reaction to the Arab uprisings across countries over time. It shows that the US response does not display a consistent pattern in terms of goals and instruments which would correspond to these role understandings (and therefore the normative actor model) or to predefined geostrategic interests (and therefore the rational actor model). Rather, the article argues in the third section, the US response suggests a pragmatic actor who has navigated through an environment conditioned by new realities on the ground on one hand and a hesitant home public and the interests of US foreign policy institutions on the other.

US Perceptions of the Uprisings and Role Understandings

Initially, like in Europe, the uprisings in the Arab world were perceived in relatively positive terms in the American public and among policy-makers. In April 2011, 42% of the public believed that the Arab Spring would lead to lasting improvements for people living in those countries (Pew Research Center for the People and the Press 2012a). President Barack Obama and Secretary of State Hillary Clinton almost immediately raised terms such as 'transition,' 'democracy,' 'liberation,' or 'freedom' in speeches on the uprisings in countries such as Tunisia, Egypt, or Libya. Most instructive is the president's landmark speech on the Middle East and North Africa at State Department in May 2011. In it, Obama interpreted the uprisings as a 'story of self-determination,' as one of the 'times in the course of history when the actions of ordinary citizens spark movements for change,' even linking the uprisings to turning points in the US' own democratic history such as the rebellion against the British in the eighteenth century or the civil rights movement of the 1950s and 1960s (Obama 2011c).

Obama also pointed out which role he thought the US should play in this 'historic opportunity': as in the past, the US would continue to pursue a 'set of core interests in the region: countering terrorism and stopping the spread of nuclear weapons; securing the free flow of commerce and safe-guarding the security of the region; standing up for Israel's security and pursuing Arab-Israeli peace.' At the same time, a set of core principles which the US stands for would similarly enjoy top priority now — opposition against the use of violence and repression, and the support for a set of universal rights, as well as political and economic reform. This would help the US to be perceived in the region as a power which welcomes change, but he also added that the US must show a 'sense of humility' which acknowledges that it is 'not America that put people into the streets of Tunis or Cairo — it was the people themselves' and it is them that 'must ultimately determine their outcome' (Obama 2011c). Thus, the US role, as understood by the president, should be dual: it should remain an *anchor of regional security* but at the same time boost its role of being *a modest advocate of democratic change*, i.e. an actor who supports democratic change, but based on local ownership not external force. Similar perceptions of the uprisings and understandings of the US role in it can be found in Obama's and Clinton's speeches in 2011 and the first half of 2012.[4]

However and again similar to the EU, this perception changed over the course of time, notably in September 2012 with the attack on the US diplomatic post in Benghazi. For the first time, the uprisings started to be connected to extremism that can hit the US. In her reaction to the bombing, then Secretary of State Hillary Clinton referred to the US normative preference for building a safe and stable world and for its role as an anchor of security when she remarked that it 'is especially difficult that this happened on 11th September. It's an anniversary that means a great deal to all Americans. Every year on that day, we are reminded that our work is not yet finished, that the job of putting an end to violent extremism and building a safe and stable world continues' (Clinton 2012a). New vocabulary entered the interpretation of the uprisings. The Secretary of State now argued that 'this is a remarkable moment in history, if we were just to step back for a time and look at what is happening around the world. But it is also a time that is fraught with *anxiety and insecurity, uncertainty, and danger*' (Clinton 2012b, italics added). Indeed, the Benghazi bombing represented a moment of reinterpretation of the uprisings and a public debate of the US role in the region lived up, not least also since it became an issue in the presidential race. Mitt Romney, the Republican presidential nominee, did not only emphasize the risks of the uprisings and the growing threat of militantIslamism,[5] but also attacked Obama's 'passivity,' 'lack of leadership,' and 'restraint' in influencing outcomes in the region (Kirkpatrick 2012). In October 2012, the percentage of the public which believed that the Arab Spring would lead to lasting improvements for people living in those countries had dropped from 42 to 25% (Pew Research Center for the People and the Press 2012a).

The perception that the Arab uprisings represented a tinderbox rather than a positive turning point for the region further increased in 2013 with the violence which followed the ouster of elected Egyptian President Mohamed Morsi in Egypt, as well as with the use of chemical weapons in Syria's civil war. In his speech at the United Nations in September 2013, Obama referred to the uprisings no longer in transition terms but focused on the issues of violence, extremists, and sectarian conflict (Obama 2013c). The public debate on the role the US should play in the region also lived up again. But except for the 'barking' of single senators such as Republican John McCain or Democrat Robert Menendez in and on Egypt, opinion surveys (Pew Research Center for the People and the Press 2013b) and the debate on the Syria intervention rather encouraged the administration to backpedal on its role as a modest advocate of democracy. In a mid-term policy review which had been pursued over the turbulent summer in the Middle East, democracy was not raised as a core interest anymore (Landler 2013). In his speech at the United Nations in September 2013, the president hardly referred to the US role as an advocate of democracy and portrayed this issue mainly as a responsibility of the international community, whereas he argued for unilaterally protecting US core interests in the region (containing external aggression, securing the flow of energy, dismantling terrorism and weapons of mass destruction). Indeed, he stated that in the remainder of his presidency the issues his administration will focus on are security issues: the nuclear deal with Iran, Israeli–Palestinian peace, and Syria (Obama 2013c). The US role as an anchor of regional security and its normative preference for a stable order clearly took priority again.

Has variance in these role understandings in the early and later phases of the Arab uprisings been mirrored in goals and instruments in the US response in practice? While this section has focused on variance in the general perception in the US of the Arab uprisings and its own role in them over time, the next section examines variance in the US response in practice over time and across five countries: Tunisia, Egypt, Bahrain, Libya, and Syria. As will be seen, the US response does not display clear patterns of goals and instruments which would fall neatly into the US self-understanding of being an 'anchor of regional security' and/or 'advocate of democracy' or the related IR paradigms of a rational or normative actor. Instead, its practice rather suggests a *pragmatic actor* whose response has been characterized by ad hoc reactions conditioned by rapidly changing and often uncertain situations on the ground on one hand and domestic and bureaucratic politics in the US on the other.

US Goals and Instruments in its Reaction to the Arab Uprisings

Tunisia

Tunisia would have been an ideal case to unconditionally support a democratic transition since the US does not have substantial security interests in the country and the small and largely homogeneous country was initially seen as an 'inspiration' (Obama in Bull 2011) for other states in the region. Therefore, the democratization–stabilization dilemma did not apply in the case of Tunisia. However and in contrast to the EU, Tunisia has not become a focal point of US foreign policy in the region. When the protests in Tunisia were gathering momentum, the US at first reacted in default mode and merely urged all sides for restraint and the regime to respect the right of assembly. It did not employ diplomatic pressure. As Secretary of State Hillary Clinton pointed out in an interview to Al Arabiya, 'we are not taking sides, but we are saying we hope that there can be a peaceful resolution. And I hope that the Tunisian government can bring that about' (Department of State 2011). Only when Ben Ali stepped down on January 14, Obama urged the 'Tunisian Government to respect human rights and to hold free and fair elections in the near future that reflect the true will and aspirations of the Tunisian people' (Obama 2011a). In the initial period, an array of high-level diplomatic visits was deployed to Tunisia, which did not, however, translate in a significant boost of US assistance. Since the revolution, the US has allocated about USD 350 million to Tunisia (Department of State 2013) with a declining tendency and with most of the money going to the security sector, followed by support to the economy and lastly democracy (Greenfield, Hawthorne, and Balfour 2013, 15).

Egypt

As in Tunisia, Washington initially reacted in default mode to the uprising in Egypt and stuck to its long-time ally Hosni Mubarak. On January 25, 2011, Secretary of State Hillary Clinton asserted that 'our assessment is that the Egyptian Government is stable' (Clinton 2011). Only when continuously increasing protests made Mubarak a liability for the US, did it support his ouster, but not revolutionary change. To the contrary, Washington began to back the idea of an 'orderly transition' — a gradual transition toward democracy that would also guarantee stability. Obama, as Martin Indyk pointed out, 'set in place a plan for the Egyptian military to play the role of midwife to a democratic transition in Egypt, preserving stability, honouring the treaty with Israel, and ensuring a peaceful transition to democracy' (Brookings 2011). Supported by the US, the Supreme Council of the Armed Forces (SCAF) staged a coup and Mubarak was removed, while the security establishment was left in place. Similar to the Bush administration's approach of gradual democratization in the region, also Obama preferred a managed process which would not endanger US security interests and be dominated by economic liberalization.[6]

To this effect, in February 2011, Washington also announced USD 100 million in economic aid and USD 65 million to support the political transition. In May 2011, Obama announced further initiatives including a USD 1 billion debt relief, USD 1 billion in OPIC loans and guarantees for infrastructure projects, USD 700 million for small- and medium-sized enterprises, the establishment of an Egyptian-American Enterprise Fund, and a Middle East trade and investment partnership (US Embassy to Egypt 2012). While this mainly focused on economic issues, actual aid delivery has been limited, since the US — like the EU — tied much of it to Egypt reaching an agreement with the International Monetary Fund (IMF).

Furthermore, US aid to Egypt was conditioned by Congress on the government meeting its obligations under the 1979 peace treaty, as well as on its transition to civilian government, free elections and respect of freedom of expression, association, and religion. The second condition, however, played a subordinated role. Aid was typically not withheld in response to Egypt's lack of meeting these democracy requirements, but when American interests were threatened.[7]

In the meantime, events on the ground took on a life of their own in a rapidly evolving situation which forced the US out of its 'default policy' toward Egypt. Robert Springborg has likened the ensuing situation to the early 1950s when the US was trying to identify the dominant political force in Egypt, shortly flirted with the Muslim Brotherhood but eventually placed its bet on Gamal Abdel Nasser (Springborg 2013). After the 2012 presidential elections, the administration assumed that the Muslim Brotherhood was the strongest political force and started to engage it, while Congress send clear signals to the new Egyptian leadership that Israeli security had to be guaranteed. In September 2012, after the Israeli embassy in Cairo was attacked, Congress used negative conditionality in holding back a first USD 450 million cash transfer being envisaged as part of a USD 1 billion debt relief payment, expressing concerns over Egypt meeting its obligation under the 1979 Egyptian–Israeli peace treaty.[8] The signal had arrived in Cairo, where the Muslim Brotherhood signaled willingness to cooperate with the US in terms of fostering a free-market economy, as well as guaranteeing status quo relations with Israel (Gerges 2013). Indeed, the US relationship with the Muslim Brotherhood, while 'work in progress,' was developing to the point that the administration prioritized its newly evolving security relations with the Brotherhood over democracy. In November 2012, when the conflict on Gaza escalated once more with Israel leading Operation Pillar of Defence, Morsi condemned the operation, but played a key role in mediating a ceasefire. US Secretary of State Hillary Clinton met Morsi in Cairo to encourage this role and largely refrained from criticizing Morsi's controversial constitutional declaration of 22 November 2012, in which the Egyptian President increased his executive power and sought to neutralize the power of the judiciary — a turning point in the societal polarization of Egypt which had been underestimated by the US.

When Morsi was ousted from power, Washington sent mixed signals to Egypt (see McInerney and Bockenfeld 2014). On one hand, Obama stated that the US 'continues to believe firmly that the best foundation for lasting stability in Egypt is a democratic political order with participation from all sides and all political parties' (Obama 2013b). He also employed some negative conditionality when he delayed the shipment of F-16 fighter jets to Egypt, cancelled a joint military exercise, and announced the withholding of some of US military aid to Egypt. On the other hand, this was undermined by Secretary of State John Kerry who defined the ouster as a restoring of democracy (Gordon and Fahim 2013), so legally enabling the continuation of US military aid to Egypt. Nonetheless, the administration still tried to limit aid in line with new Congressional legislation — only military aid related to border security in the Sinai and to counterterrorism operations continued. Egypt has since then regressed significantly in terms of democratic rights and freedoms which has become maybe most obvious in the massive arrests, as well as show trials against members of the Muslim Brotherhood, which have been sentenced to death. Nonetheless, in April 2014, Washington announced the release of USD 650 million as well as 10 Apache helicopters to Egypt. Even though these issues are controversially discussed in Congress (McInerney and Bockenfeld 2014), it currently seems that the US approach toward Egypt has reverted back to default mode.

Bahrain

In Bahrain, the US response to the Shiite uprising has been largely void of an own US approach which has fallen victim to the US prioritization of its relations with Saudi Arabia. The US has neither pursued positive or negative conditionality nor assistance policies given that the rich Gulf state never received large amounts of aid and that the US–Bahraini relationship has been traditionally based on a security relationship where the US transferred arms or military training (McInerney and Bockenfeld 2014, 16). Also diplomacy and conditionality have been limited.

The violent crackdown against Shiite protestors by the king in Bahrain was initially criticized by Washington. However, when Saudi Arabia and the United Arab Emirates (UAE) sent in military and police forces in March 2011 at the request of the Bahraini monarchy to the Gulf Cooperation Council (GCC), the White House merely issued a statement which urged restraint, respect to the rights of the people of Bahrain, and support for dialogue, but did not back up rhetoric with action. Instead, it set out to restore its relations with Saudi Arabia which had been deeply troubled by the US support for the ouster of its long-standing ally Mubarak. In April 2011, Secretary of Defense Robert Gates travelled to Saudi Arabia and in his conversation with Saudi King Abdullah, Gates did not raise the issue of Saudi troops in Bahrain, while the discussion did touch the issue of Iran abusing the uprising (Timberg 2011). Nonetheless, following a report by Amnesty International of Western arms sales to repressive countries in the Middle East, Congress members expressed concerns on an upcoming US arms deal with Bahrain and the administration suspended the deal in October 2011, but resumed it again in May 2012 shortly after its announcement of an enormous arms deal with Saudi Arabia, as well.

Libya

In contrast to Europe, the US does not have substantial security or energy interests in Libya. The instruments and goals it pursued have to a substantial degree been driven by its European allies and have prioritized security. The US response to the uprising in Libya was characterized by hesitancy both in terms of military intervention, as well as assistance. When the uprising started, the US initially imposed sanctions on the Gadhafi regime, but was wary of military intervention. While France and the United Kingdom (UK) were pushing for an intervention for which US military support was be crucial, President Obama hesitated, until Benghazi was on the verge of falling. Being backed up by a UN resolution (which was however overstretched by the intervention as Russia and China pointed out), and supported by the Arab League and the GCC Operation Odyssey Dawn began in March 2011. Following the military intervention, the US also committed USD 187 million for urgent humanitarian and security needs (Department of State 2012b) and provided targeted assistance, mainly in the area of security (issues such as securing conventional weapons, building military capacities to address specific threats, counterterrorism, border security), less for economic strengthening or for democratic transition.

Syria

Syria is a country of major interest for the US. It borders Iraq, has been Iran's closest ally since the Iran–Iraq war, has allowed Iran to transport weapons through its territory to Hezbollah, but has at the same time driven a status quo policy with Israel on the Golan over the past decades. In light of its crucial geostrategic position, the US response to the uprising and ensuing civil war in Syria has maybe most starkly illustrated the lack of an own strategic vision, and therefore, of concrete goals for the country. It has been characterized by hesitancy, ad hoc reactions, and has at times bordered mismanagement of foreign policy. Instead of a proactive policy which the Syrian opposition or Turkey lobbied for, the US has mainly reacted to an augmentation of violence in the conflict — ranging from negative conditionality through initial sanctions, to multilateral diplomacy such as the backing of an Arab League resolution which called for Assad to step down (vetoed by China and Russia in February 2012), to the indirect and limited use of force with the delivery of small arms and ammunition to the opposition (Mazzetti, Gordon, and Landler 2013) after the White House for the first time asserted that the Assad regime has used chemical weapons on a small scale and Obama stated that this was a red line in August 2012. When chemical weapons were used on a large scale in August 2013, Obama was forced to act in order to maintain his credibility. However, the initial threat of a military attack, the subsequent hesitancy of the administration to act by putting the issue to Congressional approval, and the face-saving exit option of the Russian proposal, all undermined US credibility not only in the international but also the domestic arena. A Pew poll showed that the issue did large damage to Obama's standing with for the first time negative ratings for his handling of foreign policy and with his job approval rating edging into negative territory (Pew Research Center for the People and the Press 2013b).

Thus, the US response to the Arab uprisings and their aftermath has been characterized by an incoherency within the observed country cases where ad hoc reactions have often contradicted each other in terms of goals as in Egypt or in terms of instrument as in Syria. Also, a comparison across countries (see Table 1) reveals that the response has not been characterized by a consistent pattern of instruments and goals.

RESPONSES TO THE 'ARABELLIONS'

Table 1. US response by country, goals, and instruments

	Goals	Instruments
Tunisia	Security first, but also	Low levels of aid and diplomacy
Egypt	democracy and economy	Conditionality, aid, diplomacy
Libya		Force, conditionality, low levels of aid and diplomacy
Bahrain	Good relations with Saudi-Arabia	Low levels of diplomacy and conditionality
Syria	Lack of a strategic vision, limited security goals	Low levels of force (threat of force, delivery of weapons to opposition), conditionality, multilateral diplomacy

In terms of goals, the US has continued to prioritize security in Egypt, Tunisia, and Libya, but has also tried to reconcile this goal with economic and democracy goals in those countries which has often led to a significant degree of inconsistent signaling, notably in the case of Egypt. In Bahrain, the US response was void of a goal for Bahrain as such; rather its goal has been to maintain good relations with Saudi Arabia. In Syria, the lack of a clear strategic vision for the country has led to limited security goals, such as preventing the use of weapons of mass destruction.

In terms of instruments, the US has used force in Libya, but not in Syria where no international consensus existed and the US instead resorted to the inconsistent threat of force and the limited arming of the opposition. Negative conditionality was mainly deployed in terms of sanctions in Libya and Syria, but also in terms of tying aid to conditions in Egypt. Positive conditionality was hardly applied. Frontrunners like Tunis, for example, received a fractional amount of the aid that Cairo has received, even though Egypt has regressed significantly in terms of democratic rights and freedoms. In estimates for fiscal year 2014, Egypt receives about USD 1509 million of which USD 1308 million is security assistance, while Tunisia receives about USD 56 million (McInerney and Bockenfeld 2014, 45–47). Indeed, the US has been rather hesitant to allocate aid in general to the region and has instead sought to activate multilateral channels in this respect, such as the IMF or the Deauville Partnership. Diplomacy has been used in all cases. However, often it has not been backed up by action as in the case of Bahrain which has limited the effect of this instrument.

When comparing this response to US foreign policy before the Arab uprisings, one notices a disturbance of the previous default policy of supporting autocratic allies, notably in the engagement of the Obama administration with the Muslim Brotherhood. At the same time, no new default policy has been emerging. Rather, the US reaction to the uprisings has indicated an incoherent ad hoc policy. What then explains this US response?

Explaining the US Response

The first explanatory track put forward in the introduction to this volume suggests a rational actor who follows predefined geostrategic interests as theorized by diverse variants of realism. However, the US reaction to the uprisings makes it difficult to speak of such a rational actor. The US has rather shown an uncertainty what its geostrategic interest would be, notably in the case of Syria. This uncertainty has largely been the result of the rapid and often chaotic changes in the region, during which it was not always straightforward for Washington to assess the dynamics of change and its own interests. Equally, it is not possible to speak of a normative actor who followed a clear collective role identity — the second explanatory track put forward in the introduction. While the US has changed its role identity as a foreign actor in the Arab Spring from a dual understanding of being an anchor of security/an advocate of democracy to being an anchor of security only as the first section of this article has shown, these role identities have not been translated into clear patterns of action as the second section has shown. In Bahrain, the US has not bothered at any time of the uprising to appear as an advocate of democracy, not even a modest one. In Syria, due to its inaction, the US has clearly failed to be the anchor of security it announced to be. In Egypt, in contrast, it has tried to combine both security and democracy goals during the uprisings, as well as its aftermath. Thus, while the US' role understanding changed over time, its practice in Egypt did not.

This is not to claim that these role understandings and their related normative goals such as a stable or democratic order in MENA do not exist. Rather, the US has been confronted with a new and often highly confusing situation in a region where it could not react any longer in default mode but switched to ad hoc mode and acted pragmatically as it had to maneuver through an environment conditioned by new local and regional realities on one hand and domestic constraints on the other: a home public hesitant to engagement abroad and the interests of foreign policy institutions in the US which are frequently entangled with the interests of US key allies in the region.

New Local and Regional Constraints

The US is facing new local and regional limits to action in the Middle East and North Africa. The uprisings have posed the US in front of often chaotic situations in regional key states like Egypt or Syria during which it was not only difficult for Washington to assess the dynamics of change and its own interests in them, but also to influence them. In his 2013 State of the Union, Obama stated that '(w)e cannot presume to dictate the course of change in countries like Egypt' (Obama 2013a). Indeed, as Fawaz Gerges has pointed out, it is the indigenous revolutions in the Middle East and North Africa which have revealed the limits of US power (Gerges 2011, 106). In contrast to the past, where the US could simply deal with autocratic rulers and their inner power circles, neither the US nor new regimes in the region will be able any longer to ignore the preferences of their people which will constitute an important veto power even if autocratic rule in the region continues.

Besides domestic structural change in allied states, the regional environment is transforming deeply. While it might be too early to speak of the end of the 'Sykes-Picot' order — a synonym for the Western imposition of the Westphalian state system on the former area of the Ottoman Empire — the Arab uprisings have increased the number of failed states in the region which do not hold a monopoly of power on their areas. Borders, states and security systems are breaking down in North Africa and the larger Sahel (Cristiani *et al*. 2014), as well as in the Iraq–Syria–Lebanon triangle in the Middle East. Sectarian conflict and alternative state structures built up by actors such as the Islamic State of Iraq and Greater Syria (ISIS) in the region pose new dilemmas to US action. The Syrian conflict has well illustrated this problem since the US can neither support the Assad regime nor unanimously the rebels whose ranks have increasingly included extremist forces and al-Qaeda affiliates.

Furthermore, while the US remains the most important power in the region, other states are challenging its power more than in the 1990s and early 2000s. This is, on one hand, a result of the decision of the Obama administration to reorient its focus away from the Middle East toward Asia. As the hesitant reactions to the uprisings in Tunisia and Libya (seen as the responsibility of the Europeans) or Bahrain (seen as the responsibility of Saudi Arabia) have indicated, the US will in the future more strongly rely on its allies in the region when it comes to areas that are not touching its core interests. On the other hand, this is also a result of the Iraq war and the instability it brought to the region which has led regional powers to drive more assertive and independent policies. These include Russia in the Syrian context and Iran in the Syrian, Iraqi, and Israeli context (article on Russia, this special issue), but also allies like Saudi Arabia which has been pursuing a more independent foreign policy to protect its interests in the region. It did not only offer unconditioned USD 12 billion to the new military regime in Egypt, but also announced to substitute US military aid to Egypt should it be cut, thus undermining US conditionality policies.

A Hesitant Home Public

Another conditioning factor for US action in MENA is a public fatigue to employ American troops and taxpayers' money abroad and notably in MENA. While this fatigue has followed the Afghanistan and Iraq invasions, it has further increased in 2010 with the financial crisis which Americans partially attributed to these interventions. Consequentially, as the surveys of the Chicago Council on Global Affairs has shown, public support for cutting back foreign aid and an opposition to new military entanglements has increased steadily (Smeltz 2012). For the Middle East, this has meant that for the first time in 2012 a majority of Americans (52 and 53%, respectively) has favored the reduction of economic and military aid to Egypt (Smeltz 2012, 26–27; Pew Research Center for the People and the Press 2013a), a trend that can even be found in respect to economic and military aid to Israel for which support has declined as well.[9] Numbers are even higher when it comes to military entanglements in the Middle East.

In March 2011, 63% of Americans believed that the US had no responsibility to act in Libya, seeing the over commitment of US military forces as the best argument for not using military force in Libya (Pew Research Center for the People and the Press 2011). Also in the case of Syria, the same percentage believed the US does not have a responsibility to act in December 2012 and opposed airstrikes in September 2013 (Pew Research Center for the People and the Press 2012b, 2013b). This public mood has been mirrored in Congress which has pursued cuts in the foreign aid budget in 2011 in face of a budgetary crisis — exactly when the Arab uprisings started. The Middle East and North Africa Incentive Fund proposed by the Obama administration to support the transitions in the region fast and flexibly with USD 770 million has not been passed by Congress. A scaled-down version is now included in the 2014 budget but its fate seems rather bleak at the time of writing. Furthermore, Congress also held back aid to the region that had been approved due to skepticism about new political forces in Egypt or Libya. It also appeared rather skeptical of both, the Libya and a potential Syria intervention.

Bureaucratic Politics and the Influence of Key Allies

Finally, the US response has also been inconsistent due to the actions which diverse bureaucratic institutions have taken in line with their own interests which have often become entangled with the interests of key allies of the US in the region, notably Israel and Saudi Arabia. The Israeli–US relationship is long-standing, developed already during the presidency of Harry S. Truman, and strengthened in the wake of the Six-Day War when Israel became a key ally of the US in the region. Washington acknowledged the swift victory of Israel over Egypt, Jordan, and Syria as an asset and perceived Israel as an important counterweight to balance pro-communist and, later on, fundamentalist forces in the region. The relationship became increasingly special to the extent that the security of Israel represents a core interest of the US today (Gerges 2011, 27–68; Little 1993). In this context, the Camp David Accords and the peace treaty between Egypt and Israel were a milestone success for US policy in the region. Since the US perceived the Egyptian public as hostile to the accords it became complicit in bolstering autocracy in Egypt. It 'protected Egyptian rulers from foreign threats, heavily subsidized the Egyptian armed forces, and bolstered the Egyptian security services' (Brownlee 2012, 4).

The uprisings have once more brought this to the forefront, notably also since protest movements had deep roots in the Egyptian antiwar movement of the early 2000s against the Israeli reaction to the second Intifada, the Anglo-American invasion of Iraq, Israeli operations in Gaza, as well as the 2006 Israel–Lebanon war. On one hand, the US did not want to be seen as working against the tide of history. This position was notably taken by the White House, but also Secretary of State Hillary Clinton and US Ambassador to Egypt Anne Patterson, which all showed a preference to go forward with a managed transition process and to engage the Muslim Brotherhood when it captured the revolution. On the other hand, the

Pentagon which has a long-standing institutionalized relationship with the Egyptian army, as well as the State Department under John Kerry who prioritized Israeli–Palestinian peace talks over democratization issues, took a more 'traditional' stance. While the Morsi period had shown some degree of cooperation with the US — not least also due to an economic dependence of any Egyptian government on the influence of the US in international financial institutions — cooperation on antiterrorism, notably in the Sinai Peninsula, had been smoother under military rule in Egypt. As a result, Pentagon backed up Israel's heightened lobbying efforts after the ouster of Morsi not to cut military aid to Egypt (Ben-Zvi 2013; Lis 2013), supported by Secretary of State John Kerry. Both institutions pushed internally for a continuation of aid while the White House preferred at least a partial suspension of aid. This also led to a high degree of mixed signaling. In a trip to Cairo in early November 2013, John Kerry, for example, contradicted National Security Advisor Susan Rice who had criticized the situation in Egypt while he appreciated progress made (Rogin 2013).

Similar dynamics developed in the Gulf context. Like the US–Israeli relationship, the almost 80 yearlong US–Saudi relationship intensified during the cold war, even though it has never been as consolidated as the US–Israeli relationship and has lived through several crises. As Milton-Edwards has put it 'the association between the United States and Saudi Arabia has been cultivated more by necessity than natural political affinity' (Milton-Edwards 2011, 284). Driven mainly by the US interest in Saudi Arabia oil reserves, observers have questioned the longevity of the relationship with the shale gas revolution in the US, but Saudi Arabia remains crucial for the US in terms of an ensured energy supply to a running world economy, cooperation on counterterrorism, shared concerns about the Iranian nuclear file, as well as in terms of major arms sales — in 2010 Pentagon announced military sales to Saudi Arabia with a potential value of USD 60 billion (Blanchard 2012). Indeed, Pentagon has a vested interest in the US–Saudi relationship and it was Secretary of Defense Robert Gates who travelled to Riyadh in April 2011 to restore relations after the White House and State Department had initially backed reforms in Bahrain at least rhetorically. An alarmed Saudi Arabia lobbied intensely in Washington for the view that Iran had hijacked the uprising and in May 2011, Obama stated that we 'recognize that Iran has tried to take advantage of the turmoil there, and that the Bahraini government has a legitimate interest in the rule of law' (Obama 2011c). The US has therefore sacrificed the Bahraini uprisings to its relations with Saudi Arabia which are nonetheless continuing to enter shaky water with the US–Iranian nuclear deal and alleged talks between the US and Iran on security cooperation in Iraq.

Conclusions

This article has shown that, like the EU, the US initially assessed the Arab uprisings as an opportunity and displayed a dual role understanding as an anchor of security and modest advocate of democracy. The second role understanding faded the more the US perceived the uprisings as a risk rather than an opportunity. These role understandings have, however, not neatly translated into clear patterns in terms of practice. Rather, this article has argued that the US response to the Arab uprisings has been characterized by a lack of a consistent pattern of goals and instrument (comparable to the inconsistent EU response, see Dandashly 2014). The US has switched from default to ad hoc mode in the Middle East which suggests that the US has neither been a strategic actor nor a normative power (similar to the EU, see Noutcheva 2014). Instead, it might be more appropriate to speak of a pragmatic actor who had to navigate through a region characterized by new realities and through a domestic arena where a hesitant domestic home public and the interests of foreign policy institutions and key allies have also constrained the US response.

In the longer term, it is likely that US foreign policy in the region will switch back to default mode. Washington's policy toward Egypt in the aftermath of the ouster of Morsi suggests a restoring of 'business as usual' with a military-led regime. Nonetheless, some changes which have become evident in this article might remain. The US might increasingly rely on the EU in the region, especially when it comes to areas that are not part of its core interests, such as Tunisia or Libya. Some division of labor between the US and EU has already emerged in this respect. Furthermore, there has already been more cooperation between the US and the EU, notably in Libya, but also in Egypt, where conditions attached to aid have been streamlined with those of the IMF or where the EU and the US cooperated on a diplomatic solution in the standoff which emerged after the ouster of Morsi. Nonetheless, cooperation in the areas of security, economy, and democracy could be further institutionalized which would give both the US and the EU higher bearing in a region where other actors are increasingly trying to assert their influence, as well.

Acknowledgements

The author would like to thank the editors of this volume, as well as Nathalie Tocci and Riccardo Alcaro for their comments on earlier versions of this article.

Notes

1. Note that in the remainder of this article, the terms 'stable order' and 'security' will be used in this specific US understanding, i.e. a stable order is one that the US sees as beneficial for the security of the US, Israel, and the flow of energy.
2. As Halliday (2005) has argued, paradoxically Arab countries enjoyed more freedom during the cold war than since the fall of the USSR.
3. On the pitfalls of politicizing an academic theory, see Ish-Shalom (2008).
4. Another good example is Obama's address to the nation on the situation in Libya in which he states his belief that 'this movement of change cannot turned back' and that '(f)or generations, the United States of America has played a unique role as an *anchor of global security* and as an *advocate for human freedom*' (italics added), that only the people in the region can dictate the pace and scope of change, but that the US 'can make a difference' (Obama 2011b).
5. It should be noted that US administrations have differentiated between militant and political Islam which became maybe most obvious in the aftermath of 9/11 when US politicians started to present

RESPONSES TO THE 'ARABELLIONS'

Turkey's Justice and Development Party (AKP) as a model worthy of emulation in the whole region, see Taspinar (2007) and the article of Ayata (2014).
6. In his keynote address on the Arab Spring in May 2011, Obama argued that the road to democratization would go through economic liberalization: 'We think it's important to focus on trade, not just aid; and investment, not just assistance. The goal must be a model in which protectionism gives way to openness; the reigns of commerce pass from the few to the many, and the economy generates jobs for the young. America's support for democracy will therefore be based on ensuring financial stability; promoting reform; and integrating competitive markets with each other and the global economy' (Obama 2011c).
7. After a crackdown on civil society in Egypt, the administration threatened to withhold aid not in response to the crackdown, but to press Cairo on lifting a travel ban on *American* civil society representatives which had fled in the US embassy. In March 2012, when the travel ban was lifted, Secretary of State Hillary Clinton waived new legal conditions of Congress on US aid to Egypt 'on the basis of America's national security interest' (Department of State 2012a).
8. On a detailed overview of aid delivery and Congressional legislation on the issue, see Greenfield, Hawthorne, and Balfour (2013), Sharp (2013), and McInerney and Bockenfeld (2014).
9. Forty-five per cent prefer to keep economic aid, 41% think it should be decreased or stopped (up 7% points since 2010). Regarding military aid, 15% want to increase it, 45% prefer to keep it, and 38% want to decrease or stop it (Smeltz 2012, 31).

References

Asseburg, M. 2007. *Hamastan vs. Fatahland. Fortschritt in Nahost?* http://www.swp-berlin.org/common/get_document.php?asset_id=4155.

Atlas, P.M. 2012. US Foreign Policy and the Arab Spring: balancing values and interests. *Digest of Middle East Studies* 21, no. 2: 353–85.

Ayata, B. 2014. Turkish foreign policy in a changing Arab world: rise and fall of a regional actor? Journal of European Integration 37, no. 1: 95–112.

Ben-Zvi, G. 2013. *Report: Pentagon asked* Israel to pressure Obama, congress to continue providing aid to Egypt, http://www.algemeiner.com/2013/12/25/report-pentagon-asked-israel-to-pressure-obama-congress-to-continue-providing-aid-to-egypt/

Blanchard, C.M. 2012. *Saudi Arabia: background and US* relations. Congressional Research Service. http://www.fas.org/sgp/crs/mideast/RL33533.pdf

Brookings. 2011. *Assessing Obama's Middle East policies*, http://www.brookings.edu/events/2011/11/21-obama-middle-east

Brownlee, J. 2012. *Democracy prevention the politics of the US-Egyptian alliance.* Cambridge: Cambridge University Press.

Bull, A. 2011. *Obama Hails Tunisia as inspiration of Arab Spring.* Reuters, http://www.reuters.com/article/2011/10/07/us-usa-tunisia-idUSTRE7966J520111007

Bush, G.W. 2003. *President discusses the future of Iraq*, http://georgewbush-whitehouse.archives.gov/news/releases/2003/02/20030226-11.html

Bush, G.W. 2005. *Inaugural address,* http://www.presidency.ucsb.edu/ws/index.php?pid=58745

Carothers, T. 2006. The backl ash against democracy promotion. *Foreign Affairs* 85, no. 2: 55–68.

Carothers, T. 2009. *Democracy promotion under Obama: finding a way forward.* Carnegie endowment for international peace. http://carnegieendowment.org/files/democracy_promotion_obama.pdf

Carothers, T. 2012. *Democracy policy under Obama: revitalization or retreat?* http://carnegieendowment.org/2012/01/11/democracy-policy-under-obama-revitalization-or-retreat/8z6x

Clinton, H. 2011. *Remarks with Spanish Foreign Minister Trinidad Jimenez after their meeting. Remarks.* US Department of State, http://www.state.gov/secretary/rm/2011/01/155280.htm

Clinton, H. 2012a. *Remarks on the deaths of American Personnel in Benghazi, Libya.* US Department of State, http://www.state.gov/secretary/rm/2012/09/197654.htm

Clinton, H. 2012b. *Remarks at the Saban Center for Middle East Policy 2012 Saban forum opening gala dinner.* US Department of State, http://www.state.gov/secretary/rm/2012/11/201343.htm

Cristiani, D., A. Dessi, W. Mühlberger, and G. Musso. 2014. *Africa and the Mediterranean. Evolving security dynamics after the Arab uprisings.* IAI-GMF Mediterranean Papers No. 25. http://www.iai.it/content.asp?langid=2&contentid=1056.

Dandashly, A. 2014. The EU response to regime change in the wake of the Arab revolt: differential Implementation. *Journal of European Integration* 37, no. 1: 37–56.

RESPONSES TO THE 'ARABELLIONS'

Department of State. 2011. *Interview with Taher Barake* of Al Arabiya, http://www.state.gov/secretary/rm/2011/01/154295.htm

Department of State. 2012a. *US support for Egypt,* http://www.state.gov/r/pa/prs/ps/2012/03/186709.htm

Department of State. 2012b. *US Government Assistance to Libya,* http://www.state.gov/s/d/met/releases/198354.htm

Department of State. 2013. *Tunisia,* http://www.state.gov/r/pa/ei/bgn/5439.htm

Freedom House. 2013. *Country ratings and status by region,* FIW 1973-2013. http://www.freedomhouse.org/report-types/freedom-world

Gerges, F.A. 2011. *Obama and the Middle East: The end of America's moment?* New York, NY: Palgrave Macmillan.

Gerges, F.A. 2013. What changes have taken place in US foreign policy towards Islamists? *Contemporary Arab Affairs* 6, no. 2: 189–97.

Gordon, M., and K. Fahim. 2013. Kerry says Egypt's military was 'Restoring Democracy' in ousting Morsi. *The New York Times,* 1 August. sec. World / Middle East, http://www.nytimes.com/2013/08/02/world/middleeast/egypt-warns-morsi-supporters-to-end-protests.html

Greenfield, D., A. Hawthorne, and R. Balfour. 2013. US and EU: lack of strategic vision, frustrated efforts toward the Arab transitions. Atlantic Council, http://www.atlanticcouncil.org/images/publications/US_EU_Lack_of_Strategic_Vision_Frustrated_Efforts_Toward_Arab_Transitions.pdf

Halliday, F. 2005. *The Middle East in international relations.* Cambridge: Cambridge University Press.

Hassan, O. 2012. *Constructing America's freedom agenda for the Middle East: democracy or domination,* 1st edn. Abingdon: Routledge.

Ish-Shalom, P. 2006. Theory as a hermeneutical mechanism: the democratic-peace thesis and the politics of democratization. *European Journal of International Relations* 12, no. 4: 565–98.

Ish-Shalom, P. 2008. Theorization, harm, and the democratic imperative: lessons from the politicization of the democratic-peace thesis. *International Studies Review* 10, no. 4: 680–92.

Kessler, G. 2005. Rice criticizes allies in call for democracy. *The Washington Post,* 21 June, http://www.washingtonpost.com/wp-dyn/content/article/2005/06/20/AR2005062000468.html

Kirkpatrick, D. 2012. Attack in Libya shows contrasting views of Obama and Romney. *New York Times,* 21 October, http://www.nytimes.com/2012/10/22/us/politics/benghazi-and-arab-spring-rear-up-in-us-campaign.html?pagewanted=1&_r=1&

Landler, M. 2013. Rice offers a more modest strategy for mideast. *New York Times,* 26 October, http://www.nytimes.com/2013/10/27/world/middleeast/rice-offers-a-more-modest-strategy-for-mideast.html?pagewanted=1&utm_campaign=MB%2010.28.13&utm_medium=email&_r=1&utm_source=Sailthru&ref=middleeast&utm_term=*Morning%20Brief%2010-24-13%20through%2011-04-13&

Lis, J. 2013. Washington cuts Egypt aid despite intense israeli lobbying. *Haaretz,* 10 October, http://www.haaretz.com/news/diplomacy-defense/1.551666

Little, D. 1993. The making of a special relationship: the United States and Israel, 1957–68. *International Journal of Middle East Studies* 25, no. 4: 563–85.

Mansfield, E.D., and J. Snyder. 1995. Democratization and the danger of war. *International Security* 20, no. 1: 5–38.

Mansfield, E.D., and J. Snyder. 2002. Democratic transitions, institutional strength, and war. *International Organization* 56, no. 2: 297–337.

Mazzetti, M., M. Gordon, and M. Landler. 2013. U.S. Is said to plan to send weapons to Syrian Rebels. *The New York Times,* 13 June. sec. World / Middle East, http://www.nytimes.com/2013/06/14/world/middleeast/syria-chemical-weapons.html

McInerney, S., and C. Bockenfeld. 2014. The Federal Budget and Appropriations for Fiscal Year 2015. Democracy, Governance, and Human Rights in the Middle East and North Africa. *Project on Middle East Democracy,* http://pomed.org/wp-content/uploads/2014/06/FY2015-Budget-Report.pdf

Milton-Edwards, B. 2011. *Contemporary politics in the Middle East.* Cambridge: Polity Press.

Noutcheva, G. 2014. Institutional governance of European neighbourhood policy in the wake of the Arab Spring. *Journal of European Integration* 37, no. 1: 19–36.

Obama, B. 2009. *A new beginning,* http://www.whitehouse.gov/blog/NewBeginning/transcripts

Obama, B. 2010. *National Security* Strategy 2010, http://nssarchive.us/?page_id=8

Obama, B. 2011a. *Statement on the situation* in Tunisia, http://www.presidency.ucsb.edu/ws/index.php?pid=88899&st=&st1=

Obama, B. 2011b. *Address to the nation on the situation* in Libya, http://www.presidency.ucsb.edu/ws/index.php?pid=90195&st=&st1=

Obama, B. 2011c. *Remarks by the president on the Middle East and North Africa*, http://www.whitehouse.gov/the-press-office/2011/05/19/remarks-president-middle-east-and-north-africa

Obama, B. 2013a. *Remarks by the president in the state of the union address*, http://www.whitehouse.gov/the-press-office/2013/02/12/remarks-president-state-union-address

Obama, B. 2013b. *Statement on the situation in* Egypt, http://www.presidency.ucsb.edu/ws/index.php?pid=103820&st=&st1=

Obama, B. 2013c. *Remarks by President Obama in address to the United* Nations general assembly, http://www.whitehouse.gov/the-press-office/2013/09/24/remarks-president-obama-address-united-nations-general-assembly

Pew Research Center for the People and the Press. 2011. *Public wary of military intervention in Libya*, http://www.people-press.org/2011/03/14/public-wary-of-military-intervention-in-libya/

Pew Research Center for the People and the Press. 2012a. *On eve of foreign debate, growing pessimism about Arab Spring aftermath*, http://www.people-press.org/2012/10/18/on-eve-of-foreign-debate-growing-pessimism-about-arab-spring-aftermath/

Pew Research Center for the People and the Press. 2012b. *Public says U.S. does not have responsibility to act in Syria*, http://www.people-press.org/2012/12/14/public-says-u-s-does-not-have-responsibility-to-act-in-syria/

Pew Research Center for the People and the Press. 2013a. *Public backs cutoff of military aid to Egypt*, http://www.people-press.org/2013/08/19/public-backs-cutoff-of-military-aid-to-egypt/

Pew Research Center for the People and the Press. 2013b. *Opposition to Syrian airstrikes surges*, http://www.people-press.org/2013/09/09/opposition-to-syrian-airstrikes-surges/

Rogin, J. 2013. Exclusive: John Kerry defies the White House on Egypt policy. *The Daily Beast*, 18 November, http://www.thedailybeast.com/articles/2013/11/18/exclusive-john-kerry-defies-the-white-house-on-egypt-policy.html

Sharp, J.M. 2013. Egypt: background and US relations. *Congressional Research Service*, http://www.fas.org/sgp/crs/mideast/RL33003.pdf

Smeltz, D. 2012. Foreign policy in the new millennium. *Results of the 2012 Chicago council survey of American Public Opinion and US Foreign Policy. Chicago Council on Foreign Affairs*, http://www.thechicagocouncil.org/UserFiles/File/Task%20Force%20Reports/2012_CCS_Report.pdf

Springborg, R. 2013. The Nasser playbook for dealing with Abdel Al-Sisi. *Foreign Affairs*. November, http://www.foreignaffairs.com/articles/140242/robert-springborg/the-nasser-playbook

Taspinar, O. 2007. The US and Turkey's quest for EU membership. In *Turkey and the European Union: internal dynamics and external challenges*, eds. J.S. Joseph, 191–210. Basingstoke: Palgrave Macmillan.

Timberg, C. 2011. Gates has 'warm' meeting with Saudi Arabia's King Abdullah. *Washington Post*, http://articles.washingtonpost.com/2011-04-06/world/35231673_1_saudi-troops-saudi-arabia-saudi-officials

US Embassy to Egypt. 2012. *Supporting Egypt's economy*, http://egypt.usembassy.gov/economy.html

Weisman, S.R. 2006. Rice admits U.S. underestimated Hamas strength, *The New York Times*, 30 January. sec. International/Middle East, http://www.nytimes.com/2006/01/30/international/middleeast/30diplo.html

Whitehead, L. 2009. Losing 'the force'? The 'dark side' of democratization after Iraq. *Democratization* 16, no. 2: 215–42.

Russia and the Arab Spring: Supporting the Counter-Revolution

ROLAND DANNREUTHER

Faculty of Social Sciences and Humanities, University of Westminster, London

ABSTRACT Russia's response to the Arab Spring ranged from apprehension to deep anxiety and diverged significantly from the US and the EU responses. While initially welcoming the popular demands for political reform in North Africa, the Russian reaction rapidly became more critical as a result of Western military intervention into Libya and the threat of the spread of Islamist extremism. It was these twin fears which prompted the Russian leadership to adopt an uncompromising stance towards Syria. While geopolitical factors certainly played a role in driving Russian strategy, domestic political factors were also more significant. As the Russian leadership felt internally threatened by the growing opposition within the country, conflict in the Middle East highlighted the perceived flaws of the imposition of Western liberal democracy and the virtues of Russia's own model of state-managed political order. There was, as such, a significant ideational and ideological dimension to the Russian response to the Arab Spring.

Introduction

One of the unforeseen outcomes of the tumultuous developments of the Arab Spring is that Russia has emerged as a significantly more influential and powerful strategic presence in the Middle East, reminiscent to some degree of the Soviet role during the cold war period. In relation to Syria, in particular, Russia was willing to countenance a degree of diplomatic confrontation with the West which was unparalleled since the end of the cold war and provided the background for the confrontational Russian stance towards Ukraine in 2014. Russia was willing to provide significant support to a Syrian regime which was treated as an illegitimate pariah by most other regional and international actors.

In the end, this diplomatic and political strategy proved to be astute and to reap dividends. In September 2013, when the US and its allies were on the brink of military intervention into Syria, a Russian diplomatic initiative to secure the dismantlement of Syria's chemical weapons averted the threat of military strikes. This, in turn, led to a limited US–Russian *rapprochement* and an agreement to convene the Geneva II Conference in February 2014, though this ultimately proved to be fruitless in terms of reaching a broader political settlement. The need for such a comprehensive meeting as a pre-condition to forge a peace has been the constant demand of Russia and bringing all the parties together in Geneva was perceived in Moscow as a vindication of its earlier diplomatic stance. The subsequent deterioration in US–Russian relations over Ukraine and the annexation of Crimea has revived the tensions between the US and Russia over Syria but has not derailed the continuing cooperation over the destruction of Syria's chemical weapons arsenal, which was almost fully completed by mid-2014.

The principal aim of this article is to identify and evaluate the evolution of Russia's approach towards the Arab Spring. The first part of the article assesses the initial Russian response to the developments of the Arab Spring. This was, at the start, relatively low-key, reflecting the limited economic and political ties with Egypt and Tunisia. But there was undoubtedly apprehension over these developments even at this time, which contrasted with the more positive assessments from the US, the EU and Turkey, as highlighted in other contributions to this volume. Russian anxieties did, though, intensify with the conflict in Libya which resulted in Muammar Gaddafi's removal from power in October 2011 supported by Western military intervention. This crisis led to an unprecedented internal debate within Russia where the more hardline viewpoint of Prime Minister Vladimir Putin gained ascendance, and where Western intervention into Libya was viewed as representing a fundamental challenge to core Russian national interests. Increasingly, the Russian government and Russian analysts saw the Arab Spring as strengthening and consolidating Islamist extremism which was viewed as undermining stability not just in the Middle East but also potentially within Russia itself.

This sceptical and negative perception of the Arab Spring, rejecting the idea that this was a positive process of democratization, was mirrored in the approach taken by Israel, as set out by Magen in this volume. However, unlike Israel, Russia had significantly greater capacities to promote its preferences for managing and resolving the conflict. The second part of this article assesses the policies and instruments that Russia used to promote its strategic interventions into the region, most notably in Syria. In the main, these were diplomatic in nature though there was also the cultivation of the perception that Russia could, if it so wished, escalate the crisis through arms sales or more direct support for the Syrian regime. In reality, Russia did provide substantive diplomatic, economic and political support to the Syrian regime, which led to a severe cooling of relations between Russia and the West as well as with many moderate Arab states. However, Russian strategy was always carefully calibrated and there was no desire irretrievably to damage its long-term relations with the US and other

Western and Arab states. Thus, when the opportunity came for US and Russia to work together, such as over the dismantlement of Syria's chemical weapons, Russia was keen to rebuild and improve relations and not to continue to emphasize the differences in their political positions over Syria. There was also a conscious exercise of self-restraint in Russia to limit their satisfaction and sense of *schadenfreude* that the Western strategy had failed to achieve its key strategic objective of the overthrow of the Asad regime, which actually gained in power and achieved a number of military successes during 2014.

The final section of this article addresses the main factors, which explain why Russia adopted the approach that it did to the Arab Spring and to the conflict in Syria. The main argument here is that while geopolitical factors undoubtedly played a major role in promoting Russia's distinctive stance, there were also significant domestic political factors, as well as an ideological and ideational dimension. Indeed, in this case, the domestic and ideational factors have a stronger explanatory force. Domestic factors were important as the events of the Arab Spring occurred at a time of significant electoral tension within Russia during the 2011–2012 parliamentary and presidential elections. The ideational factors include the development in Russia, particularly by official government-supporting analysts and thinkers, of a specific conceptualization of democracy which is essentially illiberal and anti-Western in its orientation, and which places much greater weight on the need for gradual stability-prioritizing and state-led change rather than the more pluralist role played by civil society inherent in the liberal democratic model. Whether or not the Russian concept of 'sovereign democracy' is really a democratic model or just a variant of authoritarianism, the sense that this model was more appropriate for promoting change in the Middle East rather than Western-supported regime change was a factor behind the stance taken by Russia. Indeed, the Russian perception is that their overarching prognosis has tended to be supported by political developments in the majority of the states affected by the Arab Spring in the period from 2012 to 2014. This, in turn, emboldened Russia to take its unprecedented actions towards Ukraine, including the annexation of Crimea, so as to undermine what Moscow saw as similar Western support for regime change in Ukraine, a country of much greater strategic importance to Russia than the countries of the Middle East.

Russian Assessment of the Arab Spring

It was, though, certainly not evident at the start of the Arab Spring that such a negative and pessimistic outcome was inevitable or pre-ordained. Most Western and popular Arab sentiment was generally optimistic that a new era was dawning and that this presaged a decisive shift towards democracy. The Russian leadership was also keen on not to be seen as a reactionary force, denying the legitimate democratic aspirations of the Arab world. Putin himself regularly affirmed that the social dynamics resulting in the Arab Spring were both positive and necessary and the 'sympathies of Russians were on the side of those struggling for democratic reforms'

(Putin 2013). The initial developments in Tunisia and Egypt also initially appeared to present no significant threat or disruption to Russian interests, given the relatively limited economic and political ties between Russia and these two countries, which had historically much closer relations with the US and the EU. Initially, at least, there did not appear to be a threat of Islamist extremism from these popular revolts.

There was nevertheless an unavoidable parallel between the expression of the democratic impulses of the Arab peoples in Cairo and Tunis and Russians who were beginning to demonstrate in their thousands in Moscow and other Russian cities. The onset of the Arab Spring occurred at a particularly sensitive moment in Russia's political cycle with the run-up to the 2011 parliamentary elections and the 2012 presidential elections. The central question of these elections was the future political role of Putin who, in the previous elections, had swapped jobs with Dmitry Medvedev and became Prime Minster while Medvedev moved to the Presidency. The big political issue which dominated Russian speculation ever since that re-shuffling in 2008 was Putin's future and whether a new leadership would emerge for the next elections. This was resolved in an abrupt, and to many Russians, highly cynical manner in the Spring of 2011 when it was peremptorily announced that Putin and Medvedev would again swap jobs and Putin would have a third term as President. The cynical stage management of this, the evidence of electoral vote rigging, and a general dissatisfaction with the corrupt and authoritarian nature of Russian politics, led to unprecedented opposition rallies during 2011–2012.

The linkage between the pro-democracy developments in the Middle East and those in Russia was picked up as a theme by Russian commentators and opposition forces (see Sokolov 2011). However, Russian analysis also highlighted the different political situation in the Middle East how what was happening there was more akin to the revolutions in 1989 in East Central Europe rather than with the 'coloured' revolutions of the 2000s. In addition, emphasis was accorded to the differing political culture in Europe compared to the Middle East, where Islam plays such a strong role in mitigating against a democratic culture. There was, as a result, a much greater scepticism and ambivalence about the democratic potential of the Arab Spring revolutions than found in most Western analyses.

This pessimism did not entail an unconditional support for the ruling secular Arab authoritarian regimes. Among Russian analysts, there was a recognition that these regimes had been in power for too long, had become too corrupt and had failed to reflect the changing nature of their societies (see Ivanov 2013a, 8–32). This contributed to the initial cautious welcoming of the revolts in Tunisia and Egypt. However, the critical divergence from Western analysis was that the Arab Spring was rarely if ever viewed as part of an inexorable process towards democracy. The dominant narrative among Russian analysts was that the Arab Spring was much more a return to the traditional values of Middle Eastern societies, incorporating a more Islamic identity, than a shift to Western-style democracy. The narrative was thus couched primarily in terms of Islamization than of democratization. This again is explicitly expressed in Putin's own reflections on developments in the Middle East when in an interview on August 2013, he argued that Russia is not, as many in the West argue, against the need for radical reform in Syria and that Russia is not just unreservedly supporting Asad but that a simplistic understanding of democracy, supported and promoted by the West, was a major factor in the violence in the region;

> In my opinion, this is happening because some people from outside believe that if the region were to be bought into compliance with a certain idea—an idea that some call democracy—then peace and stability would ensue. That's not how it works. You can't ignore the region's history, traditions and religious beliefs, and you can't just interfere. (Putin 2013)

There was, therefore, a recognition that an inevitable transformation was taking place in the Arab world and that there was a historical logic and inevitability about it, but that this change is not to be viewed through the prism of Western-style democracy but in terms of a broad-based societal yearning for a more authentic and traditional Islamic identity. This passing of an old order is viewed with some wistfulness and nostalgia by Russian analysts, even while accepting its inevitability. As one senior Russian diplomat notes, what is happening is a shift of power from the Soviet-educated secular leftist Arab generation to a younger Islamist generation that has less affection and more limited historical ties with post-Soviet Russia (Lukmanov 2013, 104). Russia was, therefore, willing to be pragmatic and to work with the Islamist government of Mohamed Morsi, when he came to power in 2012, and Moscow did not predict, though certainly welcomed, the military coup in July and August 2013. However, this did not generally affect the broader understanding of a dynamic of Islamization in the region, as confirmed in Syria and Iraq with the rise in particular of the Islamic State in Iraq and Syria (ISIS) in 2014.

Russian analyses also tend to converge on this perception that the old secular Arab nationalist model is under threat and that the struggle is increasingly between moderate political Islam, such as with sections of the Muslim Brotherhood, and radical Islamist extremism, represented by al-Qaeda and its affiliates. This conceptualization of a bifurcated internal civil war between moderate and extremist Islam is deeply embedded in Russian thinking and has its sources in Russia's own experiences of dealing with the Muslim world (Dannreuther 2010). From the Russian perspective, the Soviet/Russian state has been engaged in an almost continuous struggle against Islamist extremism from the late 1970s onwards. This extends from the Soviet experience in Afghanistan, to the Islamist civil war in Tajikistan, and to the insurgency in Chechnya in the North Caucasus, which notably shifted in the late 1990s from being a mainly nationalist secessionist to a more radical Islamist struggle. In the mid-2000s, the Islamization of the Chechen insurgency mutated further into a more generalized Islamist insurgency in the whole of the North Caucasus that continues to threaten the stability of the North Caucasus region.

In the ideological world-view of Putin and his advisers, the root cause of this serious internal threat was the 'false promise' of Western-style democracy promoted in the 1990s. Democracy became critically identified with the loss of the sovereign power of the centre through devolution and federalization, as most famously expressed by former President Yeltsin's call for the Russian regions 'to grab as much sovereignty as possible'. For Putin, it was precisely this loss of power of the central state, and the devolution of power to the periphery, which resulted in a vacuum that in the North Caucasus, led to chaos, civil war and the rise of a radical anti-Russian Islamist extremist challenge. There was, therefore, a deeply held conviction, drawn from Putin's direct experience that viewed the Western export of liberal democracy as a recipe for internal conflict, state disintegration and chaos. This significantly informed and added to the apprehension and anxiety over developments in relation to the Arab Spring.

This, in turn, confirmed the strongly held Russian opposition to postcold war Western intervention under the guise of humanitarianism. A deep suspicion and distrust of Western intervention has also been a constant theme in post-Soviet Russian strategic thinking, where Western interventions, justified on humanitarian grounds, into Bosnia in 1995 and Kosovo in 1999 were generally perceived in Russia to be a smokescreen for a deliberate strategy of NATO expansion (Dannreuther 1999–2000). The US–UK intervention into Iraq in 2003 lost, in Russian eyes, even the UN fig-leaf for its legitimation. By the mid-2000s, Russian elite suspicions extended to the perception that the West was using its 'soft power', mainly through support of Western-oriented NGOs, to foment domestic political opposition and to engineer 'coloured revolutions' among the former Soviet states. In 2011 and 2012, this domestic discontent and open opposition to the ruling regime extended right to the heart of Moscow as large opposition rallies criticized the corruption and authoritarianism of the Russian political system. There was always, therefore, a potential threat in Russian eyes that the Arab Spring might provide the West with a further opportunity to engage in regime change through the justification of 'humanitarian intervention'. Ensuring against such Western intervention was, therefore, a key goal of Russian policy-making.

Resisting Western Intervention: Russian Policies towards the Conflicts in Libya and Syria

These concerns and anxieties became increasingly acute with the evolution of events in Libya. In contrast to Tunisia and Egypt, the Libyan regime did not swiftly capitulate to the demands of the opposition, but rather threatened brutally to crush that opposition. The dilemma for Russia was if it should support a Western-sponsored resolution at the UN Security Council which aimed to provide protection for Libyan civilians under threat from Gaddafi's forces. Medvedev was inclined to support the Western initiative, believing it was critical to preserve the 'reset' agenda, including Russian entry into the WTO and the new START treaty, and that it was not worth jeopardizing this for an isolated Arab leader with almost no support in the wider Arab world (Suslov 2012). However, the Russian Foreign Ministry recommended vetoing the resolution. Vitaly Churkin, the Russian permanent representative to the UN, explicitly warned about the 'inclusion of provisions in the document that potentially open the door for large-scale military intervention' (Grigoriev 2011). The eventual compromise was that Russia abstained from Resolution 1973. Once the resolution was passed, NATO initiated air strikes and provided military support to the opposition which contributed to the overthrow of the Gaddafi regime.

This decision not to veto this resolution was, though, challenged by Putin (then Prime Minister) who noted that the resolution was 'deficient and flawed' and that it 'allows anyone to do anything they want—to take any actions against a sovereign state. Basically, all that this reminds me of is a medieval appeal for a crusade' (Ivanov and Kozlov 2011). Medvedev immediately responded saying it 'was absolutely inexcusable to use expressions that, in effect, lead to a clash of civilisations—such as 'crusades' and so forth' (Demchenko 2012). At the time, it appeared that this unprecedented clash between the two figures at the heart of the leadership duopoly might be just another example of the stage management of differences of opinion, with a message carefully calculated to meet the differing expectations of a foreign as against a domestic audience (Samarina 2011). However, in retrospect, this internal dispute can be seen as a critical turning point when Medvedev's ambition for a second presidential term was significantly weakened. The NATO air strikes in support of the Libyan opposition and thus in support, from a Russian perspective, of 'regime change' was a significant embarrassment for Medvedev and shifted elite support and public popularity towards Putin (Suslov 2012).

Taking a much more forceful and uncompromising posture towards developments in Libya was not just driven by electoral factors. There was also a strong conviction in Putin's distinctive world-view that the Arab Spring was now going badly wrong. Thus, despite his earlier support for the uprisings, Putin noted 'that it became quickly clear that events in many of these countries were not turning out according to a civilized scenario. Instead of the affirmation of democracy, instead of defending the rights of the minority, there was increasingly the expulsion of the enemy, coup d'états, where the domination of one side becomes an ever greater aggressive domination of the other' (Putin 2012). The West, if not the sole cause of this deterioration, was, according to Putin exacerbating the situation as these negative developments 'were made worse by intervention from outside in support of one side of the internal conflict and the forceful character of that intervention. It led to a number of governments under the cover of humanitarian slogans and with the aid of air power dividing the Libyan regime. And the apotheosis of this was not even a medieval but simply a brutal elimination of Muammar Gaddafi' The firm conclusion that Putin draws from this is that 'we must not allow the 'Libyan scenario' to be attempted to be reproduced in Syria' (Putin 2012).

It is this broader context of a resolute opposition to Western military intervention to support opposition forces to existing regimes which provides an explanation for why, after Libya, the Russian stance towards Syria was so uncompromising. Sergei Lavrov, the Russian Foreign Minister, argued that 'the way the Syrian crisis is resolved will largely determine the model for the international community's response to internal conflicts in the future' (Chernenko and Yusin 2012). The Syrian crisis became, as such, a litmus test for confronting the whole issue of humanitarian intervention in the similar way that the Russian intervention into Georgia in 2008 was primarily driven by the perceived need to set 'red lines' against NATO enlargement into the post-Soviet space. Syria was also, from the Russian perspective, a much important strategic ally than Libya, given the long-standing close Soviet relations with the country and Syria generally being one of the key regional Arab powers, with a direct stake in the Arab-Israeli conflict. Syria is also much closer geographically to Russia and the potential spillover from Syria to the Caucasus and Central Asia, and to Russia itself, being of greater potential significance.

The principal instruments that Russia utilized in pursuit of its objectives in Syria were primarily diplomatic rather than military or economic in nature. This included the exercise of its power of veto in the UN Security Council to block the imposition of sanctions or authorize military action against the Syrian regime. Russia managed to block votes against Syria at three critical junctures in the UN during 2011 and 2012 and then again in 2014. In ensuring the inaction of the UN, Russia was willing to be diplomatically isolated to an unprecedented degree, such as with the second major UN Resolution in February 2012 when its sole ally in not voting for the resolution was China. Russia was also willing to take the considerable risk of providing support for Asad even at times when the Syrian regime appeared close to collapse. This diplomatic strategy did, though, mean that Russia did not have to use other more confrontational and escalatory instrument. The absence of arms sanctions regime against Syria meant that Russia could continue to supply 'defensive weapons' to the Syrian regime. Russia also justified its support for Asad on the grounds that, to do otherwise, would be to pre-judge the political process in Syria and that any settlement would have to include direct talks and negotiations between the regime and the opposition.

There was certainly a politico-military as well as a diplomatic dimension to Russian policy towards the Syrian conflict. Russian warships patrolled, from time to time, waters close to Syria and used the port of Tartus, which is one of the few foreign naval bases available to the Russian navy. Russian military advisers provided support and advice to their counterparts in the Syrian army. There was also the intermittent diplomatic threat that Russia could, if pressed too far, provide weapons to Syria, such as the S-300 anti-missile system, which would significantly shift the strategic balance in the region. There was also the inevitable reality that Western policy-makers could not exclude in their military contingency planning a Russian military reaction if the West did militarily intervene in Syria.

But the Russian leadership and analysts also calculated that the actual risk of this leading to a significant military escalation with the West was limited. This was based on an underlying assessment that the West was, in reality, deeply hesitant about a military intervention into Syria. There was a calculation that the formal Western stance of supporting the opposition goals of overthrowing the Asad regime was never likely to succeed without substantial Western military support for these forces and that Western publics lacked the appetite for this. The likely result was therefore a continuing military stalemate, which would provide opportunities for Russian diplomacy to support a political resolution, given its privileged access to the Syrian government. As such, the Russian diplomatic success in 2013 over the chemical weapons issue, which expressly averted a Western intervention, followed a logic which exposed the doubts and anxieties lying below the surface of much elite and popular thinking in Europe and the US. The gains made by the Syrian regime during 2014 only served to confirm Russian calculations that Asad was likely to survive, even in a fragmented state, and Western dilemmas of whether and how to support the opposition would not be resolved.

This diplomatic success did come with some significant costs. In the Middle East, one of the legacies of Russia's Middle East policy during the 2000s was its success in courting both moderate and radical forces in the region and to advance mutually beneficial economic relations with countries, which formerly had poor relations with Russia, such as Turkey, Israel and the Gulf states (Dannreuther 2012; Katz 2012). But these mutually beneficial relations, most notably with the Gulf states, were strongly threatened by Russia's position on Syria. For example, there was a serious deterioration of relations with Saudi Arabia and Qatar, the two countries providing the strongest support to the opposition to the Asad regime. In July 2012, the Russian ambassador to Qatar was beaten up at the airport in Doha and lucrative economic deals were cancelled with both countries. Although the amount of economic trade between Russia and the Gulf region is actually quite limited, the deterioration in political relations followed a significant rapprochement which included Putin's official visit to the region in 2007, the first such visit by a Russian or a Soviet leader. The strategic objective for Russia had been to forge closer diplomatic ties so that common interests over international oil and gas markets could be promoted more effectively. These tentative initial steps to forging closer relations in the Gulf region were undoubtedly affected by the confrontation over Syria.

More generally in the Middle East, the image of Russia was negatively affected by the events in Syria. In Egypt, a key indicator of grassroots of Arab sentiments, the share of positive opinion of Russia dropped from 50% in 2007 to 16% in 2012; in Jordan the approval rate was just 25% and in Turkey it was 16%. Highly influential Islamic thinkers adopted an increasingly critical stance towards Russia, with the internationally renowned theologian, Yusuf al-Qaradawi, calling on *Al-Jazeera* for Muslims to boycott Russia which, he claimed, 'was supporting the criminal Syrian regime with weapons supplies' (al-Qaradawi 2012). As a senior Russian diplomat expresses it, at the grassroots level 'Moscow is consistently presented as one of the forces checking the 'democratic' impulses of the region's peoples; it is assumed that Russia is getting rich on weapon deliveries to the region torn apart by conflicts and on the fuel prices which went up because of the continued bloodshed in fuel-producing countries' (Lukmanov 2013, 102). Some Russian analysts also unfavourably contrasted Russia with the EU over the period of the Arab Spring, where Russia was viewed as 'arming the dictators' while the EU promotes its 'soft power' image and distances itself from the United States (Ivanov 2013b). This qualifies some of the more pessimistic assessments of the EU's role in the Arab Spring, such as those identified in the articles by Noutcheva and Dandashly in this volume, which suggests that the short-term gains by Russia might not ultimately be as effective as the long-term engagement of the EU in the region.

The seeming one-sided support for Syria and the leadership of Bashar Asad also affected Russia's relations with the West and contributed to a significant cooling in relations. One Russian analyst suggested that by early 2013 the 'wave of anti-US fervour has reached heights perhaps not seen since the reign of Joseph Stalin' (Kiselov 2013). Although this was undoubtedly exaggerated, though perhaps less so after the annexation of Crimea, the potential damage to Russia's relations with the West has been a matter of concern for Russian diplomats. While there has been a clear shift towards a more confrontational anti-Western stance with Putin's return to the Presidency in 2012, and the Syrian crisis has been a litmus test of this, Russian diplomats have consistently tried to present Russia as an external power which seeks to promote a constructive resolution of the conflict in Syria so long as Russia's core strategic interests are protected. In March 2012, Russia accepted the UN Presidential statement, which urged Syria to accept the peace plan put forward by the UN special envoy, Kofi Annan. This plan detailed an 'inclusive political process', a ceasefire and a withdrawal of forces by both sides. Russia also voted for UN Security Council Resolution 2042 which established a short-lived monitoring mission. Similarly, Russia did cooperate with the UN-supported 'Action Group' on Syria and supported the proposals for a Syrian-led transition as set out in the Geneva Communiqué of June 2012. In May 2013, Russia and the United States agreed to promote an international conference based on this June 2012 Communiqué, which was eventually convened in February 2014.

There were, therefore, precedents for a more constructive and cooperative Russian–US stance. This provided the basis for the passing of the UN Security Council Resolution 2118 in September 2013 which obligated the destruction of Syria's chemical weapons stockpiles. Russia's forceful diplomatic action to support and promote this resolution came with some significant political risks, as Russia's reputation and credibility inevitably became hostage to the Syrian government's willingness and commitment to such a process. In this regard, although the resolution did not explicitly endorse an automatic punitive response to violations of the agreement, there was nevertheless reference to a chapter seven provision, which recognized that such coercive actions would be forthcoming if there were such verified violations. The fact that there was a reference to chapter seven in the wording of the resolution did represent a significant compromise for Russia.

In the aftermath of the vote, Putin was also careful not to boast of a Russian victory and to highlight it as a collective and mutually advantageous result, which potentially heralded a more constructive and cooperative relationship between Russia and the West. There was clearly a sense in Moscow that the crisis in Syria had led to a dangerous deterioration in relations with the West and that this needed to be actively changed. Thus, the chemical weapons agreement was used to bolster US–Russian ties rather than, as could easily have been the case, to further embarrass Obama's weakness and strategic vacillation. The desire for Putin to have a good Sochi Winter Olympics in 2014 also concentrated minds in seeking to ameliorate Russia's external image, which resulted in the freeing of Mikhail Khodorkovksii and the Pussy Riot protestors. Developments in Ukraine, in early 2014, certainly undermined and revealed the fragility of any such improvement in relations with the West but, even in the case of Ukraine, Russia has also tried to balance its support for pro-Russian forces in Ukraine with ensuring that relations with the West are not irrevocably broken.

Understanding Russia's Approach to the Arab Spring

Periods of significant conflict and tension between Russia and the West inevitably highlight Russia's geopolitical approach to international relations, which is undeniably a core aspect of the Russian strategic mentality. However, this needs to be qualified by certain factors, particularly when examining Russia's role towards the Arab Spring and the crises in Libya and Syria. The first is that, as identified in much of the proceeding analysis, domestic political factors were critical in the nature and development of Russia's diplomatic stance. The tense political situation within Russia, with the need for Putin to consolidate his position against an unprecedented degree of internal opposition, was critical in understanding why a resolute and uncompromising stance in relation to the Syrian crisis was seen as politically necessary for the consolidation of Putin's domestic support. The second factor is that the Russian leadership were also conscious that there were potential costs in adopting an excessively geopolitical approach. And the third factor is that the Russian stance cannot be understood without recognizing that Russia under Putin has developed a distinctive 'Russian idea' of the sources of political order in international relations and the role that democracy, civil society and the state should play in ensuring progressive change. There is, as such, an important ideational and socially constructed element in Russian strategic thinking which needs to be incorporated.

In relation to the recognition of the tension between the undoubted attractions of a geopolitical approach as against its potential negative consequences, this is a key feature in Russia's response to the Arab Spring. It was well understood by more pragmatic elements in the Russian leadership that there is a fine line between the 'principled' opposition to certain elements of Western strategy, such as 'regime change' or Western-promoted humanitarian intervention and the promotion of a more generalized geopolitical struggle against the West, and its regional allies, which places Russia in a countervailing camp aligned with Syria, Iran and other rejectionist forces in the region. It is a fine line, however, which Russian leaders and policy analysts instinctively and regularly found themselves crossing, given the strengths of a deeper Soviet and Russian tradition of geopolitical and realist thought. For example, Sergei Lavrov, the Russian foreign minister, noted in one interview that;

> Asad has been turned into a bogeyman. But, in reality all of these groundless charges—that he is to blame for everything—are a cover for a big geopolitical game. The geopolitical map of the Middle East is once again being reformatted as different players seek to secure their own geopolitical positions. Many are concerned more about Iran than Syria. They are saying bluntly that Iran should be deprived of its closest ally, which they consider Asad to be. (Vorobyov 2012)

The depiction of a broader geopolitical struggle also played well to a domestic audience, with one Russian commentator noting that criticism of domestic politics cannot easily be controlled by those in power but that 'where Syria is concerned, geopolitics trumps objectivity ... geopolitical nationalism has deep roots. Putin himself is a product of that culture, and not just an active media manipulator' (Nekrasov 2012). Opinion polls demonstrate clearly that Putin's personal popularity increases significantly with these external confrontations with the West; his popularity increased from 58% to 68% during the year 2013, aided by his handling of the Syrian crisis, before reaching over 80% in March 2014 after the annexation of Crimea.

However, Russian diplomats remained sensitive to the limits of geopolitics, particularly in promoting the core goal of modernization and strengthening of the domestic economy. Russia is not, in this sense, the same country as the Soviet Union which was willing to sacrifice its economic interests for ideological and geopolitical commitments. Sergei Ivanov, a key political ally of Putin, presented this more pragmatic picture of post-Soviet Russia by stating that 'we don't exportideology anymore—we only export goods and capital' (Ivanov 2008). When the Middle East is viewed from this more pragmatic economic perspective, the geopolitical interest of Russia in support of Syria appears strategically relatively much less significant. Although much is made of the importance of the Tartus naval facility on the Syrian coast, the only naval base outside of the former Soviet Union, this is actually run-down and of little military significance, only permitting temporary mooring (Allinson 2013). Its importance is more one-rooted in nostalgia than the actual needs and demands of Russian naval power. Similarly, Syria is an important importer of Russian arms, representing 72% of its arms imports from 2007 to 2011, but this accounts for only 5% of Russia's total arms deliveries abroad.

More generally, from the economic perspective, it is actually with Middle Eastern countries who have strongly supported the opposition against the Asad regime that Russia has the strongest and most significant economic relations. The most important in this regard is Turkey. Turkey has always been Russia's most important trading and economic partner in the Middle East with trade rising from about \$4 billion in the 1990s to USD 15 billion in 2005 and USD 34 billion in 2012. Russia accounts for 63% of Turkish natural gas imports thanks to a dedicated gas export line between the two countries—Blue Stream—which started supplying gas in 2003. In Russia, Turkish construction companies, as well as consumer goods companies are very active and Turkish investments in Russia are estimated to total USD 5 billion (Akhmedkhanov 2008). However, the Syrian crisis threatened to put at risk these Russian economic interests in Turkey. In September 2012, Prime Minister Recep Tayipp Erdogan, the leader of the ruling Justice and Development Party, explicitly included Russia among those countries that 'history will not forgive for assisting the bloody Syrian regime'. A few weeks after that speech, the Turkish air force grounded a Russian passenger plane on a Moscow–Damascus journey (Glazova 2012). The annexation of Crimea added to tensions with Turkey, particularly over the fate of the Crimean Tatars. However, despite these political setbacks, there is no sign that economic relations have been greatly affected.

In fact, what one can draw from this is that a Soviet-style reflexive geopolitical approach no longer correlates with the actual post-Soviet 'national interests' of Russia. As such, a realist or geopolitical analysis is insufficient for understanding why Russia acted the way it did and was willing to take such potential political and economic risks. To understand, this requires recognition of the role that ideational and ideological factors played.

Critical to this was the fact that the Arab Spring and developments in Libya and Syria coincided with a shift in ideological orientation of the Russian political system and its sources of political legitimation. During Medvedev's presidency, the key overarching political agenda was defined in terms of modernization, involving the need for the Russian economy to diversify away from its dependence on raw materials and towards a more technologically advanced manufacturing and services economy. This agenda incorporated a generally favourable attitude towards both the West and the more liberal, modernizing sections of Russian society. However, with that liberalizing domestic constituency becoming increasingly vocal in its criticisms and opposition to the ruling regime during the course of 2011–2012, the electoral logic for securing Putin's re-election required involved focusing attention on consolidating the support of the more traditional and conservative majority of Russian society found in the rural and Soviet legacy industrial heartlands (Trenin, Lipmann, and Malashenko 2013). This meant not only a shift to a more openly confrontational posture towards the West but also a stronger and more forceful critique of the Western ideas perceived to be driving the opposition forces within Russian society.

In the mid-2000s, much of the ideological spadework for this anti-Western and anti-liberal critique had been completed with the development of the concept of 'sovereign democracy'. Vladislav Surkov, the key intellectual figure behind this concept, argued that the form of democracy appropriate to Russian society, and by extension to other modernizing and industrializing societies, is one where the state has the primary role in managing the transition to democracy, ensuring that the resulting societal transformation does not lead to disorder and conflict but preserves social stability and economic development (Surkov 2006). As such, the intellectual core of the concept of 'sovereign democracy' is a rejection of liberal pluralist conceptions of democracy, which requires the division of society into competing factional groups. For Surkov and other Russian elites, the danger is that, in the Russian context, this pluralistic conception would only lead to internal disorder, societal conflict and the loss of the 'sovereign' integrity of the state. Such a liberal pluralist concept of the state might be appropriate for advanced post-industrial Western societies, where the underlying political culture is sufficiently consensual to permit such open dissension without undermining the integrity of the state. However, the 'sovereign democracy' concept articulated the view that this was not appropriate for those states, including Russia, which have a different inherited historical and political culture, and where any attempt to implement this would lead to the loss of sovereignty or 'de-sovereignization' (Averre 2009, 1697).

There was also an inter-confessional and inter-ethnic dimension to this conservative statist conception of the appropriate forms of political order in complex internally divided societies, which draws from Russia's post-Soviet development. In developing Russia's strategy to deal with Islamist extremism, Putin developed a religio-political as well as a coercive military dimension. This involved a pro-active policy of supporting, both politically and financially, Muslim religious representation through a tightly regulated and hierarchically configured sphere of moderate Russian-rooted Islam. This shift towards a more differentiated conception of the secular nature of the Russian state, which accords a greater role to the religious identities in Russia, was carefully articulated so as to extend beyond the Russian Orthodox church to include the other 'traditional religions', most notably Islam. Tatar Muslims were recognised as the indigenous population of Russia and should be considered as 'co-constructors of the Russian state' (Naumkin 2006). The Russian leadership has generally been careful in articulating the multi-ethnic and multi-confessional nature of the Russian state, the importance of asserting a civic (Rossiiski) rather than an ethnic (Russkii) Russian identity, and how Russia does not subscribe to the 'clash of civilizations' thesis.

This sense that Russia is distinctive in its tolerance of religious, ethnic and confessional difference is not just an elite phenomenon but has a broader popular base, as indicated in a survey which asked Russians to identify the core values of the EU as against Russia (Figure 1). While the values of the EU were identified to be those classically aligned with liberal democracy, such as the market economy, the human rights, the rule of law and democracy, the core values of Russia were defined in terms of respect of different cultures and religions, of toleration and of preservation of cultural heritage. This survey is suggestive that there might be broad societal support for the Russian claim that, though European values of liberal democracy are something to aspire towards, they do potentially represent a threat to traditional values of toleration and respect for minority rights,

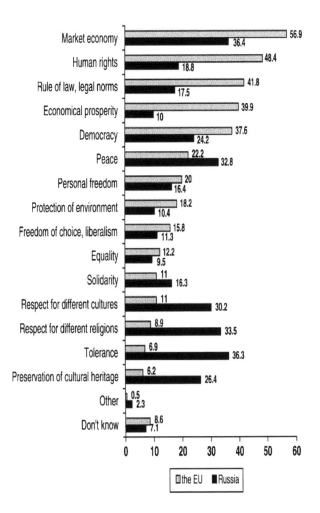

Figure 1. Values characteristic of the EU and Russia in public opinion (per cent)
Notes: The wording of the question was as follows: 'Which of the following values are most attributable to the EU (five answers maximum)?' and 'Which of these values are more attributable to your country?' The question offered the opportunity to choose several positions, so the sum of the indicators may exceed 100%.
Source: Nation-wide survey, conducted in November 2008 by the Centre for Sociological Research 'Opinio', Moscow State University, under the ESRC-funded project (RES-061–25- 0001).

particularly if promoted through external coercive intervention. The Russian model is one that is seen therefore as a potentially attractive export to the non-Western world. As one influential Russian report argues, Russia's advantage in the Middle East is that it 'comes across as a civilisationally close state, in a significant measure belonging to both Europe and Asia, the Christian and Islamic worlds, and not expressing to the world European 'hyper-secularism' which is not welcome to Middle Eastern societies, particularly in the post-Spring period' (Ivanov 2013b, 24).

There is, therefore, little that was apologetic or defensive in the Russian approach to the Arab Spring. From Moscow's perspective, the Russian experience, forged through a long association and engagement with the Muslim world, is that social stability and multi-ethnic and multi-confessional toleration in Muslim societies are fragile social commodities which can rapidly be broken apart in periods of radical social change. The political instability and fragmentation in Libya after the overthrow of Gaddafi in Libya was a confirmation of this analysis from the Russian perspective, though it should be noted that this has not stopped Russian companies from being active in Libya, including starting again arms sales. Similarly, in Egypt, the economic and political crises which led to the election of the Muslim Brotherhood and then its brutal repression and the reassertion of military rule highlighted the potential for anarchy and disorder in periods of radical change.

All of this contributed to the immediate and instinctive support for the Asad regime not just because it is a long-standing ally of Russia but also because it is seen to defend the interests of the minorities in Syria and seeks to preserve the traditions of multi-confessional toleration, despite the authoritarian nature of the regime. As such, the most effective way to resolve the Syrian crisis is not the unconditional demand for Asad's overthrow but a externally-supported process of negotiations between all the parties to the conflict. For Russia, the Western interpretation of support for democracy as meaning support for the Syrian opposition, whose principal constituency is the Sunni majority population, unintentionally but inevitably strengthens radical and extremist elements that are intolerant of all difference, seek to eliminate their opponents and unashamedly use the instruments of fear and terrorism. It is for this reason that Putin has regularly cited the rise of the extremist groups, Jabhat al-Nusra and ISIS, among the opposition and has highlighted the atrocities that these groups have committed. For Putin, the rise of such extremist forces in the Syrian conflict, and how this has intensified the brutality of the conflict more generally, is the result of a misguided and fundamentally misconceived Western policy.

Conclusion

This article has sought to identify the key factors explaining the evolution of Russia's stance towards the Arab Spring and the conflicts that developed in Libya and Syria. While recognizing that geopolitical factors were undoubtedly important for understanding the distinctive position adopted by Russia, which was both sceptical of the democratic potential of the Arab Spring and strongly opposed to any external military intervention, the article has highlighted the critical roles that domestic, political and ideational factors played in the articulation of Russia's strategic posture.

The larger and more critical message that Russia sought to present and defend in its response to the Arab Spring was a distinctive 'Russian idea' over the nature of political order which explicitly critiques and challenges the idea of Western-promoted liberal democracy. The essence of this 'Russian idea' is that democracy needs to be thought as something, which strengthens rather than fragments social stability, that preserves rather than destroys local traditions and religious cultures and that consolidates rather than breaks apart sovereign states. From this Russian perspective, the West utilizes liberal democracy as an instrument militarily to enforce their preferred 'democratic' partners through intervention on putatively humanitarian grounds. In contrast to this, Russia presents a model, which is conservative in its support of the overriding need of the state to defend its sovereign rights of state and to respond to the societal demands for reform. For this Russian perspective, such change can only come from within and cannot be imposed from outside. Compared to the 1990s or even early 2000s, Russia now feels much more confident about promoting this essentially authoritarian Russian model of statepower since it is supported by China and by a number of other emerging powers.

The Middle East is not, however, the most important site for this Russian attempt to promote its own model of the state. The struggle to articulate a convincing alternative to the Western and, in particular, the European normative idea of democracy is being much more forcefully waged in the so-called 'shared neighbourhood' in East and Central Europe and in the Caucasus. For Putin, the Middle East is a significantly less important strategic priority than the ambition to construct a Eurasian Union in the post-Soviet space which would limit and contain the perceived threat from NATO and the EU. The Russian defence of the Syrian regime can, thus, be seen as an intermediate stage between the 2008 intervention into Georgia and the annexation of Crimea and the de facto support for pro-Russian separatists in Eastern Ukraine in 2014. In all of these conflicts, which pit Russia in a struggle against the EU/West for the 'hearts and minds' of the peoples of the former Soviet Union and in the Middle East, there is no clear-cut victory for either side and the Russian preference for authoritarian order and stability will continue to be challenged by the natural impulses towards freedom and autonomy. During the Soviet period, it used to be stated that the Soviet Union could bring war but could not bring peace to the region; the same is true of post-Soviet Russia not just in the Middle East but also in Central and Eastern Europe.

References

Akhmedkhanov, B. September 2008. Turkish Union. *Profil* 33.

Allison, R. 2013. Russia and the Syria crisis: regional order and the controversy over regime change. *International Affairs* 89, no. 4: 795–823.

al-Qaradawi, Y. 2012. *Life and Shariah Program.* 5 February on http://www.aljazeera.net/programs/pages/8dd26065-1213-48fd-9ec3-40316262ce98 (accessed 23 January 2013).

Averre, D. 2009. Competing rationalities: Russia, the EU and the "Shared Neighbourhood". *Europe-Asia Studies* 61, no. 10: 1689–713.

Chernenko, E., and M. Yusin. 17 July 2012. Kremlin Wall stands behind Syria. *Kommersant.*

Dannreuther, R. 1999–2000. Escaping the enlargement trap in NATO–Russian relations. *Survival* 41, no. 4: 143–64.

Dannreuther, R. 2010. Russian discourses and approaches to Islam and Islamism. In *Russia and Islam: state, society and radicalism,* eds. R. Dannreuther and L. March, 9–25. Basingstoke: Routledge.

Dannreuther, R. 2012. Russia and the Middle East: A cold war paradigm. *Europe-Asia Studies* 64, no. 3: 543–60.

Demchenko, A. 2012. Arab Spring and Russian policy in the Middle East. *Perspectivy*, http://www.per spektivy.info/rus/desk/arabskaja_vesna_i_politika_rossii_v_blizhnevostochnom_regione_2012-09-15.htm (accessed 20 July 2013).

RESPONSES TO THE 'ARABELLIONS'

Glazova, A. 12 November 2012. Russian-Turkish Cooling. *Nezavisimaya gazeta.*

Grigoriev, E. 21 March 2011. Today Libya: tomorrow everywhere. *Nezavisimaya gazeta.*

Ivanov, S. 2008. *Where is Russia heading? New vision of Pan-European security*, http://www.security conference.de/konferenzen/rede.php?sprache\xFEen&id-217 (accessed 3 March 2009).

Ivanov, I.S. (ed.). 2013a. *Russia and the "New Elites" of the countries of the "Arab Spring": possibilities and perspectives on cooperation.* Moscow: Russian Council on International Affairs.

Ivanov, I.S. 2013b. *Russia and the greater Middle East.* Moscow: Russian Council of International Affairs.

Ivanov, M., and D. Kozlov. 22 March 2011. Resolution is ripe for Russia. *Kommersant.*

Katz, M.N. 2012. Moscow and the Middle East: repeat performance. Russia in Global Affairs 3, http://eng.globalaffairs.ru/print/number/Moscow-and-the-Middle-East-Repeat-Performance-15690# (accessed 7 October 2013).

Kiselov, E. 4 February 2013. *Russia to be downgraded on US priority list.* Moscow Times.

Lukmanov, A. 2013. Russian Muslims and the "Arab Spring". *International Affairs* 59, no. 2: 101–16.

Naumkin, V. 2006. Evroislam kak naslednik dzhadidizma [Euroislam as successor to Jadidism]. In *Forumy Rossiskykh musul'man na poroge novogo tysyacheletiya* [Forum of Russian Muslims on the Threshold of the new Millennium], ed. D.V. Mukhetdinova. Medina: Nizhnii Novgorod.

Nekrasov, A. 1 August 2012. War in Syria: A Quasi-War with the West. *Vedemosti 1.*

Putin, V. 2012. Russia and the Changing World. Rossiskaya gazeta, http://www.rg.ru/2012/02/27/putin-politika.html (accessed 7 October 2013).

Putin, V. 2013. *Putin talks NSA, Syria, Iran, Drones in Russian Television Interview*, http://rt.com/news/putin-rt-interview-full-577/ (accessed 7 October 2013).

Samarina, A. 23 March 2011. Tandem tests strength before 2012 election. *Nezavisimaya gazeta.*

Sokolov, M. 2011. *Is Russia threatened by a popular revolution as in the Arab countries*, http://www.svobodanews.ru/content/transcript/2323664 (accessed 6 June 2012)

Surkov, V. 2006. Sovereignty: it is a political synonym for competitiveness. In *Sovereignty*, ed. N. Garadzha. Evropa: Moscow.

Suslov, D. 2012. *Arab revolutions and Russian-US relations*, http://www.hse.ru/data/2011/04/27/1210609292/Apace%20peo%20%20P-CA.pdf (accessed 15 August 2014).

Trenin, D. 2013. Putin's new foreign policy has control as its true objective. *Security Times.* http://www.carnegie.ru/2013/02/01/putin-doctrine/fn12 (accessed 7 October 2013).

Trenin, D., M. Lipman, and A. Malashenko. 2013. *The end of an era in EU-Russia relations.* Moscow: Carnegie Endowment for International Peace.

Vorobyov, V. 23 October 2012. Syria under Asad Siege. *Rossisskaya gazeta.*

Turkish Foreign Policy in a Changing Arab World: Rise and Fall of a Regional Actor?

BILGIN AYATA

Department of Political Science, Freie Universität Berlin, Berlin, Germany

ABSTRACT   This article analyses Turkey's responses to the Arab uprisings in the context of its larger foreign policy transformation and regional aspirations. The AKP government seized the uprisings as an opportunity to increase its influence in the region by assigning itself a central role in the transition processes in various countries. In the process, however, Turkey faced a number of setbacks and reversals. Comparing the cases of Libya, Syria, and Egypt, the paper argues that Turkey's efforts to advance regime change in these sites were marked by inconsistency and incoherence. Furthermore, the paper argues that this trajectory of reactions can be explained only by taking both ideational and domestic factors into account. Despite the shortcomings of Turkey's actions, however, the article concludes that Turkey has consolidated itself as a regional actor, albeit a controversial one.

Introduction

The outbreak of protests in the Arab world, that resulted in a series of regime changes, was as unexpected for Turkey as for other countries, yet it did not take long for the Turkish leadership to seize the events as a golden opportunity to expand Turkey's role and influence in the region. While actors such as the EU, the US, Russia, and Israel expressed their support for the Arab uprisings but opted for a low-key profile in order not to appear too interfering from the outset (see the articles in this Special Issue), the Turkish Government took the opposite attitude by positioning itself center stage, claiming regional leadership as an actor eager to spearhead the transitions from autocratic regimes to popular democracies. Capitalizing on its improved relations with Arab countries, and the praise it had been receiving from Western leaders for the country's ascendancy after a decade of political stability and economic growth, Turkey embarked on a daring path of foreign policy involvement in response to the so-called Arab Spring. Yet this path soon evolved into a turbulent roller coaster ride, which some describe as the rise and fall of the Turkish Model in the region (Samaan 2013).

In late 2011, Turkey was referred to as the 'winner of the Arab Spring' in a public opinion poll among five Arab countries. The poll asked respondents to evaluate the international reactions toward recent events in the Arab world (Telhami 2011). The majority of the respondents listed Turkey as playing the most constructive role during the Arab uprisings, while Turkish Prime Minister (PM), Erdogan, was mentioned as the most admired global leader. Other external actors such as the US, Russia, and the UK fared relatively poorly, as did their leaders.[1] Yet, three years later, following an increased involvement in regional affairs, Turkey's popularity in Egypt fell behind that of Saudi Arabia and the United Arab Emirates, which are now named as the two most favorable countries (Zogby 2013).[2] Other opinion polls in the region point to similar tendencies: Turkey is still perceived as one of the most popular external actors in Arab countries, but the heyday of the 'Arab Spring, Turkish Harvest' (Heydarian 2011) is over.[3]

Initially, the prospects for Turkish involvement after the uprisings looked promising. Compared to other external actors like the US, the EU, or Israel — all of whose rhetoric of democracy and practice of supporting autocratic regimes undermined their credibility in the region — Turkey's status had risen, thanks to its own transformation process, which included a departure from Turkey's traditional foreign policy strictly bound to Western interests. Instead, a pro-active, value-based, and identity-driven foreign policy was now shaping Turkey's actions, with a new 'zero problem with neighbors' doctrine leading to major improvements with Arab neighbors. Particularly, after Erdogan's challenging of Shimon Perez at Davos in 2009 and Turkey's stance against Israel after the Gaza Flotilla incident, Turkey's popularity in the Arab world increased to an unprecedented level, especially compared to previously hostile Arab–Turkish relations (Jung 2001; TESEV 2011). Moreover, the fact that Turkey's AKP (*Adalet ve Kalkinma Partisi*, Justice and Development Party) managed to stay in power via democratic elections over three consecutive terms without replacing the secular order with the Sharia was perceived as a promising alternative to Iran or the Gulf countries. The AKP government's tenure helped to disprove Western claims that democracy and Islam were incompatible, positioning Turkey as a democratic role model for Muslim countries. Thus, Turkey enjoyed strong credibility and a normative advantage over other external actors, which only increased when it quickly took the side of protestors. This response was far from self-evident; however, Turkey had been developing close ties with the region's autocratic regimes for the past decade in order to improve its long-neglected relationship with the Arab world (Alessandri and Altunisik 2013).

The protests against the regime leaders carried the risk of backfiring on Turkey's large political and economic investments in the region, yet the Turkish Government wanted not only to be on the 'right side of history,' but also push for a new regional order that would change the power constellation in the Middle East (Özha 2011).

Up until mid-2012, it seemed that Turkey was indeed up to the task of asserting itself in the region as a mediator and model of stable democratic transition. It deployed a range of soft power instruments such as financial assistance, technical expertise, and civil society support to Tunisia, Egypt, Libya, Syria, and Yemen. And the already-expanding trade relations within the region intensified even more after the protests. Yet, as Syria's uprising evolved into a civil war, Turkey's reactions became increasingly erratic, confrontational, and interventionist. Diplomatic efforts to support a democratic transition in Syria were soon overshadowed by security concerns related to Turkey and Syria's shared 900 km border — a large part of which is home to many Kurds and the Kurdish conflict. Thus, in Syria, Turkey eventually pushed for military intervention — a measure it had tried to prevent in Libya. Meanwhile, in Egypt, Turkey was a fervent critic of military inventions. Its reaction to the removal of President Morsi in Egypt in July 2013 was so openly partisan on behalf of the Muslim Brotherhood that Turkey's claim to be a neutral mediator in the region dissipated just as its 'zero problem with neighbors' doctrine had in Syria. Turkey's vocal opposition to the military ouster isolated Turkey from Western actors and led to a rapid deterioration in Egyptian–Turkish relations. Since these developments, Turkey's foreign policy in the region has been increasingly criticized as sectarian and cited as a case of overstretch, even failure — not only by Western observers, but also by secular voices in the region disappointed with Turkey's partisan support for the Muslim Brotherhood (Edelman *et al.* 2013; Samaan 2013). At the time of this writing, four years after the outbreak of protests in Tunisia, Turkey has become so embroiled in the unfolding regional conflicts that its leverage has been reduced significantly and its credibility undermined. Moreover, in the course of these four years, Erdogan has vocally challenged the NATO, the US, Russia, Israel, the EU, and the UN — an attitude that is popular with his electorate, but has increasingly isolated Turkey in the international arena. Growing domestic opposition against the AKP and widening societal polarization within the country only add to Turkey's image decline in the regional and international arenas.

Despite these setbacks, this article cautions against premature conclusions and calls for a more measured assessment of Turkey's responses to the Arab Spring and its aftermath. Turkey is part and parcel of the fierce battle for a new order in the Middle East, along with Iran, Israel, Russia, Saudi Arabia, and the US (see Dannreuther 2014; Huber 2014; Magen 2014). While Turkey's rhetoric and self-understanding of its role has fluctuated from case to case and over time, it generally supported the uprisings in political and economic terms both during and after the protests, as the following sections will show. The Turkish leadership went out on a limb by getting so extensively involved in the transition processes that followed the uprisings, but in doing so, it also consolidated its status as a relevant, albeit controversial, player in the region. Compared to the EU and US, Turkey's financial capacities are too limited and its military capacities are too dependent on the NATO to implement the kind of independent and multidirectional foreign policy that is its ultimate goal. Following the uprisings, both the cornerstones as well as the limits of Turkey's foreign policy aspirations became more transparent. In cases where the political outcomes of the regime changes converged with the ideological interests of the AKP government, Turkey's reactions were extensive and constructive in support of the reform processes advancing a strong pro-democracy rhetoric. In contrast, in cases of conflict such as Syria and post-Morsi Egypt, foreign policy principles were quickly thrown overboard and replaced by a defensive, often erratic course void of a coherent strategy. In an effort to understand these shifts and variations in Turkey's foreign policy responses over time, this article focuses on the three sites of Arab uprisings that were most concerning and controversial for Turkey: Libya, Egypt, and Syria. These cases challenged not only Turkey, but also the EU, the US, Russia, and Israel — as the other articles in this issue discuss. Yet, in the case of Turkey, the contrast between these cases is particularly drastic and calls for closer examination. In what follows, the article will lay out Turkey's initial reading of the uprisings, and then analyze the shifts in both its stance and the instruments it employed, and finally explore what factors were driving these reactions.

Turkey's Reactions to the Arab Uprisings: Roles, Instruments, and Goals

Turkey's Approach and Role

Over the past two decades, Turkish foreign policy has undergone important transformations as the country seeks a powerful role in regional and global affairs as an independent actor in a multi-polar world (Ülgen 2010). Turkey has notably expanded its scope of engagement not only in its immediate neighborhood, but also in the wider Middle East, the Balkans, the Caucasus, and even a range of Muslim countries on the African continent (Aras 2013). Under the AKP rule, Turkey has set up its own visa-free zones and trade agreements, as well as entered numerous forms of bilateral and regional cooperation with neighboring Arab countries. These efforts bore fruit during the Arab uprisings and provided the Turkish government with fertile ground to assume an active role during and after the protests (Kirisci 2011).

Moreover, even though a variety of social forces came together during the protests to remove the authoritarian leaders, the fact that Islamic movements emerged as the best organized opposition in shaping the aftermath of the protests boosted Turkey's role. Turkey's AKP — a party that formed out of an Islamic movement and that adopted a range of pro-democracy reforms, curtailed the power of the military, improved the country's economy, and brought it closer to the EU than ever before — was widely discussed as a successful role model for the Middle East. The Turkish leadership benefitted from these discussions, even though PM Erdogan and

Foreign Minister (FM) Davutoglu were careful not to directly claim such a model themselves. Instead, they sought to convey self-confidence combined with sympathy for the 'brotherly peoples' of the Arab world, emphasizing common historic, religious, and cultural bonds, while at the same time highlighting Turkey's commitment to democracy, secularism, and rule of law. For FM Davutoglu, the mastermind behind the new foreign policy doctrines, the uprisings presented a historic opportunity to expand Turkey's role in the region and (re)claim a status appropriate to Turkey's imperial past and its geostrategic location (Reynolds 2012).

Thus thriving on the 'Turkey as role model' discourse and motivated by Turkey's goal of more leverage in the region, the AKP took a very active role in the Arab uprisings, asserting itself as a promoter of democracy and popular will. This was the case particularly in Tunisia and Egypt, where, following Morsi's victory in the latter, Davutoglu even spoke of an axis of democracy that spanned the region and connected the countries (Özkan and Korkut 2013). Similarly, in Libya, as well as in the first months in Syria, Turkey assumed the role of a mediator between autocratic regimes under pressure and Western actors, based on Turkey's unique position as a Muslim country with strong Western alliances. After the regime change in Libya, Turkey shifted to a guide and supporter of the transition by providing infrastructural assistance. Then, in Egypt after Morsi's removal, as well as in Syria after the Turkish government changed course toward Assad, Turkey positioned itself as a guardian of the popular will, attacking the rulers on behalf of the opposition.

While European observers tended to compare the Arab uprisings to the Eastern European protests and regime changes, Turkey offered a different reading. The Turkish leadership identified the Arab uprisings and subsequent regime changes as a replication of Turkey's own transformation spearheaded by the AKP. This was most expressively captured in May 2011 when Davutoglu stated that 'the Arab Spring is also a Turkish Spring' (Davutoglu 2001). Just as the AKP had sought to overturn Turkey's militaristic legacy that upheld an orthodox secularism through undemocratic means and Western backing, the Turkish leadership now interpreted the Arab uprisings as constituting the same process against the respective secular autocratic leaders who were also backed by the West. This reading was extended even further, when Turkey framed the protests as an uprising against the US-imposed Camp David order after 1978 in the Middle East that put the region under tutelage.[4] With the Arab uprisings, the AKP vision for a 'new Turkey' thus took on a regional dimension and expanded to a 'new Middle East,' in which the influence of the West, in general, and the US and Israel in particular would be diminished. By identifying the uprisings as a regional replication of the Turkish experience, Turkey assigned itself a unique role compared to other external actors — not unlike the position of the EU after the Eastern European transition process, but without any comparable institutional and financial means. The next section will analyze Turkey's reactions in more detail against the backdrop of this identification and self-assigned role regarding the uprisings.

Turkey's Instruments and Goals

In almost all the affected countries, Turkey employed the common range of instruments, with the exception of positive conditionality (see the Börzel, Dandashly, and Risse 2014). In every case, it emphasized and attempted diplomacy before moving to other instruments. Most notably, it attempted diplomatic persuasion in both Libya and Syria, before it employed sanctions and, finally, military force. Financial and technical assistances were employed during and after the regime transitions in Tunisia, Egypt, Libya, Yemen, and Algeria, while financial and technical assistances were also provided to the Syrian opposition. In order to highlight differences, I focus on Turkey's actions in Libya, Syria, and Egypt as it was across these cases that Turkey's actions varied the most and were most extensive in scope. In Libya, Turkey first strongly opposed military action in favor of a political solution, and then later opposed the NATO decision to carry out operations, until finally acceding to the NATO plan. In Syria, it began by trying to convince Assad to resign, but eventually shifted to pushing for an international military intervention. And in Egypt, Turkey risked extensive political and economic investments when it turned from friend to foe following the military ousting of Morsi. The attempt of using diplomacy to mediate among all parties, as implemented in Libya and Syria in 2011, was completely abandoned in 2013. Similarly, Turkey's 'zero problems with neighbors' doctrine went astray in both Syria and Egypt.

How to handle the events in these three cases was tricky, not just for Turkey but also for other actors such as the EU, the US, and Russia (see articles in this special issue). In Libya and Syria, external actors such as the EU and the US shifted their preferences from democracy to stability and similarly in Egypt, they had to reconsider their position after the mass protests of 2013 and the subsequent removal of Morsi. It was also in these three sites that Turkey entered into conflict with its former allies, first in Libya, escalating in Syria, and finally reaching its peak in Egypt. The next sections highlight the continuities and shifts in Turkey's responses and contextualize them in relation to the leadership's broadly conceived new foreign policy — a policy that found itself put to the test with the Arab uprisings.

Diplomacy Instead of Intervention in Libya

In Tunisia and Egypt, Turkey's initial reactions to the protests were similar to its Western allies, but in Libya, Turkey demarcated itself from NATO members by strongly opposing sanctions and military intervention, insinuating that France and the US were unduly motivated by Libya's oil reserves (Akbas and Düzgün 2012). For Turkey and other external actors, the speedy devolution of protests in Libya into armed conflict posed a particular challenge given Libya's economic significance. As the fourth largest oil producer in the world, unrest in Libya had an immediate effect on the global export of its resources.[5] For Turkey, additional economic concerns were at stake since Libya constitutes its second largest market after Russia in terms of work undertaken by Turkish contractors abroad. There are 215 registered Turkish companies in Libya worth about 20 billion USD (SETA 2011a), and since 1975, Turkey has provided a steady flow of Turkish workers to offset the lack of skilled labor in Libya (Ronen and Yanarocak 2013). When protests broke out, about 25,000 Turkish nationals were present in Libya.

Further influencing Turkey's reaction to events in Libya was the importance of Gaddafi for Turkey's new foreign policy. After a major political crisis between Libya and Turkey in 1996, diplomatic relations cooled off until the AKP took power and slowly made peace with Gaddafi. In November 2009, Erdogan was the first Turkish PM to visit Libya after 1996.[6] Gaddafi was important for Turkey's new foreign policy in two ways: he was an ally in Turkey's support for Palestine, and an important door opener for Turkey's ambitions in Africa. Thus, even though Turkey expressed its support for protestors in Libya just as it did in Egypt and Tunisia, it was in Turkey's interest to encourage a solution that Gaddafi would accept.

Outbreak of protests. Protests in Libya broke out on 17 February 2011, prompting the UN Security Council (UNSC) to pass a resolution on 17 March in favor of an international military intervention, and then launched that intervention only one month later. Turkish leaders voiced concerns that an intervention would lead to disintegration in Libya that would resemble the situations in Iraq or Afghanistan (SETA 2011a). Davutoglu highlighted Turkey's ability as a Muslim country to mediate between the opposition and the regime, and was already, in fact, talking with both Gaddafi and the opposition. In the short time period before the UNSC resolution, Turkey stepped up efforts to prevent military intervention and seek an alternative solution. Erdogan communicated three times with Gaddafi, as well with his son, urging him to leave (SETA 2011a). Davutoglu met with opposition leaders and external actors to prevent an intervention. According to Turkish press reports, Turkey presented an alternative plan to the US on 18 March, but to no avail; a French-led military strike commenced on 19 March (Davutoglu 2011). Turkey criticized the strike, and challenged the legitimacy of the Paris Summit where the decision was made — a summit to which Turkey had not been invited.[7] NATO took over the operation on 27 March, despite both Turkey and Germany expressing opposition. Turkey refused to supply armed forces for the operation, but it did allow NATO to use a base in Izmir, Western Turkey, to oversee the aerial mission (Akbas and Düzgün 2012).

Military intervention and regime change. After efforts to mediate with Gaddafi and propose alternative peace plans were unsuccessful, Turkey changed course and adopted a stronger stance. On 3 May 2011, Erdogan called on Gaddafi to resign and recognized the authority of the Libyan opposition's National Transitional Council (NTC) after the head of the NTC visited Turkey. During this visit, Turkey also committed USD 300 million of financial support to the NTC. Davutoglu visited Libya in July 2011, followed by Erdogan in September in the course of his Arab Spring tour, and then Turkey's minister for economy along with 225 Turkish businessmen in November (SETA 2011b).

After Gaddafi's murder and the end of NATO operations in October 2011, Turkey's actions focused on providing infrastructural assistance and expertise to the NTC. Turkey committed to provide training for 3000 soldiers of the Libyan Army (SETA 2013). Turkish businesses became actively involved in Libyan reconstruction. Over the course of 2011, Turkish exports to Libya increased from USD 500 million to USD 1.5 billion, while Turkish imports rose from USD 132 to 235 million (SETA 2012). Following elections in Libya in 2012, Turkey maintained amicable relations, but it has continued to argue that military intervention did more harm than good, pointing out that the situation there has begun to resemble that in Iraq and Afghanistan. The fact remains, however, that in spite of its strong rhetoric, Turkey did eventually give in to NATO, even facilitating its military intervention by making its airbases available. But while Turkey was fiercely critical of a NATO intervention in Libya, in Syria it became one of the most vocal advocates for military intervention. In contrast to Russia, which more consistently objects to Western intervention (see Dannreuther 2014), Turkey began calling in Syria for exactly what it opposed in Libya.

From Diplomacy to the Brink of War in Syria

Before the uprisings, Turkish–Syrian relations had improved significantly during the AKP rule, after decades of hostility, tension, and conflict (Hale 2009). In fact, Syria had become Turkey's most successful application of its new 'zero problems' foreign policy doctrine. This was achieved by building a close relationship between the two leaders, Assad and Erdogan; a steep increase of economic activity between the two countries through free trade agreements; and the lifting of visa requirements and the establishment of a high-level council of strategic partnership in 2009 (Bishku 2012). When protests broke out and turned into violent conflict, not only were these political and economic investments at stake, but the emerging instability and security threats had direct consequences for Turkey given its 900 km shared border with Syria. Consequently, Turkey's primary goal in Syria was to restore stability and security, and prevent any spillover effects the protests might have on Turkey. In particular, Turkey feared the effect Syrian unrest could have on the Kurdish movement in Turkey, given that large parts along the border cross through Kurdish territories. In recent years, Syria had cooperated with Turkey to suppress the Kurdish movement, and any deterioration of relations in Syria could fuel the Kurdish conflict. With these concerns in mind, Turkey employed a mismatch of strategies and instruments that made its reactions over the next three years look not only inept, but also erratic and contradictory. In retrospect, Turkey overestimated its leverage over Syria and underestimated the resilience of Assad's regime as well as its support from both Russia and Iran.

Outbreak of protest. In the first six months of the protests, Turkey pursued a divided strategy. It tried both to pressure Assad to make political reforms, while at the same time allowing the Syrian opposition to organize and mobilize within Turkey. Davutoglu presented this as Turkey's principle of maintaining dialog with all sides, as it had also done in Libya (SETA 2011a). Yet, these parallel efforts did not sit well with Assad. Assad did pass some reforms, such as lifting emergency rule, releasing some political prisoners, and giving citizenship back to Syrian Kurds disenfranchised in 1962 but he also continued a heavy military assault on the uprising. When events morphed into a civil war, scores of Syrians fled to Turkey: in June 2011, over 10,500 arrived, by mid-2012, the number rose to 130,000, and by the end of December 2013, it reached 800,000 (Kirisci 2013). The Turkish government hosted not only Syrian refugees but also the Syrian opposition, which held two conferences in Turkey in April and May 2011, resulting in the formation of the Syrian National Council (SETA 2011b). Irritated by Turkish support for the Syrian opposition, Assad targeted Turkey's greatest weakness: the Kurdish conflict. For two decades, Syria had hosted the PKK's (*Partiye Karkeren Kurdistan*, Kurdistan's Workers Party) leader Öcalan in Damascus and provided the PKK a safe base from which to lead its struggle against the Turkish military. The end of this support had been the precondition for Turkish–Syrian relations to improve during the AKP tenure, but in the course of the intensifying Syrian conflict, Assad played this trump card. He tacitly supported the empowerment of the Syrian Kurds — who, ironically, were also part of the Syrian opposition — first by sparing the Kurdish regions of Syria from military excess and later by tacitly allowing Syrian Kurds to build autonomous enclaves along the Turkish border. For Turkey, this was a wake-up call that shifted the leadership's focus from political reform in Syria to national security at the border.

From diplomacy to military action. In August 2011, after a final visit by Davutoglu to Syria, Turkey abandoned its diplomatic efforts with Assad. In September 2011, Erdogan declared Turkey's suspension of relations with the Syrian Government. What followed was a radical U-turn, as Turkey now switched to openly advocating for regime change. There was a grim realization that the expectations for a post-Assad Syria had been premature, despite the precedence of an externally enforced regime change in Libya. Turkey clearly underestimated and miscalculated Russia's stance on Syria (see Dannreuther 2014). To Turkey's disappointment, the US was not taking a consistent and strong stance against Syria either (see Huber in this Special Issue). The Syrian conflict hence negatively affected Turkey's relations with Iran and Russia, as well with the US, which was further irritated by Turkey's hard line (Cagaptay 2013). Turkey attempted to rally regional and international support for regime change, first by supporting the EU-drafted UN resolution to condemn Syria and impose sanctions in October 2011. But when the resolution was vetoed by Russia and China, Turkey imposed its own economic sanctions on Syria, in addition to an earlier arms embargo. Turkey also supported the second attempt at a UN resolution, this time drafted by the Arab League, which was once again vetoed by Russia and China.

Turkish–Syrian relations deteriorated further after June 2012, when Syria shot down a Turkish military fighter, bringing the countries to the brink of war (SETA 2012). Turkey announced it was changing the rules of engagement and threatened to retaliate. The Turkish strategy of pursuing a proactive, independent, and principled policy was crumbling in Syria with every day the conflict intensified. In October 2012, when the Syrian army clashed with the opposition groups, Syrian mortar fire hit a Turkish border town, killing five Turkish citizens. The Turkish army returned fire and deployed more troops to the border. A few days later, Turkey closed its airspace to Syrian planes after intercepting a commercial Syrian airplane departing from Moscow that was allegedly carrying rockets and other military supplies to Syria (SETA 2012). Alarmed by these three incidents, Turkey requested NATO's help in November 2012 asking for Patriot missiles to be set up at its border since Syria was in possession of rockets that could hit Turkey. NATO granted Turkey's request and in January 2013, Patriot batteries from Germany, Netherlands, and the US arrived in Turkey, along with soldiers to operate the missiles.[8]

This ultimately meant the countermand of the zero problem doctrine. In light of the security threat at its border, Turkey turned to NATO and the same Western powers it was so critical of during the Libyan intervention. The contrast could not have been more striking: whilst opposing military intervention in Libya, Erdogan had declared that Turkey would never drop bombs on Muslims and now in Syria, Turkey found itself ferociously calling for an international military intervention, this time trying to spur its Western allies into action. Two further bomb attacks in Turkish border towns in February and May 2013 that killed 17 and at least 52 civilians, respectively, increased Turkey's alarm.[9] Meanwhile, protests of Turkish citizens against both the presence of Syrian refugees as well as against the government's active support for some factions of Syrian opposition groups revealed that Turkey's foreign policy reactions were also being contested domestically. For both the Free Syrian Army and other opposition groups, Turkey had become a safe zone and supply route, where they could train, recruit, and operate against Syria (Edelman *et al.* 2013). Yet, by harboring such groups, the Turkish Government was actively contributing to the security threat for which it blamed Syria.

With US support for the Russia-proposed chemical weapons deal, military intervention in Syria was off the table, as were any Turkish hopes for an externally enforced regime change. This only increased its support for the Muslim Brotherhood in Syria and other affiliated Sunni opposition group — fuelling critiques that Turkey is pursuing sectarian politics (Taspinar 2012). Given the previous decade of rapprochement with Assad and the downplaying of intra-religious differences, it may well be that that current conflict in Syria has turned into a proxy war, in which many different interests and powers are clashing. Indeed, any foreseeable solution to the conflict seems unrealistic as Turkey's actions grow increasingly questionable. Furthermore, when the Islamic State of Iraq and Syria (ISIS) seized the Turkish consulate in Mosul, Iraq, in June 2014, kidnapping 49 Turkish staff members and procuring the consulate as their main headquarters, but prompting no serious response from Turkey, speculation grew that Turkey was actually arming ISIS and other organizations (Zaman 2014). Thus, despite its efforts to establish itself in 2010 as a promoter of democracy in the region, in 2014 Turkey appears as a partisan actor deeply embroiled in the power conflicts in Syria, and in repeated conflicts with the US, EU, Russia, Iran, Saudi-Arabia, and Israel. This drastic change in Turkey's reactions is demonstrated even more clearly in Egypt, where Turkey went from being a celebrated actor in the post-Mubarak transition process to an unwanted interloper attempting to interfere in Egypt's domestic affairs.

From Friend to Foe in Egypt

Outbreak of protests. In Egypt, Turkey was quick to react to the outbreak of protests in favor of regime change. While the EU and US were still hesitating, Erdogan was the first leader to call for Mubarak's resignation — a move that only increased Turkey's already-rising popularity in the region (Özkan and Korkut 2013; Salem 2011). When Erdogan and Davutoglu visited Egypt in September 2011 and were welcomed by cheering crowds, it boosted their perception of Turkey's role in the Arab uprisings. Although Erdogan's emphasis on secularism and the rule of law during his speeches in Egypt irked hardliners within the Muslim Brotherhood, still the visit carved out an important role for Turkey that was also beneficial for other contested external actors such as the US or the EU who preferred to keep a lower profile (Soler and Lecha 2011). On their visit, Erdogan and Davutoglu were accompanied by six ministers, 250 Turkish businessmen, and a large delegation of AKP members, who entered in partnership and dialogue with a number of Egyptian civil society organizations (SETA 2013). Furthermore, a 'High-level Strategic Cooperation Council' was established with Egypt on 13 September 2011 for the purpose of strengthening the economic and political partnerships of the two countries. Similar councils had been established with Iraq, Syria, and Lebanon before the Arab uprisings, and the groundwork for the council with Egypt had been initiated in 2010.

Turkish support for Morsi's presidency. The emergence of the Muslim Brotherhood as the most powerful group after the protests further motivated the AKP to intensify its efforts in Egypt. Once Morsi won the elections in June 2012, Turkey increased its foreign investment in Egypt with more business partnerships and bilateral projects, including a joint military defense project, for which Turkey provided USD 250 million to Egypt (Bekdil 2013).[10] By 2013, trade between Turkey and Egypt had reached USD 6 billion and Turkish investments rose to USD 2 billion (SETA 2013). Turkey was the first country that Morsi visited during his presidency in September 2012, when he emphasized the importance of Turkish support during the Arab revolutions. During the visit, Turkey announced that Egypt would receive a USD 2 billion loan in two installments. For Egypt, this was a very important contribution that, combined with loans from Qatar and Libya, enabled it to reject an IMF loan of USD 4.8 billion with less-favorable conditions.[11] With this large loan in particular, Turkey showed that it was not only an economic powerhouse in the region, but also that it could back up its rhetoric with money.

Turkish opposition to Morsi's removal. After the military ouster, the Turkish government became such a fervent defender of Morsi and the Muslim Brotherhood that it severely damaged its bilateral relations with the new Egyptian leadership and with other Arab populations that increasingly perceived the AKP as a Turkish branch of the Muslim Brotherhood. With the removal of Morsi, Turkey lost an important ally in its effort to establish its vision of a new Middle East. The Turkish leadership interpreted Morsi's ouster as not only an assault on the will of the Egyptian people (conveniently ignoring the masses of Egyptians who protested Morsi before his removal), but also as a conspiracy on the part of Israel and the US to prevent Qatar, Turkey, Libya, and Egypt from breaking the post-Camp David order. Erdogan, in particular, seized upon the ouster and the subsequent crackdown on the Muslim Brotherhood as a vicariously Turkish affair by frequently addressing AKP party meetings with the four-finger salute symbolizing the crackdown at Rabia Square.[12] He strongly criticized Western toleration of the military takeover, stating that military intervention was an assault on democracy, no matter where it occurs (SETA 2013). That such an ostensibly pro-democracy argument could be just as easily leveled against Turkey itself and/or its own advocacy of military intervention in, for example, Syria, was not, of course, acknowledged.

The new regime in Egypt eventually expelled Turkey's ambassador by declaring him a *persona non grata*, closed some Turkish media and cultural institutions, and terminated diplomatic relations (SETA 2013). After the military takeover, the fate of Morsi and his supporters became the single focus of the Turkish government in Egyptian relations, risking its ongoing economic investments. Yet, despite the political standstill between the two governments, neither Turkey nor Egypt have reversed any of the existing economic agreements, and business representatives confirm that projects with Egypt are continuing, relatively untainted by the current hostility between General el-Sisi and Erdogan (Bekdil 2013).[13] El-Sisi's victory in the June 2014 elections has had little effect and Turkey's cold war with Saudi Arabia and Russia — both of whom support el-Sisi — continues, leaving Qatar as Turkey's only ally.

Turkey's Reactions: What Explains the Variations?

As the previous sections have outlined, Turkey's foreign policy responses have changed over time and differed across the three cases. It shifted from generally proactive measures in the affected countries between 2011 and 2012 to relatively reactive measures first in Syria after mid-2012, and eventually to wholly defensive responses after the military coup in Egypt in July 2013. What explains these shifts and variations? What drove Turkish foreign policy in this process and has it failed to pass the litmus test of reacting to the Arab uprisings in accordance to its new foreign policy goals and doctrines?

From a realist perspective, it could be suggested that the security threats at Turkey's border with Syria and the incoming masses of refugees led Turkey to abandon its value-based foreign policy and switch to advocating military action. Such an explanation, however, fails to explain why Turkey *continues* to insist on regime change in Syria, while other actors such as the US have amended their position in this regard (see Huber 2014). A realist approach alone is even less equipped to explain Turkey's strong adverse reaction to the military coup in Egypt, where its ongoing opposition to el-Sisi risks its substantial economic interests there. This applies to Libya as well, where Turkish investments were similarly endangered by Ankara's position.

In order to explain the variation and shifts across all three cases, we need to incorporate ideational and domestic factors. In terms of the former, by drawing such a strong parallel between the uprisings and Turkey's own experiences, the Turkish leadership boxed themselves into an inflexible corner that made Turkey's reactions both extreme and erratic, and that afforded little room for more measured responses. In terms of domestic factors, it is necessary to contextualize Turkey's reactions vis-à-vis two core challenges at home: the Kurdish conflict and the secular opposition to the AKP's vision for the region.

Ideational Factors: The Arab Uprisings as Replicating Turkey's Experience

One of the biggest obstacles facing the AKP when it took power in 2002 was a military legacy that had dominated Turkey's domestic and foreign policy for much of the history of the Turkish republic. The military's power was sustained through heightened national security discourse that portrayed Turkey as surrounded by hostile neighbors and under constant threat from internal enemies, such as minorities, Islamists, or leftists. Three military coups and the armed conflict between the PKK and the Turkish army had firmly consolidated the military's putative role as the guardian of Turkey's secular order and national unity (Öktem 2011). At the domestic level, the AKP attempted to curtail the power of the military elite through a range of democratic reforms and its EU candidacy, which supported the demilitarization of civilian politics. At the foreign policy level, the AKP reversed the military's discourse of constant besiegement by developing amicable relationships with its neighbors, in particular, with Syria and other Arab countries. The 'zero problems with neighbors' doctrine led to a more cooperative and value-based foreign policy that not only curtailed the military's power externally but also provided a massive boost to the Turkish economy by opening up new markets and improving trade relations in the MENA region (Kirisci 2011).

After the outbreak of protests, Turkey further intensified its identity- and value-based foreign policy by highlighting not only its religious and cultural bonds with its Arab neighbors, but also by emphasizing their shared history of military rule (and its overthrow) in the region (Özkan and Korkut 2013). By 2011, the AKP had significantly weakened Turkey's old military guard, and replaced it with its own power, enjoying the majority of votes within Turkey and receiving international praise for establishing political stability and economic success. Thus, when uprisings began to spread throughout the region, Turkey was quick to see it as replicating its own experience and heralding the end of the status quo in the Middle East (Özha 2011). The Turkish leadership claimed that, just as Turkey had divested itself of its military legacy, now the Middle East would free itself from the political tutelage that the Camp David order had imposed on the region. Analysts close to the government to this day continue to make this link when writing about the 'new Turkey' in a 'new Middle East,' identifying the changes in the Arab world as mirroring Turkey's own transformation (Kücükcan 2013). This vision of a new regional order spearheaded by Turkey was the main driver of its proactive policies in the initial phase of the uprisings. The elections and regime changes in Tunisia, Egypt, Yemen, Morocco, and Algeria that brought Islamic parties with close links to the AKP into power only fortified Turkey's value- and identity-based foreign policy.

Domestic Factor I: The Kurdish Predicament

The limits to this value- and identity-based policy became most visible during the Syrian crisis, which not only brought masses of refugees and instability to Turkey's border, but also revealed once again the unresolved Kurdish conflict as Turkey's Achille's heel. With Assad's support for Syrian Kurds, the PKK increased its attacks on Turkish military units in 2011. As Syrian Kurds established autonomous enclaves along the Turkish border in mid 2012, Turkey's actions became increasingly reactive and nervous. In order to prevent a spillover of Kurdish empowerment in Syria, the Turkish Government responded at the domestic level by launching a peace process seeking a solution to the Kurdish conflict — ahistoric development for Turkey (Tocci 2013). The PKK began to withdraw some troops from Turkey to Syriain in May 2013, where they are now helping to consolidate the autonomous Kurdish enclaves. Yet, the government has not taken any further steps to push forward the peace process, in fact, the entire process appears more as a tactical move than a paradigm shift regarding the Kurdish conflict. If the current peace process in Turkey with the PKK comes to a halt, violence may erupt anew and possibly even worse than before, as there is now a powerful Kurdish belt around Turkey's Syrian and Iraqi borders. This explains in part Turkey's uncompromising stance against Assad, who utilized the Kurdish conflict against Turkey in addition to the larger Sunni–Shia power battle in the region.

Domestic Factor II: The Gezi Protests

Even though it is currently more rhetoric than action, the peace process was a smart domestic strategy on the part of the Turkish government to contain the spillover of Kurdish empowerment. Yet it could not prevent the outbreak of protests by dissatisfied urban dwellers in Istanbul in the spring of 2013. Mass protests in Istanbul and other cities erupted after protestors occupying a public park were brutally suppressed by police forces. Images of the police violence were broadcasted around the world, turning Turkey's image as a democratic role model upside down. The events mobilized the secular opposition in Turkey, which had been growing increasingly dissatisfied with AKP rule. Despite only two years ago being held up as the model for introducing democracy to the region, the Turkish Government now found itself rebranded as part of the problem by domestic youth fed up with Erdogan's authoritarian rule.

Rather than attempting to accommodate the domestic protest — as it had urged other Arab leaders to do in 2011 — the Turkish leadership became increasingly defensive, blaming an international conspiracy on the AKP. It was this domestic pressure from late May 2013 onward that explains the Turkish Government's fiercely negative reaction against the military ouster of Morsi in Egypt in July 2013. Turkey's outrage against the removal of Morsi has to be assessed in the context of the perceived threats to its own power at home. The Turkish Government would never have silently accepted Morsi's removal given its political and financial commitments in Egypt; however, it was this combination of domestic challenges and the renewed specter of military power that intensified the AKP's reaction. Erdogan criticized the West for having double standards vis-à-vis democracy and accused Israel of plotting against the Muslim Brotherhood (Edelman *et al.* 2013). By defensively citing Morsi's victory at the ballot boxes, the Turkish Government shifted its rhetoric from a promoter of democracy to the guardian of a lost revolution in Egypt. As noted above, this conveniently ignored the masses that protested against Morsi in the days before his removal and, ironically, replicated the same strategy at home of ignoring domestic protests. Thus, it might seem that, in contrast to the case in Syria, Turkey prioritized democracy over security in Egypt. It would be more accurate, however, to say that what Turkey prioritized in Egypt was Morsi over the military — for it was Morsi, not the military, whom the AKP government regarded as a key ally in its vision of a new Middle East.

What does this change from proactive policies to reactive and defensive policies say about Turkish foreign policy in a (partially) reconfigured Arab world? Put another way: if the Arab Spring was a litmus test of Turkey's new role in the region, did Turkey fail? The record of an ISIS-seized consulate in Iraq, a Turkish ambassador expelled from Cairo, an embassy closed in Damascus, and tense relations with Israel and Saudi Arabia in mid-2014 certainly indicate the failed 'zero problem' doctrine in the Middle East. Ultimately, the limitations of Turkish foreign policy were foregrounded after the Arab uprisings. Not only does Turkish policy contain any alternate strategy for cases in which the zero problem doctrine collapses, but its lack of credible commitment to democracy beyond victory at the ballot boxes has been revealed, undermining its value-based foreign policy. The transitions in the Arab world are ongoing, thus the long-term effects of all this remain to be seen. Yet, as an interim assessment, while Turkey has not become a regional leader, it has certainly consolidated itself as an important regional actor whose ideological and strategic commitments to a particular vision of a new Middle East demarcate it from its former allies in the EU and US. Even though this creates growing unease both at home and abroad, the current Turkish leadership continues to pursue this vision and the prominent place imagined for Turkey therein.

Conclusion

In previous decades, scholars described Turkey as an 'awkward and uneasy candidate in both European and Middle Eastern politics' (Robins 1991) or at most granted it a 'middle power' (Hale 2000) status in foreign policy. In stark contrast, policy reports on the Arab uprisings from 2011 highlighted Turkey as a potential player that could 'inspire,' 'facilitate,' or 'mediate' the process of transformation in the region (Tocci *et al.* 2011). Three years later, a different picture emerges. In Tunisia, Libya, Yemen, and Algeria, Turkey maintains close and constructive bilateral relations with the new regimes. In these cases, Turkey has managed to turn the uprisings to its advantage; its responses to and support for the uprisings in these countries are positively evaluated therein. In Syria and Egypt, however, Turkey's reactions have resulted in conflict, chaos, and political standstill. Its uncompromising stance calling for Assad's removal and its refusal to accept the military resurgence in Egypt has isolated Turkey from other actors and reduced its leverage in the region. The AKP government's strong identification with the transformations in the Middle East explains some of its confrontational and erratic responses. This article has therefore argued that while Turkey generally attempted to assert itself as an independent actor in the region after the Arab uprisings, two factors limited its efforts. First, its value- and identity-based foreign policy provided no alternative vision or strategy for conflict, leading to extreme and erratic reactions. Second, it lacks a credible commitment to democratic principles and an attendant openness to opposition and difference. Given the legitimacy crisis that the Turkish government is currently experiencing at home, this second factor may be particularly decisive in shaping the future prospects for Turkish foreign policy. If the ongoing processes set in motion with the Arab Spring do present Turkey with a litmus test, the results, while undoubtedly less triumphant than Turkey might have originally hoped, ultimately remain to be seen.

Notes

1. The poll was conducted in Egypt, Jordan, Lebanon, Morocco, and United Arab Emirates. The following external actors were listed in the question on the constructive role: Turkey (50%), France (30%), US (24%), China (20%), Britain (11%), Germany (10%), Russia (9%), and Japan (8%). PM Erdogan (38%) was listed in Egyptian poll as the leader that the next Egyptian President look like, followed by Ahmadinajad (11%), Mandela (9%), King Abdullah (8%), Sarkozy (6%), Chavez (6%), Nasrallah (5%), Obama (5%), and Putin (2%). Key findings of the poll are available at http://www.brookings.edu/~/media/research/files/reports/2011/11/21%20arab%20pub lic%20opinion%20telhami/1121_arab_public_opinion.pdf.
2. The most favorable countries in Egypt in September 2013 were listed as Saudi Arabia (58%), UAE (52%), Turkey (36%), Qatar (19%), EU (10%), Iran (9%), US (4%), and Israel (0%) (Zogby 2013, 13).
3. A poll by the Turkish Think Tank TESEV on Turkey's perception in the Middle East encompassing 16 countries shows declining approval rates from 2011 to 2013 for all listed external actors when asked about their role during the Arab Spring except for China (2011: 31%, 2013: 38%) and Russia (2011: 30%, 2013: 38%) (TESEV 2013, 18).
4. Analysts and advisors to the Turkish Government have highlighted the relationship of the Arab revolutions and the Camp David order (Kücükcan 2013; Özha 2011; SETA 2011b).

RESPONSES TO THE 'ARABELLIONS'

5. It even led to the release of emergency stock piles of oil by the International Energy Agency (IEA) — an emergency act that was only taken in 1991 during the First Gulf War (1991) and in 2005 after Hurricane Katrina http://www.bloomberg.com/news/2011-06-23/iea-will-release-60-million-barrels-of-oil-in-emergency-offset-from-libya.html.
6. For decades, Gaddafi had been a strong supporter of the Palestinian cause, criticizing Turkey and Egypt for its alliances with Israel. In fact, it was his disappointment with Arab leaders and lack of unity regarding Palestine that Gaddafi turned his attention towards African countries (Ronen and Yanarocak 2013). After PM Erdogan's critique of Israel during the Davos meeting in January 2009, the tension between Turkey and Libya was eased. In September 2009, when Gaddafi celebrated his 40th anniversary of his rule in Libya, PM Erdogan's wife and Erdogan's deputy minister Bülent Arinc followed his invitation. In November 2010, Gaddafi invited Turkey to participate in the third Africa-EU summit in November 2010 during which PM Erdogan was awarded the 'Qaddafi Human Rights Prize' (Ronen and Yanarocak 2013).
7. http://www.euractiv.com/global-europe/turkey-accuses-france-oversteppi-news-503385.
8. The mandate for the missiles has just been renewed for another year (http://www.tagesschau.de/inland/kabinett-bundeswehr100.html).
9. Turkey blamed the Syrian intelligence for the car bomb in Reyhanli, yet the case remains unresolvedhttp://www.bbc.co.uk/news/world-middle-east-22494128.
10. http://www.defensenews.com/article/20130714/DEFFEAT02/307140010/Turkish-Firms-May-Lose-Contracts-After-Egypt-Ouster.
11. http://www.reuters.com/assets/print?aid=USL5N0D41QX20130417.
12. The four finger salute emerged in mid-August 2013 symbolizing the crack down at Rabaa square. While its origin is not clear, it was Erdogan who made it popular at an international level (http://english.alarabiya.net/en/media/2013/08/21/Four-finger-salute-Egypt-rivals-use-Rabaa-symbol-to-turn-Facebook-yellow.html). In contrast, Saudi Arabia has banned its use as a sign of support for the Muslim Brotherhood (http://www.al-monitor.com/pulse/originals/2014/04/saudi-arabia-tur key-muslim-brotherhood-sunni-middle-east.html).
13. http://www.worldbulletin.net/?aType=haberYazdir&ArticleID=113023&tip = .

References

Akbas, Z., and Z.A. Düzgün. 2012. A constructivist approach to Turkish Foreign Policy oriented to the Arab Spring in Libya. *Ekonomik ve Sosyal Arastirmalar Dergisi* 8, no. 2: 57–81.

Alessandri, E., and M. Altunisik. 2013. Unfinished transitions: challenges and opportunities of the EU's and Turkey's responses to the 'Arab Spring'. Working Paper 04. *Global Turkey in Europe.*

Aras, B. 2013. Turkey's Africa Policy-Policy Brief, *German Marshall Fund.* October.

Bekdil, B. 2013. Turkish firms may lose contracts after Egypt Ouster, *Defense News*, http://mobile.de fensenews.com/article/307140010 (accessed 25 January 2014).

Bishku, Michael B. 2012. Turkish-Syrian relations: a checkered history. *Middle East Policy* 19, no. 3: 36–53.

Börzel, T.A., A. Dandashly, and T. Risse. 2014. Responses to the "Arabellions": the EU in comparative perspective – Introduction. *Journal of European Integration* 37, no. 1: 1–17.

Cagaptay, S. 2013. Ankara's Middle East Policy Post Arab Spring. Policy Notes Nr. 16. *The Washington Institute for Near East Policy.* Washington, DC.

Dannreuther, R. 2014. Russia and the Arab Spring: supporting the counter-revolution. *Journal of European Integration* 37, no. 1: 77–94.

Davutoglu, A. 2001. *Stratejik Derinlik: Türkiye'nin Uluslararası Konumu* (Strategic depth: Turkey's international position). Istanbul: Küre Yayınları.

Davutoglu, A. 2011. Arab bahari oldugu kadar TÃ¼rk bahari. *Daily Aksam*, 25 May 2011.

Edelman, E., S. Cornell, A. Lobel, and M. Makovsky. 2013. *The roots of Turkish conduct: understanding the evolution of Turkish policy in the Middle East.* Washington, DC: Bipartisan Policy Center.

Hale, W. 2000. *Turkish Foreign Policy 1774–2000.* London: Frank Cass.

Hale, W. 2009. Turkey and the Middle East in the 'New Era'. *Insight Turkey* 11, no. 3: 143–59.

Heydarian, R.J. 2011. Arab Spring, Turkish Harvest. *Foreign Policy in Focus.* September.

Huber, D. 2014. A pragmatic actor — the US response to the Arab uprisings. *Journal of European Integration* 37, no. 1: 57–75.

Jung, D. 2001. Turkey and the Arab world: historical narratives and new political realities. *Mediterranean Politics* 10, no. 1: 1–17.

RESPONSES TO THE 'ARABELLIONS'

Kirisci, K. 2011. Turkey's 'Demonstrative effect' and the transformation of the Middle East. *Insight Turkey* 13, no. 2: 33–55.

Kirisci, K. 2013. Syrian humanitarian crisis: the fundamental difficulties facing Turkey. *Journal of Turkish Weekly*. Brookings Institute. 28 December. Washington, DC.

Kücükcan, T. 2013. *Misir, Suriye, Bölgesel Düzen ve Türk Dis Politikasi* (Egypt, Syria, regional order and Turkish Foreign Policy). Ankara: SETA Foundation. 23 September.

Magen, A. 2014. Comparative assessment of Israel's foreign policy response to the 'Arab Spring'. *Journal of European Integration* 37, no. 1: 113–33.

Öktem, K. 2011. *Angry Nation-Turkey since 1989*. London: Zed Books.

Özha, T. 2011. The Arab Spring and Turkey. *SETA Foundation*. 15 October.

Özkan, M., and H. Korkut. 2013. Turkish Foreign Policy towards the Arab revolutions. *Epiphany* 6, no. 1: 162–81.

Reynolds, M. 2012. Echoes of Empire: Turkey's crisis of Kemalism and the search for an alternative policy. Analysis Paper 26. The Saban Center for Middle East Policy at Brookings. June.

Robins, P. 1991. *Turkey and the Middle East*. London: Royal Institute of International Affairs.

Ronen, Y., and C. Yanarocak. 2013. Casting off the shackles of Libya's Arab-Middle Eastern Foreign Policy: a unique case of rapproachment with non-Arab Turkey (1970s–2011). *The Journal of North African Studies* 18, no. 3: 494–508.

Salem, P. 2011. Turkey's Image in the Arab World. *TESEV*. May.

Samaan, J.-L. 2013. The rise and fall of the 'Turkish Model' in the Arab World. *Turkish Policy* 12, no. 3: 61–9.

SETA. 2011a. Isyan, Müdahale ve sonrasi: Libya'da dönüsümün sancisi. Reports No. 5. December, Ankara.

SETA. 2011b. *2011'de Türkiye* (Turkey in 2011). Reports Nr. 48. December. Ankara.

SETA. 2012. *2012'de Türkiye* (Turkey in 2012). Reports Nr. 57. December. Ankara.

SETA. 2013. *2013'de Türkiye* (Turkey in 2013). Reports Nr. 74. December. Ankara.

Soler, I., and E. Lecha. 2011. The EU, Turkey and the Arab Spring: from parallel approaches to a joint strategy? In *Turkey and the Arab Spring: implications for Turkish Foreign Policy from a transatlantic perspective. Mediterranean Paper Series*. Washington, DC: German Marshall Fund.

Taspinar, Ö. 2012. Turkey's strategic vision and Syria. *The Washington Quarterly* 35, no. 3: 127–40.

Telhami, S. 2011. *2011 Arab Public opinion poll*. Washington, DC: Zogby International.

TESEV. 2011. *2010 Ortadogu'da Türkiye Algisi* (The perception of Turkey in the Middle East). February. Istanbul: Tesev.

TESEV. 2013. *Ortadogu'da Türkiye Algisi* (The perception of Turkey in the Middle East). November. Istanbul: Tesev.

Tocci, N. 2013. Turkey's Kurdish gamble. *The International Spectator* 48, no. 3: 67–77.

Tocci, N., Ö. Taspinar, H.J. Barkey, E.S. iLecha, and H. Nafaa. 2011. Turkey and the Arab Spring: Implications for Turkish Foreign Policy from a transatlantic perspective. *Mediterranean Paper Series*. Washington, DC: German Marshall Fund.

Ülgen, S. 2010. A place in the sun or fifteen minutes of fame? *Carnegie Papers*. 1 December.

Zaman, A. 2014. Islamic State uses Turkish consulate in Mosul as headquarters. *Al-Monitor*. 17 July.

Zogby. 2013. Egyptian attitudes. *Zogby Analytics*. September. Washington, DC.

Comparative Assessment of Israel's Foreign Policy Response to the 'Arab Spring'

AMICHAI MAGEN

Lauder School of Government, Diplomacy and Strategy, IDC, Herzliya;
Governance and Political Violence Programme, ICT, IDC, Herzliya;
Hoover Institution, Stanford University

ABSTRACT   This article analyses Israel's foreign policy response to the 'Arab Spring' in comparative perspective. Following the analytical framework shared by all contributions to this Special Issue, the article addresses four main dimensions in as many parts. Part I examines Israel's initial reactions to the advent of the popular upheavals and regime changes in the Arab world in 2011–2014 and explores how those reactions have evolved over time. Part II identifies Israel's main policy objectives in relation to events in the region and particularly its immediate neighbours: Egypt, Jordan, Syria and Lebanon. Part III examines the instruments which Israel has used, and eschewed, in pursuit of its policy objectives. Finally, part IV undertakes a theoretically informed analysis with the aim of explaining Israel's distinctive strategic posture and policy responses to the events of the 'Arab Spring' thus far.

Introduction

Few states in the world not enduring the upheavals of the 'Arab Spring' themselves have a higher, more immediate stake in its causes, convulsions and consequences than Israel. This article analyses, in comparative perspective, Israel's response to the wave of anti-regime uprisings and popular revolts that erupted in parts of North Africa, the Levant and Arabian Peninsula since December 2010.

Based on original interviews with Israeli officials, documentary materials and media sources, it applies the analytical framework shared by all contributions to this Special Issue to address: Israel's assessment of the 'Arab Spring' and its self-perception vis-à-vis the regional tumult; its strategic objectives and goals; policy instruments used and avoided; and explanatory factors accounting for Israel's reactions. By doing so, the article sheds light on the variable responses of key regional and global actors, including the EU, to the unfolding events of the 'Arab Spring' and so, contributes to a finer grained, better-grounded understanding of EU international actorness. Moreover, the article adds to a nascent corpus of scholarship examining the EU and Israel comparatively (Magen 2012a; Tovias and Magen 2005).

Part I examines Israel's assessment and institutional reaction to the advent of the wave of anti-regime uprisings and popular revolts that erupted in parts of North Africa, the Levant and Arabian Peninsula in the period between December 2010 and mid-2011. Unlike the EU, US, Turkey and Russia, Israeli officials consciously avoided a regional approach to the upheavals, focusing attention on their most immediate neighbours, particularly Israel's most populous and important southern neighbour: Egypt. It then traces the evolution of Israeli assessments since the onset of civil war in Syria in mid-2011, identifying internal dilemmas about how best to handle the Syrian crisis and its spillovers into Lebanon and Jordan. It distinguishes between three main phases of Israeli assessments of cross-cutting trends affecting its national security, and identifying periods of heightened and reduced Israeli anxiety about regional dynamics.

Israel's initial interpretation and evolving evaluations produced a comparatively coherent set of policy objectives relatively early on. These are examined in Part II. Significantly, policy do's and don'ts were derived as part and parcel of the structured policy deliberations undertaken by the country's security and foreign policy establishment, under the aegis of the National Security Council in early to mid-2011, and adjusted incrementally since. The evidence gathered indicates policy chiefs conceive of the country's strategic objectives in terms of three broadly hierarchical policy priorities. These are meant to be mutually reinforcing but are, in reality, not free of internal tensions. In this context, Israel stands out in adopting overwhelmingly, but not exclusively, defensive, non-idealist goals designed to insulate its population and economy from the tumults in its vicinity.

Part III undertakes a theoretically informed analysis of the policy instruments Israel has deployed, considered deploying or avoided in its strategic posture vis-à-vis regional events. Here too, the evidence indicates that Israel constitutes a significant outlier, both in its use of military force and deliberate avoidance of policy instruments heavily relied upon by other external actors, especially the US, EU and Turkey.

Finally, Part IV draws upon the three main theoretical traditions pertaining to state action in international politics, in an effort to explain Israel's policy responses. To accurately capture the motivations and limitations of Israel's reaction, it argues, it is necessary to not only appreciate the country's defensive Realism, but also its self-understanding as an actor and the constraints imposed by domestic popular and elite preferences.

Taken together, Israel's posture is essentially designed to insulate itself from the regional upheaval and is driven primarily by lack of faith in its neighbour's ability to liberalize and its own capacity to influence them positively.

Israel's Assessment of the 'Arab Spring'

The burst of popular protests and anti-regime uprisings in Tunisia, Libya, Yemen and Egypt, which took place in the six-week period between late December 2010 and Hosni Mubarak's resignation on 11 February 2011, threw the Israeli national security and foreign policy system into a whirlwind of reflection and strategic assessments. Much like their American, European, Russian and Turkish counterparts (see respective articles in this special issue), Israeli analysts did not predict either the timing or ferocity of the eruptions, and were surprised both by the scale and seemingly contagious nature of the revolts, and the apparent ease with which protesters managed to dislodge from power two of the Arab world's most prominent and experienced dictators, presidents Ben-Ali and Mubarak.[1]

The Analytical Challenge and Initial Assessment

Senior Israeli officials describe what amounts to a three-phase initial assessment process that took place within the country's security and foreign policy establishment during the several tumultuous months following December 2010 — a process whose broad institutional and methodological legacy has endured.

While the anti-regime uprising in Tunisia did not instantly jolt Israeli officialdom, the spread of mass protests to Israel's immediate southern neighbour in January 2011 and the events leading to the fall of Mubarak in February, grabbed the attention of policy-makers' time at the highest echelons of the government — including the prime minister himself, his national security advisor and military secretary. This early involvement of the prime minister and his most intimate circle of advisors is indicative of the seriousness attributed by Israel to the events in Egypt and, from 15 February 2011, the advent of civil war in Libya.

According to Maj. Gen. (ret.) Yaakov Amidror,[2] the most immediate phase of official response involved an institutional recognition that a potentially monumental event was in motion, and deciding upon the appropriate governmental infrastructure and methodology needed for gathering and analysing the large amount of disparate information that was flowing from both open and clandestine sources.[3]

The institutional configuration selected to manage this epistemological and analytical challenge involved three main circles: first, the NSC was tasked with coordinating the gathering of information and intelligence estimates from Israel's various security and foreign policy agencies; with conducting independent analysis; and creating policy briefs for the prime minister which were then discussed by him and the national security advisor. A second, purposefully separate process of consultation directly vis-à-vis the prime minister, occurs through the PM's military secretary (*Mazkir Tzva'i*), who funnels to the prime minister the estimates of the military and clandestine services, Mossad and the Israel Security Agency. Finally, a portion of the government cabinet, often referred to as the security political cabinet and composed of the PM, the minister of defence, minister of foreign affairs and two or three additional ministers, confers and guides binding government decisions.

The second phase of initial assessment entailed intensive discussions, organized under the aegis of the NSC, with the participation of the main national security and foreign affairs agencies, as well as external experts. Between February and June 2011, for example, Prime Minister Netanyahu met twice with ad hoc groups of some 20 prominent Israeli analysts and academics — regional experts, economists, historians, political scientists and lawyers. Collectively, these deliberations are described by Israeli officials who took part in the consultations as 'broad-ranging', 'rich' and 'unbounded' strategic assessment exercises.[4]

The third and final phase of initial assessment described by officials involved a conscious, structured initiative to define Israel's national interests vis-à-vis events in the region, and to distil a clear set of strategic principles that would help translate those interests into concrete 'policy do's and don'ts'.[5] Indeed, it was decided that, once defined and clearly articulated, the strategic principles would bind all relevant agencies in the country — from the military and clandestine security forces to the diplomatic service — in order to promote tight coherence in what were understood to be highly sensitive matters.[6] Inconsistency in official Israeli statements and signals (not ordinarily an unheard of phenomenon) was perceived to be unacceptable in this context, given the conditions of high volatility and the risk of unintended consequences leading to unwanted entanglements.[7]

It is noteworthy that unlike their American, European and perhaps Turkish counterparts (see Ayata 2014; Dandashly 2014; Huber 2014; Noutcheva 2014), Israeli policy-makers appear to have concluded early on that while the upheavals in Tunisia, Libya, Egypt, Bahrain, Yemen and Syria displayed some common features, treating the events of the 'Arab Spring' as a region-wide phenomenon was a mistake because the apparent similarities were superficial, likely to be ephemeral and risked distorting policy analysis. Accordingly, Israeli officials emphasize that as the Western media was speaking about the 'Arab Spring' in broad regional terms, they were warned 'to resist homogenizing events' and to examine each arena — especially Egypt, Syria, Lebanon, Jordan and Palestinian territories — separately.[8]

Israeli decision-makers drew several conceptual guidelines from their initial assessment process. The first was a keen sense that Israel's immediate geopolitical environment has in fact entered a profound transformative process, whose causes, dynamics and outcomes were poorly understood and needed to be carefully examined as a matter of national security priority. As protests and uprisings proliferated from Tunisia, Egypt and Libya to Oman, Bahrain, Yemen, Morocco and then Syria in the spring of 2011, Israeli analysts noted both the fluidity of the situation and the possibility that the Middle East that would emerge from the tumult would be very different from the one that existed prior to January 2011. As one official put it: 'It was clear we were witnessing a singular, historic event and that new elements, new dynamics were entering [reality in the Middle East] that no one really understood, or even knew how to analyze'.[9] In this respect, at least, initial Israeli reactions were not dissimilar from those of their counterparts' in Europe and the US (Dandashly 2014; Huber 2014; Noutcheva 2014).

Among the new elements and dynamics identified by Israeli analysts as being novel and significant were the mobilizing forces of social media, particularly in Tunisia and Egypt, and questions about the nature and relative power of opposition groups challenging the Ghaddafi regime in Libya and Assad regime in Syria.[10]

More distinctively, official assessments emphasized the need for Israel to conduct itself with extreme caution. Unlike Turkey in particular (Ayata 2014), the Israeli establishment's reflexive posture was one of tense observation and circumspection, not open-handedness or readiness for engagement. The assumption undergirding this position was that the breaking of the regional status quo was essentially hazardous for Israel and that, since the dangers were still poorly understood, Israel must first avoid strategic blunders by adopting a 'wait and see' approach.

Where Israeli assessments diverged most sharply with American and European perceptions of the same events is in relation to prospects of democratization in the MENA region (Dandashly 2014; Huber 2014; Noutcheva 2014). As a general rule, Israeli policy chiefs did not perceive the revolts as harbingers of political liberalization and were alarmed by what they viewed as dangerously naïve American readings to the contrary. As early as 2 February 2011, for example, Israeli officials reportedly warned that the unfolding revolution in Egypt resembled 'Tehran 1979', rather than 'Berlin 1989' (Zacharia 2011). After conducting a specific consultation on the language to be used to refer to events in the region, the military intelligence branch of the IDF officially rejected the term 'Arab Spring', deeming it misleading and decreed that the military use the phrase 'the regional upheaval' (*Ha'Taltala Ha'Ezorit*), instead (Harel and Issacarov 2011). Many Israeli commentators referred to the events as the 'Arab Winter' or the 'Islamist Winter' (Lars 2013, 7).

Israel's interpretation of the regional upheavals was set most forcefully by Prime Minister Benjamin Netanyahu himself. In his first comment on the anti-regime uprising in Tunisia, on 16 January 2011, Netanyahu eschewed any reference to democracy, emphasizing the dangers inherent in an unstable Middle East: 'the region we live in is unstable ... we see that in several places in the geographical space where we live' (Hugi 2011). Netanyahu reiterated the danger of instability and the need for vigilance in a speech marking the opening of the Knesset winter session in October 2011 (Netanyahu 2011a).

Netanyahu's statements regarding the Arab Spring display significant variance, depending both on whether he addressed domestic or international audiences, and the nature of international audience addressed. For example, Netanyahu did refer to the possibility of democratization in the MENA region and adopted more optimistic, conciliatory language in his September 2011 speech before the UN General Assembly, declaring:

> I extend [a hand in peace] to the people of Libya and Tunisia, with admiration for those trying to build a democratic future ... I extend it to the people of Syria, Lebanon and Iran, with awe at the courage of those fighting brutal repression. Netanyahu 2011b)

In contrast, in a May 2013 joint press conference with Russian President Vladimir Putin, Netanyahu again made no reference to prospects of democratization, instead stating: 'the region around is us very stormy, unstable and explosive' (Israel Ministry of Foreign Affairs 2013).

Other Israeli leaders expressed different interpretations. Former President Shimon Peres opined that Arab nations faced a profound choice: 'to join the new global age of democratic peace and liberal economy, or to stay clinging to its history of closed societies and autocracy' and stated that 'Israel welcomes the wind of change and sees a window of opportunity' (Peres 2011). In a similar vein, former Israeli Deputy Prime Minister Natan Sharansky challenged the idea that authoritarian stability was good for Israel and called upon Israel and the West to 'bet on freedom in Egypt' (Sharansky 2011). These more open-handed, risk-tolerant voices were a distinct minority already in 2011, and largely petered out as the initial hope of the 'Arab Spring' turned increasingly sour in 2012–2014.

Evolving Assessments: mid-2011 to mid-2014

Though hardly self-contained or neatly demarcated, Israel's evolving assessments of events in the region since mid-2011 can be broadly divided into three phases: a period of high-anxiety marked by the rise to power in Egypt of the Muslim Brotherhood and seeming strengthening of the Iran-Syria-Hezbollah-HAMAS axis; a phase of reduced anxiety resulting from the return of the old guard in Egypt, and the weakening of Hezbollah and HAMAS and, most recently, the emergence of new concerns focused on the proliferation of areas of limited statehood in the MENA region — especially Iraq and Syria — the growing presence of Global Jihad organizations on Israel's borders and resurgent HAMAS rocket fire, culminating in a third round of major HAMAS–Israel hostilities in July 2014.

In the 17-month period between the fall of Mubarak in February 2011 and the Egyptian military's ousting of the Muslim Brotherhood from power in July 2013, Israeli officials and analysts were generally rattled by regional dynamics, particularly by what they saw as three pernicious potential consequences of the Egyptian — and, to a lesser extent, Tunisian and Libyan — revolutions.

First, the Israeli establishment assumed — wrongly as it turned out — that the convincing electoral victories of the Muslim Brotherhood and *Salafist* Al-Nur party in Egypt in 2011/2012 meant that well-organized

Islamist political movements have 'hijacked the revolution' and would inspire other Islamist revolutions throughout the MENA region (Heller 2012). Ennahda's convincing October 2011 electoral victory in Tunisia strengthened this view. Once entrenched in power, Israeli officials feared the rule of the Islamists would become authoritarian, virulently anti-Israel and irreversible. Analysts warned that the wave of electoral victories for the Muslim Brotherhood — which they saw as having begun already with the election of the AKP in Turkey in 2002 and continued in the 2006 HAMAS electoral victory in Gaza — would prove that when Islamists win elections, MENA countries end up in a 'one man, one vote, one time' outcome (Brom 2012, 19).

Second, with the election of Mohamed Morsi to the presidency in Egypt in June 2012, Israeli strategists feared that the new rulers of Egypt — inexperienced, emboldened by their new electoral victories and eager to prove their anti-Zionist *bona fides* — would become daring, even reckless, in their anti-Israel policies. Some Israeli officials went as far as expressing concern that under Morsi, Egypt would renege upon the Egyptian–Israeli peace treaty and would support the HAMAS government in Gaza at the expense of the Palestinian authority — thus both energizing HAMAS's armed attacks and weakening those Palestinians factions willing to engage in peace negotiations with Israel (Brom 2012).

Throughout 2012 and early 2013, Israeli concerns were exacerbated by negative signals from Cairo. Unlike Mubarak, Morsi refused to deal directly with Israeli officials or even refer to Israel by name. In March 2012, HAMAS was permitted to open offices in Cairo and in October 2012, the Muslim Brotherhood's Supreme Guide, Sheik Mohammed Badie, called for 'Jihad to liberate Jerusalem from the Israeli occupation' (Karmon 2013, 113)

Finally, Israel saw the weakening of Cairo's central authority as enabling non-state armed groups to exploit power vacuums, particularly in the Sinai Peninsula, and increase weapon smuggling from Iran, Sudan and Libya to HAMAS and Palestinian Islamic Jihad (PIJ) in Gaza. Lack of effective Egyptian control of Sinai, Israel feared, would create an even tenser regional environment in the Sinai–Gaza–Israel triangle, increase threats of cross-border terror attacks and rocket fire and, most dangerously, enhance the risk of confrontation between the Egyptian and Israeli militaries as a result of strategic miscalculation (Heller 2012; Inbar 2012).

Israel's anxiety reduced markedly in the latter half of 2013 and early 2014, as the result of three developments, none of which it foresaw or actively shaped. The demise of the Muslim Brotherhood and return of the Egyptian military to power in August 2013 produced a quiet but unmistakable sigh of relief in Israel. The stunning political defeat suffered by the Muslim Brotherhood in the Arab world's most populous and important nation — a defeat consolidated by the overwhelming victory in presidential elections of Mubarak's former Defence Minister Abdel Fattah el-Sisi, in May 2014 — stemmed what until then appeared like an uninterrupted wave of success for Islamist parties in the region.

El-Sisi's rise also spurred the Egyptian military to take determined action against what it saw as a growing threat to Egypt's own security and stability from radical Islamist groups based in Sinai (see Yaari 2012; Kirkpatrick 2013). Cooperative security ties between Israel and Egypt have been bolstered to unprecedented levels, the new–old Egyptian regime has placed unprecedented pressure on HAMAS and the risk of Egyptian–Israeli military confrontation has all but evaporated (Yaari 2014).

As mass protests spread from Tunisia and Egypt to Libya, Jordan, Bahrain and even Saudi Arabia in 2011, Israeli observers were alarmed by what they saw as the disproportionate, adverse impact of the Arab Spring on the more moderate, pragmatic Sunni Arab states of the region, and the parallel empowerment of the Shi'a dominated Iran–Syria–Hezbollah–HAMAS axis. Implicit in this analysis was the perception that the MENA was in the midst of a grand Sunni–Shi'a struggle; that it was overwhelmingly Sunni Arab states that were vulnerable to the regional tumult; and that the weakening of those states would greatly worsen Israel's security situation by strengthening the hand of Iran and its allies in their three-decade shadow war with Israel (Katz and Hendel 2012).

For Israel, the grim 'moderates down, extremists up' calculus altered considerably since early 2012. As Syria degenerated into violence and as its civil war metastasized into a regional conflict that increasingly sapped the energies of both Assad and his Iranian-backed Lebanese ally, Hezbollah, Israel saw the regional strategic balance shifting in its favour (Elliott 2014). Moreover, the elimination by June 2014 of the Assad regime's deadly arsenal of chemical weapons — under the auspices of the Organization for the Prohibition of Chemical Weapons — has reduced the danger of a future Syrian WMD attack on Israel.

Regarding the question of the desirability of the survival of the Assad regime itself, Israel faces a thorny dilemma. On the one hand, the fall of the Allawite regime would constitute a strategic blow to Iran and would effectively cut supply routes from Iran to Hezbollah in Lebanon — both, highly desirable outcomes from Israel's perspective. On the other hand, Israel has learned to live with 'the devil it knows' (Jones and Milton-Edwards 2013) and there are those in Israel who fear that what will emerge from the ashes of a post-Assad Syria will be either a powerful and hostile Sunni Islamist regime or a chaotic power vacuum that would favour radical Salafi Islamism (see Spyer 2013).

Like their American, European and Russian counterparts (Dandashly 2014; Dannreuther 2014; Huber 2014; Noutcheva 2014), Israeli analysts were initially split on the question of the effectiveness of the Syrian opposition and whether it will be able to topple the Assad regime, with or without external assistance.[11] However, the longer Assad remains in power, the stronger the assumption that his regime will ultimately survive. For hard-nosed Israeli strategists who do not see the possibility of a more liberal, peaceful regime emerging in Syria, a scenario in which the Assad regime clings on to power but is militarily weakened, serves Israel's security interests rather well.

In the meantime, Hezbollah's mobilization in support of the Assad regime has cost the Iran-sponsored Shi'a militia dearly, both in Syria and increasingly, at home in Lebanon. To date, Hezbollah has committed some 5000 fighters to safeguard Assad's rule and as of late December 2013, between 650 and 700 Hezbollah fighters are estimated to have been killed in the Syrian war (*Ya Libnan* 2013). Moreover, since early 2014, Hezbollah strongholds in northern Lebanon and Beirut have come under increasing car and suicide bomb attacks from *al-Qaeda* rebel groups in Syria and Lebanon (see Kalin 2014).

Most recently, Israeli security chiefs are warning about the emergence of new threats in the rapidly changing geopolitical realities of the Levant. Indeed, Israeli observers are increasingly alarmed by the proliferation of areas of limited statehood in the MENA region (Gaub 2014; Magen 2012b) and the growing ambition and influence of Global Jihad organizations with links to *al-Qaeda*, notably in Iraq and Syria (Schweitzer 2012). In a region increasingly characterized by porous borders, unsupervised arms flow and weak or collapsed central governments, radical Salafist armed groups are becoming substantial power brokers. Since the withdrawal of US forces in Iraq, *al-Qaeda* in Iraq (AQI) has accelerated its insurgency against the Shi'a-led government of Prime Minister Nuri al-Maliki and has extended its reach into neighbouring Syria. In April 2013, AQI announced that it was changing its name to the Islamic State of Iraq and al-Sham — taking control of the strategic Idlib province town of Saraqe on the Aleppo–Damascus highway in December 2013 — and announcing the rebirth of an Islamic Caliphate in June 2014.

More ominous still for Israel is the emergence of indigenous Salafi jihadist groups, such as the Al-Nusra Front, Abdullah Azzam Brigades and Fatah al-Islam, in Syria, Lebanon and Jordan. Unlike AQI or *al-Qaeda* affiliates in Yemen, these groups demonstrate considerable sophistication in managing popular perceptions and gaining resonance with disrupted local communities by stepping in to provide essential public goods where the state recedes. With the approach of these organizations to Israel's borders, Israeli security chiefs are increasingly worried about the rise of a new 'Salafi Crescent' (Shay 2014) in Israel's vicinity that would seek to both perpetrate attacks against Israel from Lebanon, Syria, Sinai and Jordan, and penetrate Palestinian territories in the West Bank and Gaza (Karmon 2014).

Lastly, Israeli analysts worry that HAMAS's isolation in the aftermath of the fall of Muslim Brotherhood rule in Egypt, coupled with the success of extremist groups in Iraq and Syria, spurs HAMAS to exacerbate its rocket attacks from its Gaza stronghold, partly in an attempt to recapture its role as the vanguard of armed resistance against Israel. As of August 2014, Israel and HAMAS are embroiled in another round of large-scale armed hostilities, the third since 2009 (see Booth and Witte 2014).

Policy Objectives

The top-down mobilization of Israel's small security and foreign policy establishment in response to the outbreak of the 'Arab Spring', resulted in the articulation of a relatively coherent set of policy objectives relatively quickly, especially when compared with the more cumbersome experiences of the EU (Dandashly 2014; Noutcheva 2014) and the US (Huber 2014). Documentary evidence and interview materials indicate Israeli policymakers defining the country's overarching policy objectives in terms of three mutually reinforcing sets of goals. These are broadly hierarchical, with clear priority accorded to hard security and economic interests, reflecting survivalist values.

The Tricky Quest for Non-Entanglement: Avoiding Conflict Spillage and Conflict Distraction

According to former National Security Advisor Amidror, the primary guiding principle that emerged from the 2011 assessments is 'non-entanglement'. As he put it: 'Our first priority is not to allow chaos to spill [into Israel] or unacceptable security threats to endanger us ... This means enforcing red lines when absolutely necessary but not becoming embroiled in confrontation if at all possible'.[12]

The goal of insulating Israel from the regional tumult contains a number of distinguishable components. First, Israeli policy-makers emphasize the objective of preventing the 'spillage' of negative externalities, particularly from the Syrian conflict, Lebanon and Sinai, into nearby Israeli territory. This was meant to safeguard not only domestic security and maintain the normalcy of the nation's economic and social life in the face of proximate arenas of instability, but also to reduce the risk of potential friction with neighbouring countries that could flow from unwanted cross-border movement of fighters or civilian refugees.

Second, insulating Israel's borders and population from proximate threats entails the delicate — not always successful — balancing of non-involvement with deterrence.[13] Security chiefs have attempted to achieve this balancing act by emphasizing Israel's reluctance to become embroiled in regional events, and at the same time, its determination to act defensively if compelled to do so. In September 2013, Defense Minister Ya'alon declared: 'We're not involved in the Syrian civil war unless our interests are harmed or the red lines we set [are crossed]' (Lappin 2013). Ya'alon and other senior Israeli officials have articulated three 'red lines' in this context: (1) attempts by Syria or Iran to transfer 'quality weapons' to terrorist organizations, with an emphasis on Hezbollah; (2) the transfer of chemical weapons; and (3) violation of Israeli sovereignty (Lappin 2013).

In marked contrast with the EU, US and Turkey (Ayata 2014; Dandashly 2014; Huber 2014; Noutcheva 2014), Israel's objective of non-entanglement also manifests itself in the deliberate avoidance of rhetoric. One of the earliest guidelines to emerge from the NSC-led deliberations on how to respond to the Arab revolts was an instruction that government ministers, diplomats and officers exercise 'strategic silence' vis-à-vis competing political forces in neighbouring Arab countries.[14] Official Israel was not to express its preferences for a given party, candidate or regime outcome, so as not to undermine moderates and avoid, as far as possible, being accused of meddling in the internal affairs of its Arab neighbours.

Finally here, Israeli policy chiefs view the objective of non-entanglement in neighbouring arenas as an essential component in Israel's struggle with Iran (Katz and Hendel 2012). Indeed, Israel is leery of allowing the upheavals of the 'Arab Spring' to obfuscate — for itself, as well as for the international community — what it views as an existential threat, namely the acquisition of military nuclear capabilities by the Islamic Republic of Iran.[15]

Preserving Positive and Negative Assets

Entwined with the goal of non-entanglement is Israel's overarching objective of preserving three main strategic assets in its immediate vicinity — two broadly positive, cooperative set of relations and a third set based on military deterrence.

The first, arguably most important, is peace with Egypt. From its independence in 1948 until the 1979 Egypt–Israel Peace Treaty, Egypt was Israel's most potent enemy, with the two countries fighting no fewer than five wars over this period (Quandt 1986). The American-brokered peace treaty never evolved into the warm people-to-people peace. Yet formal peace has held, and for over 30 years, Egypt and Israel cooperated reasonably well on counter-terrorism, relations with the Palestinians, energy and maritime issues. Israeli leaders were deeply alarmed by the prospect that the rise to power of the Muslim Brotherhood would deconstruct this central pillar of regional security arrangements and were enormously relieved by the return of the Egyptian military to power.

Similarly, Israel views the preservation of the Hashemite Kingdom of Jordan and the endurance of the 1994 Israeli–Jordanian Peace Treaty as critical strategic objectives, and are deeply concerned about any signs of regime instability in Jordan (Eran 2012). Like his father and predecessor King Hussein, King Abdullah of Jordan has maintained discrete but intimate security and diplomatic relations with Israel, especially on managing relations with the Palestinians; mediating between Jerusalem, Cairo and Damascus; and preventing the infiltration of foreign fighters and weapons into the West Bank. Moreover, Israeli security chiefs emphasize the unique value of Jordan as a cooperative buffer zone insulating Israel from instability in Iraq and as an increasingly rare stabilizing agent in the region (Gilad 2012).

Lastly, Israel views its ability to effectively deter belligerent neighbours — especially the Syrian army, rebel groups in southern Syria, Hezbollah and HAMAS — as a vital 'negative' strategic asset, essential for non-entanglement and the insulation of its civilian population and economy. In this, it has been partially successful, with deterrence broadly maintained towards its northern neighbours in 2011–2014, but increasingly unsuccessful towards HAMAS and PIJ in Gaza and Sinai. In its tense signalling game with the embattled Assad regime, Israel has not only reportedly struck Syrian military assets repeatedly, but has also publicly warned Assad that if attacked, Israel will act to topple his regime (Ravid 2013a). Israel has also been able to maintain the delicate deterrence it has achieved vis-à-vis

Hezbollah since the 2006 Lebanon War. However, the opening of large-scale hostilities with HAMAS and PIJ in Gaza in July 2014 — the third such round since 2009 — has prompted a heated debate in Israel about the efficacy and sustainability of its deterrence posture vis-à-vis more radical Palestinian groups, with some analysts calling for an international campaign to disarm HAMAS, and others insisting that Israel must seek to topple HAMAS's rule.[16]

Searching for New Friends and Alliances

The regional upheaval has also prompted Israel to strengthen ties and seek new alliances with actors on the peripheries of the Middle East. Israeli diplomats speak of the emergence of a 'periphery strategy 2.0' — a twenty-first-century revival of David Ben-Gurion's influential 1950s stratagem designed to break the nascent state's regional isolation and improve its international standing by forming ties with non-Arab African and Middle Eastern states, notably Iran, Turkey and Ethiopia — and national minorities such as Kurds in Iraq and Christians in Sudan (Shlaim 1999).[17]

The impetus for Israel to reach out to actors beyond the Arab–Turkish–Iranian spheres is compelling and is fuelled by both 'push' and 'pull factors'; by the loss of traditional allies and the emergence of new opportunities for enhanced ties with alternative ones. From its independence in 1948 until the fall of the Mubarak regime in 2011, Israel could always count on at least one of the strong, pivotal states in the Middle East (Chase, Hill, and Kennedy 1996) — Egypt, Iran or Turkey — to act as its ally, at least tacitly. Between 1948 and the overthrow of the Pahlavi dynasty in the 1979 Islamic Revolution, Israel enjoyed close ties with Iran. The rise of the Iranian Mullocracy severed those ties, but the strategic loss of Iran was more than offset by the successful conclusion of the Camp David Peace Accords with Egypt and the largesse bestowed on both former foes by the Carter and Reagan administrations (Quandt 1986). Similarly, relations with Ankara, which had reached levels of intimate cooperation in the 1990s, declined precipitously following the election of the AKP in 2002, falling to an unprecedented nadir in May 2010 with the *Mavi Marmara* affair, in which Israeli commandos killed nine Turkish activists seeking to break the naval blockade placed by Israel on Gaza (Ayturk 2011). Security and intelligence cooperation between Turkey and Israel were suspended following the incident, and despite fence-mending steps taken by both sides, Israeli analysts do not expect full restoration of ties with an AKP-dominated Turkey; nor do they discount entirely the possibility of a dangerous rift re-emerging in the foreseeable future between the two erstwhile allies.[18]

The catalyst for the formation of new alliances between Israel and its non-Arab–Iranian–Turkish neighbours also stems from the realignment of those neighbours' interests in response to the regional tumult. Several countries in Southern Europe, the Mediterranean basin and Caucuses share Israel's concern about waning US presence and growing Iranian influence in the region; Turkey's turn away from the West; and the proliferation of violent Jihadist networks, particularly in Libya, Sinai, Iraq and Syria. At the same time, neighbours such as Cyprus, Greece, Bulgaria, Romania and Azerbaijan recognize Israel's growing relative weight as an advanced, pro-Western actor in a region increasingly devoid of stable, functioning partners, and the potential for intelligence, technological and economic benefits in closer cooperation with it.[19]

Over the past four years, Israel found responsive partners to overtures of intensified ties in Azerbaijan, Bulgaria, Cyprus, Croatia, Greece, Romania, Serbia, Montenegro, Macedonia and the fledgling new state of South Sudan (Guzansky and Lindenstrauss 2012). These have been primarily, though not exclusively, security oriented. Despite both Iranian and Turkish pressure to distance itself from Israel, for example, Azerbaijan has intensified already convivial ties with Israel. A USD 1.6 billion arms deal was signed between the two countries in February 2012, in which Azerbaijan acquired advanced satellite and weapons systems from Israel (see Cohen 2012), and the Azeris have reportedly stepped up intelligence cooperation with Israel, including the arrest in October 2013 of an Iranian national, Hasan Faraji, suspected of planning an attack on Israeli diplomats in Baku (Ben Solomon 2013). Similarly, with Turkish airspace closed to the Israel Air Force (IAF) for training manoeuvres, Romania has become an alternative venue where the IAF routinely practices attacking targets at long distances and intercepting weapons-smuggling convoys (Ben-Yishai 2011; Katz 2011).

Beyond hard security ties *stricto sensu*, relations have intensified most prominently with Turkey's rivals, Greece and Cyprus. Greece was the last non-Arab Mediterranean country to normalize diplomatic ties with Israel and until recently, relations between Greece and Israel were lukewarm. In late 2010, George Papandreou became the first Greek premier to make an official visit to Israel and a first comprehensive government-to-government meeting took place between the two countries in September 2013. In the period between the two visits, 10 new Greek–Israeli agreements were concluded, ranging from intelligence sharing and public security to tourism and culture, and large-scale joint naval and aerial exercises have become routine (Keinon 2013; Ravid 2012). In August 2013, they signed a three-side agreement with Israel intended to interconnect their electricity grids, protect natural gas deposits in the eastern Mediterranean and cooperate on desalinizing of sea water. If fully implemented by 2016 as planned, the project would be one of the largest of its kind in the world and make Israel a significant energy player in Europe (*The Algemeiner* 2013).

Policy Instruments Used and Avoided

Looked at comparatively, Israel stands out most notably both in its willingness to deploy coercive means and in its avoidance of rhetorical action meant to influence the trajectory of political developments inside Arab societies. At the same time, like the EU, US, Turkey and Russia, Israel has made use of an array of diplomatic, economic and humanitarian-assistance tools, though it lacks the economic weight and linkages with its Arab neighbours necessary to engage in conditionality or state capacity-building (Levitsky and Way 2005).

The Obama Administration's threat to use military force against the Assad regime for use of chemical weapons on its own civilian population notwithstanding, Israel has so far been the only external actor to actually deploy coercive means to enforce 'red lines' in Syria. Though Israel has declared it would view the use of chemical weapons as a transgression of those red lines, in practice it has reportedly carried out military strikes against the Assad regime not as punishment for use of chemical weapons, but as a preventive measure meant to stymie the transfer of 'game-changing' weapons from Russia and Iran to Assad in Syria or Hezbollah in Lebanon.

Though official Israeli sources neither confirm nor deny such action, according to American officials and media reports both in Israel and internationally, since mid-2011, the Israeli Air Force (IAF) and Navy have carried out approximately a dozen covert strikes on weapon convoys or depots. On the night of 29 January 2013, for example, 12 IAF planes reportedly struck a convoy of trucks carrying Russian made SA-17 anti-aircraft missiles from Syria to Hezbollah in Lebanon (Ravid 2013b). In May, Israel reportedly took out a shipment of Iranian-made Fateh-110 missiles at a Damascus airport (*The Guardian* 1 November 2013). In late October, Israeli warplanes attacked a shipment of SA-125 anti-aircraft missiles inside a Syrian Government stronghold (*The Algemeiner* 2013). And on the morning of 5 July 2013, Israeli Dolphin submarines reportedly targeted an arms depot of Russian-made Yakhont P-800 anti-ship missiles that were recently transferred to the Assad regime and held in the Syrian Navy barracks at Safira, near the port of Latakia (Hartman 2013). The official silence surrounding these events is meant both to minimize the risk of Israeli entanglement in Syria and to help President Bashar Assad 'save face' in view of repeated Israeli strikes.

Israel's apparent willingness to use military force in Syria and Lebanon contrasts with its refusal to do so in Egypt. According to Yaakov Amidror, in the period between the demise of the Mubarak regime in February 2011 and the return of the army to power in Egypt in July–August 2013, there were those in the security establishment who urged Israeli leaders to carry out proactive military operations in Sinai in order to foil rocket attacks on the Israeli city of Eilat, and stymie the flow of sophisticated arms from Iran and Libya to the hands of HAMAS and the PIJ in Gaza. Conscious of the fact that any Israeli military action in Sinai would contravene, and possibly, undermine its peace treaty with Egypt, Israeli leaders consistently rejected the use of force in Sinai. Instead, Israel has quietly but sternly warned the Egyptian military that it expects it to take effective action against terrorist nests in Sinai; has stepped up intelligence sharing with Egyptian security forces; and has lobbied its American counterparts to pressure Cairo to fully exercise its sovereignty in Sinai.[20]

Israel has also turned to its own criminal justice system to discourage its own nationals from getting involved in the Syrian conflict. On 9 February 2014, an Israeli court in Lod sentenced 27-year-old Israeli Arab citizen, Abed Al-Kader Tallah, to 15 months imprisonment for entering Syria and joining the *al-Qaeda* affiliate, Al-Nusra Front, before changing his mind and returning to Turkey, where he was arrested (Huri 2014). Fifteen Israeli Arab men are reportedly fighting on the side of the Syrian rebels, while a handful of Druz youth have apparently joined pro-Assad forces. The criminal prosecution of Tallah is meant to deter other young Israeli Arab men from entering Syria where Israeli police fear they will become further radicalized or may assist al-Qaeda in planning and implementing attacks on Israeli targets.

Elsewhere, Israel turned to economic instruments, albeit in a limited way. In line with its concern to preserve the stability of the Hashemite Kingdom, Israel has sought to ease the transport of Jordanian exports through its Mediterranean ports of Haifa and Ashdod, and has increased the amount of water it supplies to Jordan from the Sea of Galilee and its desalination plants on the Mediterranean coast.[21] These steps — which were undertaken discretely — are meant to help bolster the Jordanian economy and offset the pressures caused to Jordan's public utilities by the flood of refugees from Syria.

Israel has also engaged in extending limited humanitarian assistance to victims of the Syrian war. As of mid-2014, over a thousand Syrian citizens, most of them injured in the civil war, have received medical treatment in Israel. Figures published in late January 2014 record some 490 Syrian national inpatients at hospitals in northern Israel (Ashkenazi 2014; see also Connolly 2013). Since June 2013, IsraAID, an Israeli development and humanitarian assistance NGO, has worked in collaboration with Jordanian and international aid organizations to provide food and other essential needs to Syrian refugees in Jordan (Kamin 2013).

In comparison with other external actors, Israel stands out, on the softer edge of the spectrum of engagement instruments, in its avoidance of pro-democratization rhetoric or engagement in communicative action (Risse 2000) with its Arab neighbours. Unlike Turkey (Ayata 2014), Israel did not seek to position itself as a model to be emulated by those in the MENA region seeking a new path towards political liberalization and economic success.

Unlike the EU and US, Israeli officialdom has generally avoided expressing preferences for what kind of political regimes it would favour in the region, and has been highly reticent to be accused of meddling in the internal political choices facing its Arab neighbours than its American, European or Turkish counterparts. In line with its 'strategic silence' policy and in marked contrast with the positions of the EU, US and Turkey, Israel has avoided calling for President Bashar Assad to step down from power. Similarly, Israeli officialdom remained conspicuously silent both when the Muslim Brotherhood rose to power and when the Egyptian military ousted Mohamed Morsi from the country's presidency. Regarding the latter, former Israeli Ambassador to Egypt, Eli Shaked, explained in July 3013: 'Israel is trying to keep its distance from what is going on in Egypt and not say too much, because anything it says on this issue will be used as a weapon against one side or the other' (quoted in Eglash 2013).

Explaining Israel's Policy Response

Broadly speaking, the guiding assumptions, goals and instruments used (and avoided) by Israeli policy-makers in response to the Arab revolts and their aftermath sit comfortably with theoretical axioms advanced by the realist tradition (Morgentahu 1948; Snidal 2002; Waltz 1979). Yet the exegetical picture would be lacking without accounting for the self-understanding and collective-identity of key Israeli foreign policy and security actors — dimensions that resonate more strongly with a social-constructivist view of world politics (Adler 2002; Katzenstein 1996; Klotz and Lynch 2007; Wendt 1999) — and, to a lesser extent, liberal theory (Moravcsik 1997; Gourevitch 2002), pertaining to the peculiar nature of Israel's security establishment and coalition parliamentarianism.

The overarching posture shaped by Israeli decision-makers in response to the Arab revolts can be summarized as defensive, conservative, non-idealist and extensively reliant on purposefully discrete military and diplomatic instruments. To a considerable degree, this posture is explainable with reference to the high stakes involved for Israel and the generally hostile nature of its geostrategic environment. Israel's primary focus on physical security stems from its inherently narrow margin of survival; the geographical proximity and multiplicity of security threats in its immediate regional vicinity — notably rocket attacks from Lebanon, Syria, Gaza, Sinai — the seriousness of those threats; and their proven tendency to materialize.

Israel's 'defensive Realist' (Jones and Milton-Edwards 2013, 405) approach to the Arab revolts — its emphasis on caution, discrete prevention, non-entanglement and insulation — is undergirded by compelling economic interests. As a small, consumer-driven, export- and investment-dependent economy, Israel is highly vulnerable to economic disruption stemming from internal, Palestinian or cross-border attacks. The national economy sustained severe losses during the 2001–2004 Intifada and, to a lesser but still significant extent, the 2006 Lebanon War and two major rounds of confrontation with HAMAS and PIJ in 2010 and 2012. Israeli leaders have therefore become highly sensitive to the need to safeguard economic normalcy in order to preserve consumption, trade, foreign investment and tourism. This socio-economic imperative too helps explain the fine balancing act sought by Israel between active prevention of potential attacks, on the one hand, and discrete non-entanglement, on the other.

Another central facet of Israeli realism is its basic conservatism. In view of its military and economic superiority in the region; ongoing competition with revolutionary Iran; and generally comfortable symbiosis with the Sunni Arab dictatorships of Egypt, Jordan and Saudi Arabia, Israel is essentially a status quo actor in the MENA region — inclined towards preserving the old, not taking a bet on the new. This helps explain Israel's emphasis on safeguarding established strategic assets (positive and negative), offsetting erosion of old alliances with the strengthening of existing ties, but avoiding sharp breaks from conventional arrangements or the going-out-on-a-limb with some new initiative towards the Palestinians or the Arab League, for example.

Israel's posture is further explained by its distinct non-idealism regarding prospects of democratization in the Arab world. When pressed on the question of whether, at least at the advent of the Arab Spring in early 2011, there existed a school of thought within the Israeli establishment that saw democratization as a reasonable possibility, the answer is an overwhelming 'no'. As Amidror put it:

> There were elements [within the security and foreign policy community] that said this is a process that could lead to democracy in eighty or a hundred year's time ... but there was no one who had the illusion that the Facebook kids [in Tahrir Square] would become a significant political actor. Not for one moment.[22]

Israel's strategic posture, policy objectives and choice of instruments are explainable in considerable part by its disbelief in prospects for rapid democratization and its assumption that the political openings created by the Arab revolts will quickly be seized by anti-democratic and anti-Israel Islamist forces, to the exclusion of Arab liberals.

Self-understanding also plays an important part in explaining Israel's posture. In marked contrast with Turkey, Israel's choice of exercising 'strategic silence', relying on covert military and diplomatic activity, and avoiding offering itself as a democratic model to be emulated by Arab reformists, is indicative of a self-image that is both keenly aware of being a regional misfit and lacks any confidence in its own ability to promote positive political and economic change among its Arab neighbours. This is reflected, for example, in the statements of Israeli diplomats that Israel must assiduously avoid expressing preferences about political currents in Arab countries because any Arab reformer saddled with Israeli sympathies — let alone support — would be branded a Zionist collaborator and undermined by alleged association.[23]

As a young, small, oil-poor, non-Arab League country that has only recently achieved a modicum of economic prosperity and trades primarily with the US, Europe and South East Asia (Magen 2012a), Israel lacks both the ethos and institutions necessary to engage its neighbours on issues of governance or economic development. Unlike the US and Europe (Magen, Risse, and McFaul 2009), Israel has never been in the business of promoting democracy abroad and is inclined to view such American and European efforts as at best Polianish, and at worst dangerously naïve (Byman 2011). This helps explain Israel's non-use of economic conditionality or state capacity-building instruments (Magen and McFaul 2009; Magen and Morlino 2009).

Lastly, Israel's policy response also needs to be read in light of domestic popular and elite preferences (Gourevitch 2002; Moravcsik 1997). Extensive media coverage of the suffering of Syrian civilians and an established tradition of providing medical assistance regardless of conditions of belligerency help explain Israel's official and NGO humanitarian activity vis-à-vis Syrian casualties and refugees. At the same time, Israel's focus on hard security and its choice of hard security instruments are perpetuated, and perhaps exacerbated, by the special weight accorded to the security establishment in Israeli decision-making circles and the prevalence of former senior military officers in civilian institutions (Barak and Sheffer 2006). Moreover, Israel's peculiar brand of parliamentary democracy, which placed an unusually high premium on representation for different ideological and sectarian factions in the Knesset and produced perennially unstable coalition governments, helps explain Israel's tendency towards non-engagement. Indeed, some domestic analysts have criticized the Netanyahu Government's 'freeze instinct' as an excuse for inaction, even paralysis, at a time of great regional fluidity and, therefore, according to the critics, opportunities for peace (Ravid 2011).

Notes

1. Author's notes from the workshop 'Governance, Development and Security in the Contemporary Middle East: A Crisis of Sovereignty?' organized by the Konrad Adenauer Stiftung (KAS) and The Lauder School of Government, Diplomacy and Strategy, IDC, Herzliya, 11–12 October 2012.
2. Maj. Gen. (ret.) Yaakov Amidror headed the Israeli National Security Council (NSC) and was Prime Minister Benjamin Netanyahu's national security advisor from January 2011 until November 2013.
3. Author interview with Maj. Gen. (ret.) Yaakov Amidror, national security advisor (2011–2013), Ra'anana, Israel, 10 November 2013.
4. Author notes from a group discussion with members of the political research and policy planning departments of the Israeli Ministry of Foreign Affairs, Jerusalem, 27 November 2013.
5. Supra, note 2.
6. The policy objectives articulated by this process are discussed in Section II of this article.
7. Supra, note 3.
8. Supra, notes 1 and 3.
9. Supra, note 3.
10. Supra, note 1.
11. Supra, note 2.
12. Supra, note 2.
13. On the origins and evolution of Israel's deterrence strategy vis-à-vis non-state actors, see Rid (2012).
14. Supra, notes 1 and 3.
15. Supra, notes 1 and 2.
16. See, for example, former Israeli Cabinet Secretary's proposal to remove HAMAS's missile arsenal in Gaza: Zvi Hauser, 'Take care of missiles, not Hamas', ynet news, 7 July 2014 (http://www.ynetnews.com/articles/07340L-4541799,00.html); former Israeli Ambassador to the US, Michael Oren, 'A smart way out of the Gaza confrontation', CNN Opinion, 13 July 2014 (http://edition.cnn.com/2014/07/13/opinion/oren-mideast-crisis-solution/).
17. Supra, note 3.
18. Supra, note 1.
19. Supra, note 3.
20. Supra, note 2.
21. Supra, notes 2 and 3.
22. Supra, note 2.
23. Supra, note 2.

References

Adler, E. 2002. Constructivism and international relations. In *Handbook of international relations*, eds. W. Carlsnaes, T. Risse, and B.A. Simmons, 95–118. London: Sage.
The Algemeiner. 2013. *Israel, Greece, Cyprus Reach 'Historic' energy cooperation agreement*, 8 August.

RESPONSES TO THE 'ARABELLIONS'

Ashkenazi, E. 2014. Some 700 Syrians treated in Israeli hospitals since early 2013. *Haaretz*, 30 January.

Ayturk, I. 2011. The coming of an ice-age? Turkish-Israeli relations since 2002. *Turkish Studies* 12, no. 4: 675–87.

Ayata, B. 2014. Turkish foreign policy in a changing Arab world: rise and fall of a regional actor? *Journal of European Integration* 37, no. 1: 95–112.

Barak, O., and G. Sheffer. 2006. Israel's 'security network' and its impact. *International Journal of Middle East Studies* 38, no. 2: 235–61.

Ben Solomon, A. 2013. Azerbaijan arrests Iranian suspected of planning an attack on Israeli embassy in Baku. *Jerusalem Post*, 21 November

Ben-Yishai, R. 2011. Training Moves from Turkey to Romania. *Ynet*, 27 July.

Booth, W., and G. Witte. 2014. Gazans flee homes as Israel promises to press the fight. *Washington Post*, 14 July.

Brom, S. 2012. Egypt after Morsi's victory in the presidential elections. *INSS Strategic Assessment* 15, no. 2: 19–26.

Byman, D. 2011. Israel's pessimistic view of the Arab Spring. *The Washington Quarterly* 34, no. 3: 123–36.

Chase, R.S., E.B. Hill, and P. Kennedy. 1996. Pivotal states and U.S. strategy. *Foreign Affairs* 75, no. 1: 33–51.

Cohen, G. 2012. Israel signed large scale arms deal with Azerbaijan. *Haaretz*, 26 February.

Connolly, K. 2013. The victims of Syria's war finding care in Israel. *BBC*, 25 November

Dandashly, A. 2014. The EU response to regime change in the wake of the Arab revolt: differential Implementation. *Journal of European Integration* 37, no. 1: 37–56.

Dannreuther, R. 2014. Russia and the Arab Spring: supporting the counter-revolution. *Journal of European Integration* 37, no. 1: 77–94.

Eglash, R. 2013. Israeli government tigth-lipped as events unfold in Egypt. *Washington Post*, 4 July.

Elliott, K. 2014. The Syrian conflict and its impact on Hezbollah's authority. *Small Wars Journal* http://smallwarsjournal.com/jrnl/art/the-syrian-conflict-and-its-impact-on-hezbollah%E2%80%99s-authority

Eran, O. 2012. The end of Jordan as we know it? *Israel Journal of Foreign Affairs* 6, no. 3: 15–20.

Gaub, F. 2014. A Libyan recipe for disaster. *Survival* 50, no. 1: 101–20.

Gilad, R. 2012. Address of Maj. Gen. (ret.) Amos Gilad, director of policy and political-military affairs. *Israel Ministry of Defence. IDC.* Herzliya, 11 October.

Gourevitch, P. 2002. Domestic politics and international relations. In *Handbook of international relations*, eds. W. Carlsnaes, T. Risse, and B.A. Simmons, 309–28. London: Sage.

The Guardian. 2013. Israel strikes Russian weapons shipment in Syria. (Associated Press, Beirut), 1 November.

Guzansky, J., and G. Lindenstrauss. 2012. Revival of the periphery concept in Israel's Foreign policy? *INSS Strategic Assessment* 15, no. 2: 27–40.

Harel, A. and A. Issacarov. 2011. Intelligence Modesty. *Haaretz*. [Hebrew], 11 December.

Hartman, B. 2013. US officials: Israel is responsible for Syrian missile depot attack. *Jerusalem Post*, 14 July.

Heller, M. 2012. Israeli responses to the Arab Spring. In *One year of the Arab Spring: global and regional implications*, eds. Y. Guzansky and M. Heller, 75–7. Tel-Aviv: INSS Memorandum 113.

Huber, D. 2014. A pragmatic actor — the US response to the Arab uprisings. *Journal of European Integration* 37, no. 1: 57–75.

Hugi, J. 2011. Netanyahu: Tunisia proof that we must safeguard security. *IDF Radio*. [Hebrew], 16 January.

Huri, J. 2014. 15 months imprisonment for Taybe resident who joined rebels in Syria. *Haaretz* [Hebrew], 9 February

Inbar, E. 2012. The 2011 Arab uprising and Israel's national security. *BESA Mideast Security and Policy Studies Papers* 95. http://www.biu.ac.il/Besa/MSPS95.pdf

Israel Ministry of Foreign Affairs. 2013. *PM Netanyahu meets with Russian President Putin*, 14 May.

Jones, C., and B. Milton-Edwards. 2013. Missing the 'devils' we knew? Israel and political Islam amid the Arab Awakening. *International Affairs* 89: 399–415.

Kalin, S. 2014. Suicide bomber kills three in Lebanese Hezbollah stronghold. *Reuters Press*, 1 February.

Kamin, D. 2013. For Syrian refugees in Jordan aid from Israel comes in a whisper. *Time of Israel*, 20 October.

RESPONSES TO THE 'ARABELLIONS'

Karmon, E. 2013. Hamas in dire straits. *Perspectives on Terrorism* 7, no. 5: 111–26.

Karmon, E. 2014. Al-Qaida and Palestinian Jihadists. *Jerusalem Post*, 29 January.

Katz, Y. 2011. IAF to return to return to Romania for training in August. *Jerusalem Post*, 15 June.

Katz, Y., and Y. Hendel. 2012. *Israel vs. Iran: the shadow war*. Washington, DC: Potomac Books.

Katzenstein, P. 1996. *The culture of national security: norms and identity in world politics*. New York, NY: Columbia University Press.

Keinon, H. 2013. Greek PM calls ties with Israel 'strategic', 'long term'. *Jerusalem Post*, 10 September.

Kirkpatrick, D. 2013. Egypt reports gains against militants in Sinai. *The New York Times*, 15 September.

Klotz, A., and C. Lynch. 2007. *Strategies of research in constructivist international relations*. Armonk, NY: M. E. Sharpe.

Lappin, Y. 2013. Ya'alon: Israelis can continue with their routine holiday plans, despite Syria tensions. *Jerusalem Post*, 8 September.

Lars, L. 2013. The Israeli discourse about the 'Arab Spring'. In *Israel and the Arab Spring: opportunities in change*, eds. N. Goren and J. Yudkevich, 7–20. Mitvim — The Israeli Institute for Foreign Policy. [Hebrew], http://www.fes.org.il/src/IsraelArabSpringHebrew2013.pdf

Levitsky, S., and L. Way. 2005. International linkage and democratization. *Journal of Democracy* 16, no. 3: 20–34.

Magen, A. 2012a. Israel and the many pathways of diffusion. *West European Politics* 35, no. 1: 98–116.

Magen, A. 2012b. On Political order and the Arab Spring. *Israel Journal of Foreign Affairs* 6, no. 1: 9–21.

Magen, A., and M. McFaul. 2009. Introduction: American and European strategies to promote democracy — shared values, common challenges, divergent tools? In *Promoting democracy and the rule of law*, eds. A. Magen, T. Risse, and M. McFaul, 1–33. Basingstoke: Palgrave-Macmillan.

Magen, A., and L. Morlino. 2009. Methods of influence, layers of impact, cycles of change. In *International actors, democratization and the rule of law: anchoring democracy?* eds. A. Magen and L. Morlino, 26–52. London: Routledge.

Magen, A., T. Risse, and M. McFaul (eds.). 2009. *Promoting democracy and the rule of law: American and European challenges*. Basingstoke: Palgrave-Macmillan.

Moravcsik, A. 1997. Taking preferences seriously: a liberal theory of international politics. *International Organization* 51, no. 4: 513–53.

Morgentahu, H.J. 1948. *Politics among nations*. New York, NY: McGraw.

Netanyahu, B. 2011a. *Prime Minister Benjamin Netanyahu Address to the Knesset*. [Hebrew], 31 October.

Netanyahu, B. 2011b. *Prime Minister Benjamin Netanyahu Address to the United National General Assembly*, 24 September.

Noutcheva, G. 2014. Institutional governance of European neighbourhood policy in the wake of the Arab Spring. *Journal of European Integration* 37, no. 1: 19–36.

Peres, S. 2011. We in Israel welcome the Arab Spring. *The Guardian*, 1 April.

Quandt, W.B. 1986. *Camp David: peacemaking and politics*. Washington, DC: Brookings Institution.

Ravid, B. 2011. The Arab Spring and Israel's winter hibernation. *Haaretz*, 8 December.

Ravid, B. 2012. Israel and Greece Hold Naval and aerial exercises in the eastern mediterranean. *Haaretz*, 1 April.

Ravid, B. 2013a. Israel publicly warns Assad: if you attack us we will topple your regime. *Haaretz*, 15 May.

Ravid, B. 2013b. Foreign sources: the attack today was carried out against trucks carrying SA-17 anti-aircraft missiles. *Haaretz*. [Hebrew]. 30 January.

Rid, T. 2012. Deterrence beyond the State: the Israeli experience. *Contemporary Security Policy* 33, no. 1: 124–47.

Risse, T. 2000. Let's argue! communicative action in world politics. *International Organization* 54, no. 1: 1–39.

Schweitzer, Y. 2012. Global Jihad: approaching Israel's Borders? *INSS Strategic Assessment* 15, no. 3: 59–71.

Sharansky, N. 2011. The West should bet on freedom in Egypt. *The Washington Post*, 17 December.

Shay, S. 2014. The threat of the 'Salafi Crescent'. *BESA Perspectives Paper* No. 235.

Shlaim, A. 1999. Israel, the great powers, and the Middle East crisis of 1958. *The Journal of Imperial and Commonwealth History* 27, no. 2: 177–92.

Snidal, D. 2002. Rational choice and international relations. In *Handbook of international relations*, eds. W. Carlsnaes, T. Risse, and B.A. Simmons, 73–94. London: Sage.

Spyer, J. 2013. *The Israeli Debate over Syria*. 16 May, http://jonathanspyer.com/2013/05/16/the-israeli-debate-over-syria/

Tovias, A., and A. Magen. 2005. Reflections from the new near outside: an Israeli perspective on the economic and legal impact of EU enlargement. *European Foreign Affairs Review* 10: 399–425.

Waltz, K. 1979. *Theory of international politics*. Reading, MA: Addison-Wesley.

Wendt, A. 1999. *Social theory of international politics*. Cambridge: Cambridge University Press.

Ya Libnan. 2013. *Over 650 Hezbollah fighters killed in* Syria, Al-Qabas, 19 December.

Yaari, E. 2012. Sinai: a new front. *Washington Institute for Near East Policy. Policy Notes*. no. 9. http://www.washingtoninstitute.org/policy-analysis/view/sinai-a-new-front

Yaari, E. 2014. The new triangle of Egypt, Israel, and Hamas. *Washington Institute for Near East Policy*. Policy Watch 2193.

Zacharia, J. 2011. Israel wary of transition in Egypt, concerned about regional stability. *The Washington Post*, 2 February.

The EU, External Actors, and the Arabellions: Much Ado About (Almost) Nothing — Conclusion

TANJA A. BÖRZEL, THOMAS RISSE & ASSEM DANDASHLY

Otto-Suhr-Institute for Political Science, Freie Universität, Berlin, Germany; Department of Political Science, Maastricht University, Maastricht, The Netherlands

ABSTRACT This article summarizes the findings from the special issue. The EU, the US, and to some extent Turkey are the only actors considered in this special issue who not only explicitly try to promote human rights and democracy, but also employ specific instruments and resources for this purpose. But all external actors prioritized stability and security over democracy as the events unfolded. Despite all the discussions about EU actorness, we did not find any difference between the EU, on the one hand, and the four states we looked at in this special issue (the US, Russia, Turkey, and Israel), on the other. In fact, the US arguably pursued the most incoherent and inconsistent foreign policy toward the MENA region in response to the Arabellions. Among the three explanations considered in the introduction to this special issue, realism scores worst. 'Objective' geostrategic interests cannot account for the variation in policy responses by the external actors. The authors in this special issue point to domestic politics in the various countries and inside the regional organization (the EU) considered here. Self-understandings and collective identities provide a complementary explanation for why external actors have acted against their economic and security goals. As to the effects of the external actors' policies in the target countries, the main drivers of events during the Arabellions have been domestic so that external actors could only assume subsidiary roles. Tunisia might be the only case in which external democracy promotion—in this case by the EU—played an auxiliary role.

Less than four years after the beginning of the 'Arabellions,'[1] the initial euphoria has faded away. Tunisia remains by and large the only country of the five Arabellion states considered in this special issue which has seen some significant improvements in the democratic quality of its regime. Bahrain has become more repressive rather than less, while Egypt is quickly reaching pre-rebellion levels of repression with a military dictatorship in power. Libya, which was exposed to external military intervention backed by the UN Security Council, underwent a regime change but has turned into a failing state. So has Syria with one part of the country still being governed by the repressive Assad regime, while other parts are under control of Islamic State (IS) and various other Jihadist groups.

The results of the Arabellions are certainly unsatisfactory from a democratization perspective. Yet, the uprisings still represent a critical juncture in world history, since they demonstrated the aspirations of hundreds of thousands of people in the Middle Eastern and North African (MENA) regions for human rights and political freedom. At the same time and irrespective of the disappointing outcomes, the Arabellions provide a unique opportunity to explore the foreign policies of the EU and other external actors in response to the events. This is what this special issue has been about. We tried to examine how the EU and other external actors assessed the Arabellions, which goals and instruments they pursued toward the MENA region, and—particularly—how they dealt with conflicting goals, such as supporting human rights and democracy, on the one hand, and preserving security and stability, on the other.

This concluding article summarizes the findings from the special issue. In particular, we compare the reactions of the EU and other external actors, and suggest some generalizable results. Our argument can be summarized in the following points:

(1) The EU, the US, and to some extent Turkey are the only actors considered in this special issue who not only explicitly try to promote human rights and democracy, but also employ specific instruments and resources for this purpose (see also Magen, Risse, and McFaul 2009). But all external actors (including the EU and the US) have prioritized stability and security over democracy as the events unfolded. Particularly, the rise of variants of Islamism became a major common concern. Even the Turkish AKP government under Erdogan did not appreciate the rise of Salafist movements in Tunisia and Egypt, let alone the growing influence of the Islamic State (IS) movement in Syria. When it comes to prioritizing security over democracy, neither the EU nor the US is a special case, but behaved as 'normal' powers who seek to balance security with human rights and democracy goals.

(2) Yet, we also observe considerable variation in how external actors tried to pursue their goals with regard to the Arabellions. As mentioned above, the EU and the US are unique to the extent that they employed their instruments for human rights and democracy promotion in response to the events. Moreover, the US was the only one which actively participated in the military intervention in Libya. In contrast, Israel was an 'active bystander' which first and foremost concentrated on Egypt and Syria being

concerned about preventing potential spillover effects for its security from its neighbors in terms of cross-border movements of fighters or refugees. Turkey first promoted its model of democratically embedded moderate Islamism. With the rise of radical Islamism, however, it became increasingly concerned with security and stability in the region, too. Russia, finally, has not been concerned with democracy and human rights. Still, it has not pursued a coherent policy towards the MENA region. While it tolerated military intervention in Libya, President Putin has vetoed any attempt of the international community to use coercion in Syria.

(3) Despite all the discussions about EU actorness (Concecao-Heldt and Meunier 2014; Hill 1993; Thomas 2012) and the EU's 'normative power' (Manners 2002, 2006; Sjursen 2006), we did not find any difference between the EU, on the one hand, and the four states we looked at in this special issue (the US, Russia, Turkey, and Israel), on the other. Lack of cohesion or incapacity to act is not what distinguishes the EU from other external actors. In fact, the US arguably pursued the most incoherent and inconsistent foreign policy toward the MENA region in response to the Arabellions compared to all other external actors in this special issue. Moreover and unlike other external actors, including the US, the EU has devoted considerable resources to help consolidate Tunisia's transition to democracy, the only success case so far among the Arabellions.

(4) Interestingly enough, among the three explanations considered in the introduction to this special issue, realism scores worst, even though it would appear to have an easy task given that all external actors prioritized security and stability goals in response to the Arabellions. 'Objective' geostrategic interests cannot account, however, for the variation in policy responses by the external actors. Time and again, the authors in this special issue point to domestic politics in the various countries and inside the regional organization (the EU) considered here. This ranges from Putin's domestic problems during an election campaign to Erdogan's attempt in Turkey to establish a hegemonic position for the AKP, Obama's constraints stemming from the growing domestic opposition against an interventionist foreign policy, and Israel's overemphasis on security and stability due to the fragility of its governing coalition. Likewise, the EU only speaks with one voice when there is a consensus and a shared view among the member states. Self-understandings and collective identities, finally, provide a complementary explanation for why external actors have acted against their economic and security goals. As a moderate Islamist party, the AKP government under Erdogan supported the Muslim Brotherhood in Egypt, and, consequently, opposed the military coup against the Morsi government, ignoring its strong economic interests in the country. The EU's identity as a norma-

tive power and the US self-perception as the world-leading democracy made them promote democracy and human rights in the first place. While realism accounts well for Israel's exclusive focus on security and stability, its self-perception as a democracy under siege provides the normative justification for neglecting issues of democracy and human rights. Russia's self-understanding as an anti-Western power, finally, provides an alternative account for a realist interpretation of its (inconsistent) foreign policy in the MENA region.

(5) While this special issue did not deal with the effects of the external actors policies in the target countries, its findings lend themselves to some preliminary conclusions. First, the main drivers of events during the Arabellions have been domestic so that external actors could only assume subsidiary roles. In Egypt, for example, the US withdrawal of support for Mubarak and his cronies might have provided the final straw that broke the camel's back. But the uprising on Tahrir square and the refusal of the Egyptian military to put it down by violent means were certainly more important. Second, only the US and the EU actively tried to promote human rights and democracy in the region, but the effects have been limited (see Figure 1). Tunisia might be the only case in which external democracy promotion—in this case by the EU—played an auxiliary role. Third, counterproductive effects should also be considered. The NATO-led military intervention in Libya did help remove one of the most repressive regimes in the region. But it also created a failing state. In contrast, doing nothing—e.g. the restraint by external actors in Syria which was widely justified by geostrategic reasons—made Western powers indirectly complicit in massive human rights violations and led to another failing state in the region.

(6) The absence of coherent strategies of external actors in responding to the Arabellions and their limited and ambivalent effects on the unfolding events do not only confirm the supremacy of domestic factors in shaping the success and failure of democratization processes (Carothers 2002; Linz and Stepan 1996; Lipset 1994; Whitehead 2001). The findings of the special issue call into question the equation of democracies promoting democracy and autocracies promoting autocracy (Bader, Grävingholt, and Kästner 2010; Burnell 2010). Russia prioritizes stability as much as the EU, the US, and Israel do. Unlike for Russia, however, this may undermine the credibility of the EU and the US as democracy promoters when they end up supporting a military *coup d'état* against a democratically elected government, as they did in Egypt, or standby massive human rights violations by a repressive regime, as they do in Syria. This yields some important policy implications we will discuss at the end of this conclusions.

The remainder of this article proceeds in three steps. First, we compare the EU's response to the Arabellions with other external actors. Second, we focus on explaining the variation in responses by external actors to the Arabellions. Third, the article looks at the potential effects of the policy reactions by external actors in the target countries. This task can only be speculative at this stage. We conclude this article with some policy considerations.

The EU's Response to the Arabellions in a Comparative Perspective

The EU has been heavily criticized for its approach to the MENA region. Its failure to respond to the events of the Arabellions unfolding is seen as yet another piece of evidence for its incapacity to play an international role (inter alia Behr 2012; Hill 1993; Pace and Cavatorta 2012; Teti 2012; Teti, Thompson, and Noble 2013, etc.). This special issue largely confirms that the EU has not lived up to its aspirations of being a 'normative' or 'transformative' power (cf. Börzel and Risse 2009). Yet, the contributions also show that the EU's marginal impact is not unique. Comparing its response with those of the US, Russia, Turkey, and Israel, demonstrates that other international and regional players have faced similar challenges in developing a consistent and effective foreign policy. These findings have not only important implications for debates on the EU's actorness, or the lack thereof. They also point to the limits of what external actors can and should do when trying to influence the domestic politics of third countries.

The failure of the EU in bringing about democratic change in third countries, in general, and in the MENA region in particular, is often attributed to its lack of actorness (Baracani 2009; Concecao-Heldt and Meunier 2014; Hill 1993; Laatikeinen and Smith 2006; Meunier 2005; Youngs 2009). Actorness has been conceptualized along four dimensions (Jupille and Caporaso 1998): authority, autonomy, external recognition, and internal cohesiveness. This special issue has replaced the fourth dimension, internal cohesiveness, by capabilities (see the introduction to this special issue). The EU has enjoyed and still enjoys recognition by the various MENA countries. Among the international and regional actors, it has the highest legitimacy (see IEMed 2013; Malmvig and Tassinari 2011). However, its authority in terms of delegated competences from the member states and its autonomy to use them, are indeed limited. This has undermined the capabilities of the EU to formulate internally and represent externally a consistent response to the Arabellions, speaking with a single voice.

The EU institutions have been given the task to define the main goals within dealing with its neighbors. The lack of consensus and common view among the EU member states pushed them to delegate 'the management of the neighbourhood to the Brussels bureaucracy which has crafted a slow but predictable response to unfolding events, offering the usual mix of incentives (money, mobility and market access) on the strength of vague expectations of reforms in partner countries' (Noutcheva 2014). Bureaucratic and institutional governance in the EU has influenced its reaction to the Arabellions and even caused some confusion at the beginning of the events.

While the EU institutions were given the task to frame the EU response to the Arabellions, they could not do that as freely as they can in some areas involving external policy and allocating of EU resources. This created a discrepancy between the EU's rhetoric and action. On the one hand, the EU promised in the aftermath of the Arabellions more support for democracy, access to the single market, and economic development. On the other hand, its promises were vague on issues related to people's mobility and visa facilitation. In the areas of shared interest to the member states, such as border's security, migration, terrorism, and trade, EU involvement and support is high. In other areas, which were deemed less important or lacked agreement among member states, including democratic reforms and political conflicts, no coherent action has been taken (see Dandashly 2014). So, in drafting the policies in response of the Arabellions, consensus among member states has been the main reason behind EU action since it gave the EU institutions more or less freedom to speak with a single voice.

When it comes to implementation and utilization of the EU instruments, again, EU actions seemed to reflect the major concerns of the member states focusing mainly on security. Despite the EU commitment to support democracy in the reformed ENP, a gap between practice and rhetoric prevails when it comes to the implementation. Its security concerns made the EU focus on helping the MENA countries restore the pre-Arabellion stability and economic performance. Thereby, the EU sought to protect its borders from the illegal migrants who are trying to escape from the lack of security or difficult economic situation. Depending on the degree of stability and security in the targeted country, the EU has utilized different instruments, which explains why we have seen different EU reactions (see Dandashly 2014).

Disagreements among the member states notwithstanding, the EU's effectiveness in responding to the Arabellionshas suffered from a substantive inconsistency in its foreign policy, which results from an inherent trade-off between the goals of democratization and the stability (Börzel and van Hüllen 2014). There is hardly any dissent within the EU over prioritizing security and stability over democratization. However, this balancing act between the desire for stability, on the one hand, and normative principles, on the other, has also shaped the responses of other external actors. The *US* behaved as inconsistent and incoherent as the EU in many instances (see Huber 2014). The Obama administration, like the EU, viewed the Arabellions as an opportunity for democracy without forgoing its security concerns especially when it came to Egypt and Syria. The US responses to the events have lacked consistency and showed confusion in the Obama Administration. The US had to deal with new uncertainties in the MENA along with the domestic politics characterizes by a hesitant public and a Republican majority. Furthermore, the US has been restricted in its action due to its external alliances with some major regional powers such as Saudi Arabia where the US was not as vocal regarding the conflict in Bahrain. However, the US did risk a major conflict with one of its top allies in the region, Saudi Arabia, when it withdrew support for the Mubarak regime in Egypt. In addition, the US relations with Israel played a major role in its reaction to the Egyptian events. Thus, the US conditioned its support on Egypt commitment to the 1979 peace agreement with Israel—especially under the rule of the Muslim Brotherhood.

The US reaction varied across countries as well depending on its specific interests in the target countries. It was rather active in Egypt and changed its course of action frequently in this case—from withdrawing support for the Mubarak regime to establishing a dialogue with the Muslim Brotherhood and the new President Morsi, to—finally—standing by and tacitly applauding the military coup under now President el-Sisi. The US was equally active at first with regard to Libya—without its military support, the NATO-led intervention could not have been accomplished. It then became a rather passive by-stander of events—as was the case in Tunisia. The same holds true for Syria in which the US changed position several times without any clear indication of what the administration wanted to accomplish. Last not least, in the case of Bahrain, the US did nothing to prevent the Saudi-led repression of the uprising.

What holds true for the US (and the EU) also applies to *Turkey* under the leadership of Prime Minister Erdogan and the Justice and Development Party (AKP). Initially, Turkey tried to push its model of democratically embedded moderate Islamism for its Arab neighbors. In fact, Turkey was widely regarded as a role model for the Arab world after the Arabellions (see Ayata's article). This positive view was due to its higher credibility compared to the EU and the US whose support for the authoritarian regimes for decades contradicted their democratic rhetoric. However, the Turkish 'honeymoon' with the Arabellions came to an end rather quickly. Particularly, the civil war in Syria became a major security and humanitarian concern for the Turkish government as a result of which it also started to prioritize stability and security goals, undermining its value-based foreign policy (see Ayata 2014).

In contrast particularly to the EU and the US, *Israel* never considered the Arabellions as a window of opportunity for regime change and progress toward human rights and democracy (see Magen 2014). Rather, the Israeli government continuously prioritized security at its borders over any other goal being an 'active bystander'. During the early months of the Arabellions, Israeli officials did not have a regional comprehensive approach to the events. Rather, their main focus was on its close neighbors: Egypt in early 2011 and Syria from mid-2011 onwards. Both upheavals were of great concern due to the strong ties with the Moubarak regime who managed to keep the borders controlled from weapons' smugglers to Hamas in Gazah, and the spillover effect of the Syrian crisis to its neighbors Lebanon and Jordan. In a way, Israel's foreign policy toward the Arabellions was much more coherent and consistent than the reactions by the EU, the US, and Turkey.

This special issue also looked at the reactions of a non-democratic power to the Arabellion, namely *Russia* (see Dannreuther 2014). Unlike the EU or the US, Russia did not have to balance security goals with efforts to promote human rights and democracy. Nevertheless, there was also little consistency in—first Prime Minister, then President—Putin's response. At first and similar to the US and the EU, Russia estimated that the MENA region was undergoing major transformations. But Russia interpreted these developments more 'in terms of Islamization than of democratization' (Dannreuther 2014). Nevertheless, Russia has not pursued a consistent and coherent foreign policy toward the Arabellions either. In the case of Libya, for example, it allowed the UN Security Council resolution authorizing the use of force to pass, while it remained adamant that no such outside interference should be legitimized with regard to its long-term ally in the region, Assad's Syria.

This brief survey of the various responses by external actors toward the Arabellions allows for some general conclusions. First, what often looks like inconsistent and incoherent policies is to a large extent explained by the need of outside actors to quickly react to developments on the ground as they unfold. None of the actors discussed in this special issue saw the Arabellions coming—despite all the warning signs identified by the literatures on autocratic and repressive regimes, slow economic growth, and high (youth) unemployment. Moreover, the external actors discussed here did not develop any master plan how to react to quickly changing circumstances after the initial events.

Second, and this observation speaks to the literature on EU foreign policy trying to understand its pitfalls and challenges, the EU is not that different from other external actors, after all. Apparently, it does not matter much whether we deal with a state or with a multi-level governance system, such as the EU: inconsistency and incoherence is not the privilege of a multi-actor system that lacks a phone number, to paraphrase Henry Kissinger. Arguably, the most inconsistent and incoherent foreign policy toward the Arabellions was carried out by Kissinger's own country, the most powerful state in the international system with tremendous economic, military, and ideational resources at its disposal, the United States (see Huber 2014; Magen, Risse, and McFaul 2009). Semi-democratic Turkey and semi-autocratic Russia were also unable to pursue policies with clearly defined goals and instruments (see articles by Dannreuther 2014; Ayata 2014). The only half-way consistent policy was carried out by the one stable democracy in the region, Israel which did not aim at promoting human rights and democracy at any moment during the course of events.

As a result, a lot that has been written on the EU's foreign policy should be reconsidered. This concerns, for example, its 'capabilities- expectations' gap (Hill 1993), its double standards with regard to 'normative power' (Manners 2006; Sjursen 2006), and its general inconsistency and incoherence. The empirical observations are certainly right, but they suffer from a lack of comparison in foreign policy analysis. Once one compares the EU with other foreign policy actors—states in this special issue –, one notices that its internal contradictions are standard features of any foreign policy of any great or middle-range power. To assume, therefore, that one day the EU will pursue a rationally designed, consistent foreign policy with a clear prioritization of goals and instruments, if only it could speak with one voice, is illusionary. In principle, the US, Turkey, or Russia should have the institutional capacities to speak with one voice in their foreign policies, too. They rarely do, as this special issue demonstrates.

If actor type does not explain similarities and differences in their responses to the Arabellions, which of the three standard International Relations explanations discussed in the introduction to this special issue does?

Explaining the Responses to the Arabellions: Geostrategic Interests, Identities, or Domestic Politics?

The various contributions to this special issue analyze the responses of international and regional actors according to three explanatory factors drawn from the field of foreign policy analysis: geostrategic interests as theorized by realism and its variants; self-understandings of actors including their collective identities as suggested by social constructivist approaches; and domestic as well as bureaucratic politics as privileged by liberal approaches.

Realism and Geostrategic Interests

At first glance, foreign policy accounts based on realist thinking do a good job at explaining the various external responses to the Arabellions. All actors considered in this special issue prioritized security and stability over any other foreign policy goals which should be in line with *Realpolitik* thinking. A second look reveals, however, that realist analysis might explain the goal orientations, but specific policy choices are either hard to reconcile with *Realpolitik* or realism is too indeterminate to account for them. Let us go through the five external actors under consideration here one by one.

The *European Union* and its member states certainly have geostrategic—security and economic—interests in the MENA region as a whole (see Noutcheva 2014; Dandashly 2014). In this sense, realism can indeed explain the prioritization of stability over human rights and democratization in general. The more specific responses to the various Arabellions are not as easy to reconcile with a *Realpolitik* outlook, though. Among the five Arab countries considered in this special issue, Egypt, Syria, and Libya are arguably most important for the EU from a security-related standpoint. With regard to Egypt and Syria, however, the EU did not have a clear foreign policy strategy to begin with, but rather reacted (and continues to react) in an ad hoc fashion. Particularly in the Syrian case, the EU and its member states did little to prevent state failure and massive human rights violations, both resulting in negative externalities for stability and security. As to Libya, a majority of EU members supported the military intervention on humanitarian grounds (Germany did not) which was led by France and the UK, and resulted in regime change. Regime change, however, does not belong in the realist foreign policy tool box. From a *Realpolitik* perspective, the EU and its members should have calculated the costs and benefits of regime change against the costs and benefits of tribal warfare in Libya resulting in state failure. Last not least, the considerable EU support for Tunisia's transition to democracy is equally hard to reconcile with realist thinking given the strategic insignificance of the country.

A quite similar picture emerges with regard to the *United States,* the only military and economic superpower with significant interests in the Arab region (see Huber 2014). While it behaved according to the realist script in Bahrain implicitly supporting the Saudi-led military intervention, its geo-strategic interests should have dictated consistent and clearly articulated foreign policies toward both Egypt and Syria. But US foreign policies toward Egypt and Syria were both ad hoc and mostly driven by short-term reactions to events on the ground. As to Libya, it makes little sense from a realist point of view that the US became actively involved in the military intervention (even if only 'leading from behind,' as Obama put it). Finally, the US—subdued—support for the Tunisian transition does not even appear on the realist screen, given that the country is irrelevant for American strategic interests.

Russia is an interesting case insofar as Putin's foreign policy outlook appears to be dominated by realist and geostrategic thinking (see Dannreuther's article). The Russian strong support for the Assad regime in Syria, a longstanding ally, fits the picture. So does Russian brokerage of the agreement to destroy Syria's chemical weapons as an attempt to alleviate the security situation in the country. Concerning Libya, a realist foreign policy would have suggested that Moscow should have vetoed the UN Security Council resolution authorizing military action. As to Egypt, Russia did not consider it vital to its interests even though a realist would strongly disagree given the pivotal role of Cairo in the Middle East. Last not least, Tunisia and Bahrain are too insignificant from a Russian geostrategic perspective to warrant any particular foreign policy.

While Russia's foreign policy toward the Arabellions is at least partly consistent with realism, *Turkey's* reactions mostly do not fit with this perspective, except when the situation in Syria started to become a serious security threat for the country (see Ayata 2014). However, Prime Minister Erdogan's strong support for the regime changes in Tunisia and Egypt, his support for Morsi and the Muslim Brotherhood in Egypt, and the opposition to the subsequent military coup are inconsistent with Turkey's strong economic interests in Egypt. While Turkish opposition to the military intervention in Libya can be regarded as anti-Western balancing behavior, a more prudent approach would probably have warranted that Ankara kept out of this case given its dependence on NATO support for responding to any instability at its Southern borders.

Israel constitutes the one actor considered in this special issue whose immediate security interests were directly at stake if not threatened by the Arabellions. Therefore, the Israeli responses to the Arabellions are mostly consistent with realist foreign policy behavior (see Magen 2014). Israel prioritized security over any other foreign policy goal and conducted a more consistent policy of 'active bystander' than any other actor considered in this special issue. It perceived itself in an acute security dilemma vis-à-vis its neighbors (if not open hostility)—and acted accordingly.

Constructivism and Collective Identities

To what extent can the various responses to the Arab spring be (better) accounted for by a social constructivist reading emphasizing collective identities and self-understandings? The articles in this special issue suggest that foreign policy identities go a long way to understand the variety of responses including some of the inconsistencies.

Let us start with the EU and the US (see articles by Noutcheva 2014; Dandashly 2014; Huber 2014). Both actors expose strong self-understandings as liberal and democratic systems, and both seek to externalize these collective identities in their foreign policy behavior. As a result, the EU and the US have developed active programs of human rights and democracy promotion, and strongly support democratic movements and civil society organizations worldwide, at least rhetorically (Magen, Risse, and McFaul 2009). This verbal support was visible again in their reactions to the Arabellions, and partly in their practices with regard to Tunisia (see Dandashly 2014) and—initially—to Egypt. The initiation and strong support for a military intervention in Libya by the US and a majority of EU member states (the EU itself could not take a stance because of mostly German opposition) is also consistent with these collective self-understandings.

At the same time, however, as shown in the articles of this special issue, neither the EU nor the US ever prioritized human rights and democracy in their foreign policies toward the region, but also pursued more mundane security and economic interests. As a result, both actors faced almost irreconcilable conflicts of interests and moral dilemmas. How to square a democratic foreign policy identity with equally valuable security and stability goals in the cases of Egypt and Syria? We suggest that neither the EU nor the US ever developed a strategy on how to balance these conflicting foreign policy goals and interests in their responses to the Arabellions in these cases. As a result, they both pursued rather inconsistent and incoherent policies largely reacting to rather than trying to pro-actively shape the situation on the ground.

In contrast to the EU and the US, *Russia* and *Turkey* were much less faced with these kinds of 'democratization-stability' dilemmas (Jünemann 2003, 7) and tough choices (see articles by Dannreuther 2014; Ayata 2014). Nevertheless, collective understandings and identities—at least on the elite level—go a long way to accounting for their responses to the Arabellions. Putin's Russia exposes a self-understanding of an increasingly 'anti-Western' great power and a different type of 'sovereign democracy' (Dannreuther 2014, 12). The main message Moscow has presented to the world was a distinctive Russian vision of 'the nature of political order which explicitly critiques and challenges the idea of Western-promoted liberal democracy' (Dannreuther 2014, 14). Russia's policies toward the Arabellions are largely consistent with this foreign policy outlook providing an alternative account to realism.

As to *Turkey*, Erdogan and the AKP's self-understandings as potential role models for the Arab world also have a lot of power to explain the initial responses to the Arab spring and, particularly, the strong support for the opposition against the autocratic Arab rulers in Tunisia, Libya, Egypt, and Syria. It also explains the backing of moderate Islamism in Tunisia (*En-Nahda*) and Egypt (Muslim Brotherhood) including the opposition against the military coup against elected President Morsi (see Ayata 2014).

As in the case of Russia, realism and social constructivism go together in explaining the *Israeli* responses to the Arabellions (see Magen 2014). Israel's collective self-understanding as a 'security state' which is surrounded mostly by enemies or by countries with which it holds a 'cold peace' (Egypt, Jordan), provides a strong explanation for its rather consistent prioritization of security over any other goal in its response to the Arabellions. Israel's other identity as a liberal democracy receded on the backburner given this dominant 'securitized' mindset (on securitization see Buzan, Waever, and Wild 1998; Waever 1995). This may explain why Israel never faced the kind of moral dilemmas experienced by the EU and the US between their support for human rights and democracy, on the one hand, and concerns for security and stability, on the other. Unlike them, Israeli readings of the Arabellions never assumed that there was a window of opportunity for a democratic Middle East.

Regime Type and Domestic Politics

Finally, what about liberal explanations for foreign policy behavior, focusing on regime type, on the one hand, and on domestic politics, on the other? As to regime type, our sample of external actors includes three consolidated democratic systems (the EU, the US, and Israel), one semi-democratic (Turkey) and one semi-autocratic country (Russia). However, the variation of regime types can obviously not explain the similarities among the external reactions to the Arabellions, namely the prioritization of security and stability over other goals in most cases. But the variation among the cases does not correspond to the variation of regime types, either.

At the same time, domestic and bureaucratic politics accounts do explain some of the specific variations in responses to the Arabellions, as our authors emphasize. In particular, domestic and bureaucratic politics provide an alternative account to the one emphasizing conflicting identities and interests for some of the inconsistencies in the behavior of both the EU and the US. The lack of substantive policy change in the EU's approach to the MENA region is largely explained by member state differences over how to deal with non-democratic regimes, how to manage illegal migration to the EU and which conflicts in the region should the EU prioritize, on the one hand, and the limited freedom EU institutions have to act on behalf of the member states, on the other (see Noutcheva 2014). Moreover, the lack of domestic security and stability severely constrained the EU's support for economic recovery and democratic reforms (see Dandashly 2014).

In the *US* case, one has to take into consideration the increasingly strong opposition against foreign military interventions and demands for cutting-back foreign aid, both in public opinion and in US Congress (see Huber's article). This opposition explains why the US refused to explicitly led the military intervention in Libya and—more important—the botched reaction to the use of chemical weapons by the Syrian Assad regime. When Obama announced that he would put a military intervention to a vote in Congress, he stood little chance to win because of a strange coalition of right-wing Republicans and left-wing Democrats. Ironically, the Russians saved the US President when they negotiated the agreement on the Syrian renunciation of chemical weapons. Some of the inconsistencies in US foreign policy in the Egyptian case can be accounted for by bureaucratic infighting by the Pentagon and the State Department (see Huber's article).

In the cases of Israel, Turkey, and Russia, domestic politics seemed to play a minor role, however. As to *Israel*, the fragility of the governing coalition and the instability of the political system in general have to be taken into account to explain its consistent policy of non-engagement (see Magen 2014). Israeli governments usually stay on the safe side and overemphasize security over taking diplomatic initiatives. In the *Turkish* case, two factors are counter-balancing Prime Minister Erdogan's value-based foreign policy from the domestic side, the risk of the Syrian civil war stirring the Kurdish conflict in Turkey, on the one hand, and the secular opposition which does not support the AKP's vision for a new regional order, on the other (see Ayata 2014).

With regard to *Russia*, the start of the Arabellions coincided with high levels of domestic opposition against Putin's regime and with discontent surrounding the 2011–2012 parliamentary and presidential elections which were widely perceived as encountering serious fraud (see Dannreuther's article). As a result, Putin in particular stepped up his efforts at articulating a counter-vision to Western democracy which then impacted upon the Russian reactions to the Arabellions. President Medvedev had refrained from vetoing the UN-sanctioned military intervention in Libya in order to avoid an international isolation of Russia, ignoring Putin's objections when he still was prime minister. After they reversed roles, President Putin has successfully opposed any Western intervention in Syria, risking Russia's relations with the Gulf states (Saudi Arabia and Qatar, in particular) and Turkey over his support for the Assad regime.

To sum up this section: Our interpretation of the articles in this special issues suggests the following picture with regard to explaining the foreign policies of the various actors toward the Arabellions. First, realism and an emphasis on geostrategic interests might explain why all external actors prioritized security and stability over democracy and human rights, albeit to various degrees. However, realism does a poor job in accounting for the specific foreign policy choices undertaken by the various actors. The EU, the US, and Turkish policies have been inconsistent with *Realpolitik* accounts, while Russia fits the bill to some extent. Only Israel's reactions are more or less compatible with realist theory.

Second, collective self-understandings and identities—mostly on the elite levels—offer a better explanation than realism in almost every single case. With regard to Russia and Israel, such a social constructivist interpretation provides an alternative account to realism. Concerning the EU and the US, emphasizing collective identities does not explain the specific policy choices. But social constructivism helps to elucidate why both actors faced severe conflicts of interests including moral dilemmas which then resulted in inconsistent and incoherent foreign policies toward the Arab world.

Third, while regime type explains neither the similarities nor the differences among the responses of external actors to the Arabellions, domestic politics offers a complementary account to the social constructivist emphasis on identities. This refers to the inner workings of the EU between the Commission, the Council of Ministers, and the member states, to bureaucratic politics in the US, and the fragility of governing coalitions in Israel. But domestic politics even played a role in Russia and Turkey, two countries outside the realm of consolidated democracies.

We now turn to a discussion of the potential effects of the reactions by external actors to the Arabellions. This part remains largely speculative, since this special issue did not specifically focus on this question.

Neither Good nor Bad or Ugly: The Limited Effect of External Actors

The capacity of external actors to influence democratic change is highly contested in the literature (*inter alia* Magen, Risse, and McFaul 2009; Whitehead 2001). The only two polities that have sought to support democratic transition in the MENA region are the EU and the US. Both have adopted a rather comprehensive or embedded concept of democracy (Linz and Stepan 1996; Merkel 2004; Wetzel and Orbie 2011). They do not only promote stable institutions guaranteeing democracy, the rule of law, and human rights. Their conditionality and capacity-building also aims at improving the structural conditions for democracy, focusing on governance capacity and socioeconomic development.

Comparing the Arabellion countries with regard to democracy, governance capacity, and socioeconomic development, we do not see much improvement (Figures 1–3). Bahrain, assisted by Saudi Arabia, managed to suppress the democratic uprisings as a result the non-democratic quality of its regime declined even further. In a similar vein, the attempts of Syria's Assad regime to stay in power triggered a civil war, involving rivaling Jihadist groups, which turned the presidential elections of 2014 into a farce. It deprived large parts of the population of their political and civil rights, and left the economy devastated. In Egypt, the military coup against the democratically elected government of the Muslim Brotherhood returned the country to its pre-Arabellion level of authoritarianism with much weaker governance capacities and no economic growth. Libya appears to be an interesting case. Despite tribal warfare turning the country into a failed state, its democracy scores, measured by a combination of Freedom House political and civil rights and Polity IV, have been substantially improving. While it came from a very low level under Mouammaral-Gaddafi, one may

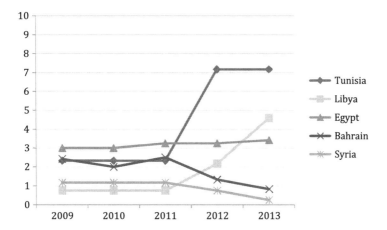

Figure 1. FH * Polity IV Index (0–10)
Notes: This figure combines the political rights index from Freedom House with the Polity IV index, whereby the averages have been re-scaled to a 0–10 scale.
Sources: Freedom House (2009–2013): Freedom in The World: Aggregate and Subcategory Scores.http://www.freedomhouse.org/report/freedom-world-aggregate-and-subcate gory-scores#.U-HpJrE1TLx (accessed 6 August 2014); Mashall, M. G., Project director. 2013. Polity IV Project: Political Regime Characteristics and Transitions, 1800–2013. http://www.systemicpeace.org/polity/polity4x.htm (accessed 6 August 2014).

still wonder to what extent Libyans can enjoy their democratic rights and freedoms given that the government lacks control over large parts of its territory, has virtually no governance capacities, and has not been able to generate much economic growth. The only success case is Tunisia which has undergone some real democratic change. To what extent this will be sustainable remains to be seen given the low level of economic growth and the weakened governance capacity.

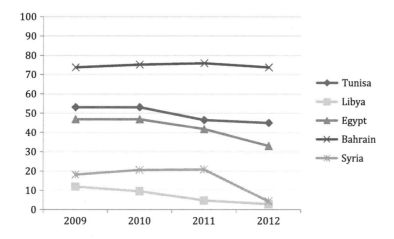

Figure 2. Regulatory quality (percentile rank)
Notes: World Governance Indicators (2013). http://info.worldbank.org/governance/wgi/index.aspx#reports (accessed 15 August 2014).

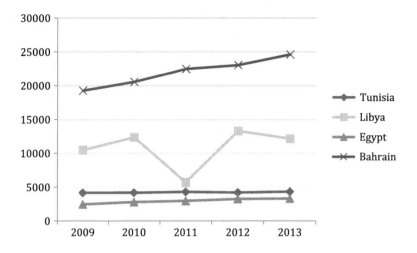

Figure 3. Development of GDP per capita (in US $)
Notes: The World Bank (2014). GDP per capita (current US$). http://data.worldbank.org/indicator/NY.GDP.PCAP.CD (accessed 15 August 2014).

What do these trends tell us about the impact of the EU and external actors on the MENA region? While the democratization literature does not give much credit to the role of external actors anyway, none of them engaged in consistent democracy promotion either. Tunisia is the only case in which the EU in particular managed to support democratization processes (see Dandashly's article). This may be explained by the democratization-stability dilemma being less pronounced. Unlike the other MENA countries, Tunisia does not only have pro-democratic forces the EU can empower. The moderate Islamist government also has sufficient governance capacity left to respond to the EU's conditionality and assistance (Börzel and van Hüllen 2014). While democratic external actors have done little to promote democracy in the other cases, they have helped stabilize non-democratic regimes in Egypt and did not prevent authoritarian regimes from seeking to restore their power in Bahrain and Syria. In these cases, their behavior does not differ from semi-democratic Turkey and semi-authoritarian Russia (see above). They all pursued stability and security. Claims about autocracies promoting autocracy undermining the efforts of democracies to promote democracy are, hence, overdrawn. While democracy promotion in the Arab region has remained limited, we have not found evidence for autocracy promotion, either.

Conclusions

The Arabellions provide a fruitful case to study the EU as a foreign policy actor and compare it to other external actors with a stake in the region. The findings of the special issue demonstrate that there is nothing special or unique about the EU, either with regard to the (conflicting) goals it pursues or its capacity to pursue them. The EU's actorness is not necessarily less developed than the one of democratic states, where decision-making powers are shared between different institutions and levels of government, such as the US. But even non-democratic states, like Russia, do not pursue a more coherent and consistent foreign policy than the EU. Nor is the EU the only actor in the region that seeks to promote democracy. The US grounds the foreign policy in similar norms and values as the EU does. At the same time, not all democracies always promote democracy. Similar to semi-democratic and semi-authoritarian states, the EU, the US, and Israel prioritize security and stability over the perils of democratic change. Regime type, hence, does not account for the similarities and differences the contributions to this special issue found with regard to the responses of the various external actors to the Arabellions. Regime type, however, is part of the self-understanding and collective identities that shaped how external actors perceived the Arabellions. The self-understanding as a model liberal democracy (the US, the EU), a democracy under siege (Israel), a Muslim democracy (Turkey), or an non-Western democracy (Russia) accounts—together with the domestic politics of these actors—for the specific foreign policy goals they have pursued and the instruments they have employed in responding to the unfolding events of the Arabellions.

Our findings yield some important policy implications, particularly for the EU and the US which seek to pursue both moral goals and geostrategic interests. Clearly, not all good things always go together (Grimm and Leininger 2012). The more instable a country is and the less democratic, the more difficult it will be to reconcile the protection and promotion of human rights and democracy with ensuring security and stability. While the democratization-stability dilemma seems to be somewhat unavoidable, democratic external actors should acknowledge it and develop strategies on how to balance the different goals. Otherwise reproaches of double standards and hypocrisy will undermine their credibility and legitimacy.

Moreover, domestic politics matter. The case of Tunisia forcefully demonstrates that external actors can support democratization processes if the conditions on ground are right. Democracy promoters should focus on countries that are sufficiently stable, have some substantial governance capacity and feature some pro-democratic forces which external conditionality, financial assistance, or military intervention can empower. Where such conditions are absent, democracy promotion often amounts to a waste of time and tax payers' money. Even worse, it can turn a rogue state into a failed state where people are not necessarily better off.

At the same time, however, stabilizing autocratic regimes by providing aid and trade should find its limits where dictators engage in massive human rights violations. For all the criticism of the EU and the US for supporting Hosni Mubarak of Egypt and Ben Ali of Tunisia, both treated Muhamar Gaddafi of Libya and Bashar Assad of Syria as pariahs. But only in the case of Libya did they intervene militarily, while they did nothing to remedy the massive human rights violations by the Assad regime.

It follows that democracy promotion and humanitarian interventions to prevent massacres and gross violations of human rights enacting the 'responsibility to protect' (R2P) are two very different foreign policies. Implementing the R2P can only be a stopgap measure, as the two cases of

Libya and Syria demonstrate. While genocide was prevented in Libya, the military intervention did not lead to democracy. Democracy promotion from the outside, however, is a much more demanding strategy which can only be effective if the conditions on the ground are right.

Note

1. A justification for the use of the term 'Arabellions' in this special issue, can be found in the introduction to this special issue.

References

Ayata, B. 2014. Turkish foreign policy in a changing Arab world: rise and fall of a regional actor? *Journal of European Integration* 37, no. 1: 95–112.

Bader, J., J. Grävingholt, and A. Kästner. 2010. Would autocracies promote autocracy? A political economy perspective on regime-type export in regional neighbourhoods. *Contemporary Politics* 16, no. 1: 81–100.

Baracani, E. 2009. The European neighbourhood policy and political conditionality: double standards in EU democracy promotion? In *The external dimension of EU justice and home affairs: governance, neighbours, security*, ed. T. Balzacq, 133–53. Basingstoke: Palgrave Macmillan.

Behr, T. 2012. The European Union's Mediterranean policies after the Arab spring: can the Leopard change its spots? *Amsterdam Law Forum* 4, no. 2: 76–88.

Börzel, T.A., and T. Risse. 2009. Venus approaching Mars? The European Union's approaches to democracy promotion in comparative perspective. In *Democracy promotion in the US and the EU compared*, eds. A. Magen, M. McFaul and T. Risse, 34–60. Houndmills: Palgrave Macmillan.

Börzel, T.A., and V. van Hüllen. 2014. One voice, one message, but conflicting goals: cohesiveness and consistency in the European neighbourhood policy. *Journal of European Public Policy* 21, no. 7: 1033–49.

Burnell, P. 2010. *Is there a new autocracy promotion?* FRIDE Working Paper 96, Madrid.

Buzan, B., O. Waever, and J.D. Wild. 1998. *Security. A new framework for analysis*. Boulder, CO: Lynne Rienner.

Carothers, T. 2002. The end of the transition paradigm. *Journal of Democracy* 13, no. 1: 5–21.

Concecao-Heldt, E.d., and S. Meunier. 2014. Speaking with a single voice: internal cohesiveness and external effectiveness of the EU in global governance. *Journal of European Public Policy* 21, no. 7: 961–79.

Dandashly, A. 2014. The EU response to regime change in the wake of the Arab revolt: differential Implementation. *Journal of European Integration* 37, no. 1: 37–56.

Dannreuther, R. 2014. Russia and the Arab Spring: supporting the counter-revolution. *Journal of European Integration* 37, no. 1: 77–94.

Grimm, S., and J. Leininger. 2012. Not all good things go together: conflicting objectives in democracy promotion. *Democratization* 19, no. 3: 391–414.

Hill, C. 1993. The capability-expectations gap or conceptualising Europe's international role. *Journal of Common Market Studies* 31, no. 3: 305–28.

Huber, D. 2014. A pragmatic actor — the US response to the Arab uprisings. *Journal of European Integration* 37, no. 1: 57–75.

IEMed. 2013. Euromed survey of experts and actors (2012). *Barcelona*, http://www.iemed.org/publica cions-en/historic-de-publicacions/enquesta-euromed/euromed-survey-of-experts-and-actors-2012 (accessed 15 August 2014).

Jünemann, A. 2003. Security building in the Mediterranean after September 11. In *Euro-Mediterranean Relations after September 11. International, Regional and Domestic Dynamics*, ed. A. Jünemann, 1–20. London: Frank Cass.

Jupille, J., and J.A. Caporaso. 1998. States, agency, and rules: the European Union in global environmental politics. In *The European Union in the world community*, ed. C. Rhodes, 213–29. Boulder, CO: Lynne Rienner.

Laatikeinen, K.V., and K.E. Smith (eds.). 2006. *The European Union at the United Nations: intersecting multilateralisms*. Basingstoke: Palgrave Macmillan.

Linz, J.J., and A. Stepan. 1996. *Problems of democratic transition and consolidation: Southern Europe, South America, and Post-Communist Europe*. Baltimore, MD: Johns Hopkins University Press.

Lipset, S.M. 1994. The social requisites of democracy revisited. *American Sociological Review* 59: 1–22.

Magen, A. 2014. Comparative assessment of Israel's foreign policy response to the 'Arab Spring'. *Journal of European Integration* 37, no. 1: 113–33.

Magen, A., T. Risse, and M. McFaul (eds.). 2009. *Promoting democracy and the rule of law. American and European strategies*. Basingstoke: Palgrave-Macmillan.

Malmvig, H., and F. Tassinari. 2011. The 'Arab Spring' and the external actor's role within the Euro-Mediterranean region. In *Euromed Survey 2011*. Barcelona.

Manners, I. 2002. Normative power Europe. A contradiction in terms? *Journal of Common Market Studies* 40, no. 2: 235–58.

Manners, I. 2006. Normative power Europe reconsidered. Beyond the crossroads. *Journal of European Public Policy* 13, no. 2: 182–99.

Merkel, W. 2004. Embedded and defective democracies. *Democratization* 11, no. 5: 33–58.

Meunier, S. 2005. *Trading voices: the European Union in international commercial negotiations*. Princeton, NJ: Princeton University Press.

Noutcheva, G. 2014. Institutional governance of European neighbourhood policy in the wake of the Arab Spring. *Journal of European Integration* 37, no. 1: 19–36.

Pace, M., and F. Cavatorta. 2012. The Arab uprisings in theoretical perspective – An introduction. *Mediterranean Politics* 17, no. 2: 125–38.

Sjursen, H. 2006. What kind of power? *Journal of European Public Policy* 13, no. 2: 169–81.

Teti, A. 2012. The EU's first response to the 'Arab Spring': a critical discourse analysis of the partnership for democracy and shared prosperity. *Mediterranean Politics* 17, no. 3: 266–84.

Teti, A., D. Thompson, and C. Noble. 2013. EU democracy assistance discourse in its new response to a changing neighbourhood. *Democracy and Security* 9, no. 1–2: 61–79.

The World Bank. 2014. *GDP per capita (current US$)*. http://data.worldbank.org/indicator/NY.GDP.PCAP.CD (accessed 15 August 2014).

Thomas, D.C. 2012. Still punching below its weight? Coherence and effectiveness in European union foreign policy. *Journal of Common Market Studies* 50, no. 3: 457–74.

Waever, O. 1995. Securitization and desecuritization. In *On security*, ed. R.D. Lipschutz, 46–86. New York: Columbia University Press.

Wetzel, A., and J. Orbie. 2011. Promoting embedded democracy? Researching the substance of EU democracy promotion. *European Foreign Affairs Review* 16, no. 5: 565–88.

Whitehead, L. (ed.). 2001. *The international dimensions of democratization: Europe and the Americas*. Oxford: Oxford University Press.

World Governance Indicators. 2013. http://info.worldbank.org/governance/wgi/index.aspx#reports (accessed 5 August 2014).

Youngs, R. 2009. Democracy promotion as external governance? *Journal of European Public Policy* 16, no. 6: 895–915.

Index

Note: Page numbers in *italics* represent tables
Page numbers in **bold** represent figures
Page numbers followed by 'n' refer to notes

Abdullah, King of Jordan 123
Abu-Shagour, M. 54n
action plans 54n
actorness 8, 11–12; EU 15, 19–23, 33, 34;
   EU international 114; national 20
actors 1–12, 52, 96, 124, 135, 142–4,
   151; domestic 11; external 1–8, 12,
   96, 99–101, 114, 126, 135–53; foreign
   68; foreign policy 142; global 114;
   independent 98, 110; international 7,
   37, 40, 77, 139; legitimate 42; non-
   state 130n; normative 68; political 10;
   pragmatic 57–75; rational 57; regional
   37, 77, 95–112, 114, 139; security 128;
   societal 10; strategic 19, 34; traditional
   21; unitary 11, 22; Western 2–3, 99
Afghanistan 58, 69, 81, 101–2
Africa 101
Africa-EU Summit (2010) 111n
aid: economic 73n; financial 45–6, 52;
   humanitarian 45–6, 53; military 73n
Al-Jazeera 85
Al-Nusra Front (Syria) 126
Al-Qaeda 6, 58, 69, 121, 126–7
Al-Qaeda in Iraq (AQI) 121
Algeria 100, 108–10
Ali, B. 38, 41–4, 63, 115, 151
allies: autocratic 67; Western 100, 104
American identity 10
Amidror, Y. 115, 122, 126, 129, 130n
Ankara (Turkey) 124, 144
Annan, K. 86
anti-Western power 138

Arab League 103, 128
Arab Revolt 37–56, 122, 128–9
Arab Spring 15n, 19–36, 37–41, 50–3,
   59–61, 73n, 110n, 145–6
Arab states 78–9
Arab uprisings 95, 98–9, 106–8
Arab world 1–2, 15n, 19–22, 57–60, 119,
   129, 146–8; and Turkish foreign policy
   95–112
Arabian Peninsula 113–14
Arinc, B. 111n
Ashton, C. 28, 48–9
Asia 23, 60, 69, 84, 129
Asia-Pacific 60
al-Assad, B. 2, 69, 84–8, 99–102, 120–1,
   126–7, 136, 151
asylum seekers 41–6
authoritarian nature 80, 92
authoritarian order 93
authoritarian regimes 39, 80, 141, 150
authoritarian rule 4, 22, 109
authoritarian stability 118
authoritarianism 79, 82, 148
autocracy 58, 118, 138, 150
autocratic allies 67
autocratic regimes 96, 142
autonomy 8, 11–12, 22, 33, 139; EU 31;
   operational 33
Ayata, B. 14, 95–112
Azerbaijan 125; Baku 125

Badie, M. 119
Baghdad Spring 59

INDEX

Bahrain 2–6, 38–9, 65–71, 116, 136, 140–1, 148–50, **149–50**; Shiite Muslims 5, 65; Sunni Muslims 5
Baku (Azerbaijan) 125
Balkans 98
Beirut (Lebanon) 121
Belarus 28
Ben-Gurion, D. 124
Benghazi (Libya) 44, 61, 66
Berlin (Germany) 117; fall of Berlin Wall 19
bilateral relations 110
border crossing: EU illegal 46, *46*
Börzel, T.A.: Dandashly, A. and Risse, T. 1–17, 135–53; and Risse, T. 40
Bosnia 82
Bouazizi, M. 1
Brahimi, M. 4, 41
Brussels (Belgium) 21–3, 29, 32–3, 48; bureaucracy 139
Bulgaria 125
bureaucracy 11, 21, 29; Brussels 139
bureaucratic politics 8–13, 52–3, 57, 62, 70–1, 146
Bush, G. 58–60, 63

Cairo (Egypt) 48–9, 58–61, 71, 73n, 80, 119, 126, 144
Camp David Peace Accords 124
Caporaso, J.A.: and Jupille, J. 11–12
Carter, J. 58, 124
Cavatorta, F.: and Pace, M. 39
Chechnya 81
chemical weapons 120, 126, 144–7
Chemical Weapons Convention 6
Chicago (USA) 69
China 6, 84, 93, 103, 110n
Christianity 91, 124
Churkin, V. 83
citizenship 103
civil rights 60, 148
civil society 24, 27, 43–5, 58, 79, 87, 97, 145; organizations 10, 105
Civil Society Neighbourhood Facility 24
Clinton, H. 60–4, 70, 73n
collective identity 8–11, 52, 68, 128, 135–7, 145–6
community: international 31, 62, 84, 137; local 121

conflict: distraction 122–3; management 27, 29–30, *29*; spillage 122–3
constraints: local 68–9; regional 68–9
constructivism 145–6; social 11, 146–8
Copenhagen (Denmark) 10
counter-revolution 77–94
counterterrorism 22, 64–6, 123
coups: military 107, 141, 144–8
credibility 86, 96–7, 138, 151
crime: organized 40
Crimea 78–9, 86–9, 93
Croatia 125
cross-border movements 137
cultural heritage 90
culture: democratic 80; political 90; religious 92
Cyprus 125

Damascus (Syria) 109, 123, 126
Dandashly, A. 13, 37–56, 86; Risse, T. and Börzel, T.A. 1–17, 135–53
Dannreuther, R. 14, 77–94
Davos (Switzerland) 96, 111n
Davutoglu, A. 99–105
de-sovereignization 90
Deauville Partnership 67
debt crisis: European 4
Deep and Comprehensive Free Trade Areas (DCFTAs) 26–7, 31, 42–3, 48
demilitarization 107
democracy 1–15, 20–4, 27, 28–31, *29*, 37–53, 135–52; external 135; liberal 9, 19–21, 51, 145–6, 151; Muslim 14, 151; non-Western 151; parliamentary 130; sovereign 13, 145; stable 12; Western 147
democratic governance 20
democratic legitimacy 24
democratic rights 149
democratization 13–14, 52–3, 62–3, 71, 73n, 117–18, 136–43, 150; pro- 127
Denmark: Copenhagen 10
Dialogue for Migration Mobility and Security (EU and Southern Mediterranean countries) 43
dictatorship: military 136
difference: intra-religious 104
differential implementation 37–56

INDEX

diplomacy 7, 28, 48–9, 52–3, 65–7, 100–3; multilateral 66; Russian 85
diplomatic relations 101, 106, 123
Doha (Qatar) 85
domestic actors 11
domestic factors 95
domestic politics 8–13, 40, 52–3, 57, 62
domestic security 5

economic aid 73n
economic development 26–7, 27, 28, 29, 33
economic growth 43–4, 96, 142, 148–9
economic liberalization 63, 73n
economy: free market 64; liberal 118
Egypt 2–6, 13–14, 47–53, 54n, 59–72, 73n, 78–80, 96–101, 105–10, 113–23, 136–50, **149–50**; Cairo 48–9, 58–61, 71, 73n, 80, 119, 126, 144; el-Sisi 2–5, 47, 106–7, 119–20, 141; *Salafist* (Al-Nur party) 118
Egyptian-American Enterprise Fund 63
Egyptian-Israeli peace treaty (1979) 64, 119, 123
eighteenth century 60
empowerment 103, 108, 151
En-Nahda Party (Tunisian government party) 41, 54n
Erdogan, R.T. 3, 11–13, 96–8, 101–6, 109, 111n, 136–7, 141, 144–7
Et-Takatol (Tunisian government party) 41
Ethiopia 124
Eurasian Union 93
Europe 20–3, 42, 49, 58–60, 80, 91–3, 124–5, 129
European Commission 28–33
European Court of Auditors (ECA) 47–8
European Endowment for Democracy (EED) 24
European External Action Service (EEAS) 10, 23, 29–32, 53
European Instrument for Democracy and Human Rights (EIDHR) 29
European Investment Bank (EIB) 48
European Neighbourhood and Partnership Instrument (ENPI) 28, 46
European Neighbourhood Policy (ENP) 13, 19–36, 38–9, 53, 140; institutional governance of 19–36
European Parliament (EP) 45, 48–9

European Security Strategy (2003) 22, 40
European sovereign debt crisis 4
European Union (EU) 1–15, 27–33, 42–7, 50–3, 54n, 61–3, 77–80, **91**, 95–100, 105–9; actorness 15, 19–23, 33, 34; -Africa Summit (2010) 111n; autonomy 31; Frontex 24–5; illegal border crossing 46, 46; international actorness 114; Lisbon Treaty (2009) 23–5, 28; member states 25–6, 30–4
external actors 1–8, 12, 96, 99–101, 114, 126, 135–53
external democracy 135
extremism 61; Islamist 3, 14, 77–81, 90

Facebook 129
Faraji, H. 125
federalization 82
financial aid 45–6, 52
financial crisis: global (2008) 4
foreign actors 68
foreign aid 42–3, 147
foreign policy 21–5, 99–102; identity-based 107, 110; identity-driven 96; Israel 113–33; multidirectional 98; Turkish 95–112; value-based 106–10
France 32, 65, 100, 143; Paris 101
free market economy 64
Free Syrian Army 104
Freedom House Polity Index 148, **149**
Frontex 24–5
Füle, S. 48
fundamentalism 41

Gaddafi, M. 5–6, 25, 44, 53, 65, 82–3, 101–2, 111n, 151
Gates, R. 65, 71
Gaza 70, 119–21, 124–8, 130n, 141; Palestinian Islamic Jihad (PIJ) 119, 124–8
Geneva (Switzerland) 78
genocide 152
geopolitical environment 116
geopolitical factors 14, 79
geopolitical nationalism 88
geopolitical realities 121
Georgia (USA) 84
geostrategic interests 3–4, 8–11, 50–1, 57, 60, 67–8, 143–8; objective 135–7

157

INDEX

geostrategic thinking 144
Gerges, F. 68
Germany 101, 104; Berlin 19, 117
Gezi protests (Turkey) 108–10
global actors 114
global financial crisis (2008) 4
global Jihad organizations 118
governance: democratic 20; institutional
    19–36
Great Britain 32
Greece 20, 47, 125
gross domestic product (GDP) 26, 150
Gulf 1, 58–60, 65, 71, 85, 96, 147
Gulf Cooperation Council (GCC) 5, 13,
    47–50, 65–6

Halliday, F. 72n
HAMAS 59, 118–28, 130n, 141
Hashemite Kingdom 123
Hauser, Z. 130n
hegemony 59
heritage: cultural 90
Hezbollah 6, 66, 118–26
Huber, D. 14, 57–75
human rights 1–2, 21–4, 38–40, 48–9,
    60–3, 135–8, 141–8, 151
humanitarian aid 45–6, 53
humanitarian interventions 87, 151
humanitarianism 82
Hurricane Katrina (USA) 111n
Hussein, King of Jordan 123
hyper-secularism 91

ideational factors 14, 79, 95, 107–8
identity: American 10; collective 8–11, 52,
    68, 128, 135–7, 145–6; Islamic 80
identity-based foreign policy 107, 110
identity-driven foreign policy 96
ideology 58
illegal border crossing: EU 46, 46
illegal migration 32, 38–41, 44–5, 140, 146
illegal refugees 6
immigration 24
independent actors 98, 110
Indyk, M. 63
instability 2, 22, 41, 117, 122, 144;
    political 7
institutional governance 19–36
institutionalization 40

international actorness 114
international actors 7, 37, 40, 77, 139
international arenas 97
international community 31, 62, 84, 137
International Energy Agency (IEA) 111n
international military intervention 101, 104
International Monetary Fund (IMF) 63, 67,
    72, 105
international politics 114
international relations 8–9, 62, 143
interventions: humanitarian 151;
    international military 101, 104; military
    136–7, 144–7, 151–2
Intifada (2001–4) 128
intra-religious differences 104
Iran 5–6, 13, 28, 31, 69–71, 96–7, 102–5,
    118–28; Tehran 117
Iran-Syria-Hezbollah-HAMAS axis 118–20
Iranian Mullocracy 124
Iraq 2, 58–60, 66, 69–71, 102, 105, 109,
    121–5; Mosul 104
irregular migration 52
Islam 13–14, 59, 72n, 80–1, 90
Islamic identity 80
Islamic Justice and Development Party
    (AKP) (Turkey) 3, 13, 73n, 95–102,
    105–10, 119, 124, 136–7, 146
Islamic Revolution (1979) 124
Islamic State of Iraq and Greater Syria
    (ISIS) 69, 81, 92, 104, 109, 136
Islamism 11, 136–7, 146; militant 61;
    radical 137; radical Salafi 120
Islamist extremism 3, 14, 77–81, 90
Islamization 80–1, 142
IsraAID 127
Israel 1–6, 15n, 61–4, 69–71, 95–9, 105–6,
    111n, 136–41, 147–8, see also Gaza
Israel Air Force (IAF) 125–6
Israel Defence Forces (IDF) 117
Israel-Lebanon war (2006) 70
Israeli-Egyptian peace treaty (1979) 64,
    119, 123
Istanbul (Turkey) 108
Italy 20, 47, 50
Ivanov, S. 88
Izmir (Turkey) 101

Jebali, H. 4
Jerusalem (Israel) 119, 123, 130n

INDEX

Jihad organizations: global 118
Jihadist networks 125, 148
Jordan 25, 38, 42, 70, 85, 113–16, 120–3,
    127–8, 141
Jupille, J.: and Caporaso, J.A. 11–12

Al-Kader Tallah, A. 126–7
El-Keib, A. 54n
Kerry, J. 64, 71
Khodorkovksii, M. 87
Kissinger, H. 142
Kosovo 28, 82
Kurdish people 124, 147
Kurds: Syrian 103
Kuwait 47

Lavrov, S. 84, 88
Lebanon 59, 105, 113–22, 126–8, 141;
    Beirut 121
Lebanon War (2006) 124, 128
left-wing Democrats (USA) 147
legacy: military 108
legal migration 32
legitimacy 20, 110, 151; democratic 24
legitimate actors 42
Levant 113–14
liberal democracy 9, 19–21, 51, 82, 90–2,
    145–6, 151; Western 77
liberal economy 118
liberalism 11
liberalization 27, 30, 42, 117; economic
    63, 73n; political 117, 127; trade 29,
    32–3, 42
liberation 60
Libya 2–6, 44–50, 54n, 65–72, 72n,
    95–106, 111n, 115–20, 136–8, 141–7,
    149–50, 151–2; Benghazi 44, 61, 66;
    National Transitional Council (NTC)
    101–2
Lisbon Treaty (EU, 2009) 23–5, 28
local communities 121
local constraints 68–9
Lukashenko, A. 28

McCain, J. 62
Macedonia 125
Magen, A. 14–15, 78, 113–33
Al-Maliki, N. 121
Malmström, C. 44

Malta 20
media: social 117; Western 116
Mediterranean 20, 24, 37–9, 42–6, 46, 50,
    124–7
Medvedev, D. 80–3, 89, 147
Menendez, R. 62
middle class 41
Middle East 8–12, 57–65, 77–81, 88–93,
    97–9, 106–9, 110n, 144–6
Middle East and North Africa (MENA)
    1–12, 15n, 37–41, 50, 51, 68–9, 107,
    117–21; Incentive Fund 70
migration 7, 21–5, 27, 29–30, 33–4, 40–7,
    50, 140; illegal 32, 38–41, 44–5, 52,
    140, 146; irregular 52; legal 32
militant Islamism 61
military aid 73n
military coups 107, 141, 144–8
military dictatorship 136
military intervention 101, 136–7, 144–7,
    151–2; international 101, 104
military legacy 108
military power 109
Milton-Edwards, B. 71
mobility 21, 24–5, 27, 29, 34, 43–4, 46–7,
    140; physical 49; social 49
mobilization 120–1
modernization 88
Montenegro 125
Morocco 25, 38, 42, 108, 116
Morsi, M. 47–8, 54n, 62–4, 71–2, 97–100,
    105–6, 119, 127, 146
Morsihas, M. 48
Moscow (Russia) 78–82, 85–7, 91, 104,
    144–5
Mosul (Iraq) 104
Mubarak, M.H. 5, 47, 63, 105, 115, 118,
    124–6, 138, 141, 151
Mullocracy: Iranian 124
multidirectional foreign policy 98
multilateral diplomacy 66
Muslim Brotherhood 2–5, 47–52, 64–7,
    104–6, 111n, 118–21, 137, 144
Muslim democracy 14, 151
Muslims 85, 91–2, 97–8, 104; Tartar 90

Nasser, G.A. 64
national actorness 20
National Forces Alliance 54n

INDEX

national security 107, 114–16; Israel 115
national unity 107
nationalism: geopolitical 88
NATO (North Atlantic Treaty
 Organization) 44, 82–4, 93, 97–104,
 138, 141, 144
Netanyahu, B. 116–18, 130, 130n
Netherlands 104
Nisaa Tounes (Tunisia) 54n
Noble, C.: and Teti, A. and Thompson, D. 39
non-governmental organizations (NGOs)
 43, 127–9; Western-oriented 82
non-idealism 129
non-state actors 130n
non-Western democracy 151
normative actors 68
normative power 136–9, 142
North Africa 1, 20–3, 32, 37–41, 50–3,
 58–60, 77, 113–14
North Caucasus 81–4, 93
Noutcheva, G. 13, 19–36, 53, 86
Al-Nusra, J. 92

Obama, B. 57–63, 66–71, 72–3n, 87, 137,
 147; Administration (USA) 126, 140
objective geostrategic interests 135–7
Oman 116
ontology 9
operational autonomy 33
Oren, M. 130n
Organization for the Prohibition of
 Chemical Weapons 120
organized crime 40
orthodox secularism 99
Ottoman Empire 69

Pace, M.: and Cavatorta, F. 39
Palestine 59, 101, 111n
Palestinian Islamic Jihad (PIJ) 119, 124, 128
Papandreou, G. 125
Paris (France) 101
parliamentarianism 128
parliamentary democracy 130
Partnership for Democracy and Shared
 Prosperity 20
Patterson, A. 70
Pentagon (USA) 71, 147
Peres, S. 96, 118
Perthes, V. 49

physical mobility 49
physical security and stockpile management
 (PSSM) 45
Pinxten, K. 47
PKK (*Partiye Karkeren Kurdistan*) (Syria)
 103, 107–8
pluralism 21
Poland 43
polarization: societal 97
political actors 10
political culture 90
political instability 7
political liberalization 117, 127
political stability 96, 107
political tutelage 108
politics: bureaucratic 8–13, 52–3, 57, 62,
 70–1, 146; domestic 8–13, 40, 52–3, 57,
 62; international 114
power: military 109; normative 136–9,
 142; transformative 139; vacuum 120;
 Western 2–6, 138
pragmatic actors 57–75
pro-democratization 127
protectionism 73n
Pussy Riot protestors (Russia) 87
Putin, V. 11–14, 78–89, 92, 118, 137, 142–7

Al-Qaradawi, Y. 85
Qatar 85, 105–6; Doha 85

radical Islamism 137; Salafi 120
radicalism 41
rational actors 57
Reagan, R. 58, 124
realism 3, 11, 68, 114, 137–8, 143–8
realist thinking 143–4, 147
Realpolitik thinking 143, 147
refugees: illegal 6
regional actors 37, 77, 95–112, 114, 139
regional constraints 68–9
regional stability 60
religious cultures 92
responsibility to protect (R2P) 151
Rice, C. 58–9
Rice, S. 71
right-wing Republicans (USA) 147
rights: civil 60, 148; democratic 149;
 human 1–2, 21–4, 38–40, 48–9, 60–3,
 135–8, 141–8, 151

INDEX

Risse, T.: and Börzel, T.A. 40; Börzel, T.A. and Dandashly, A. 1–17, 135–53
Romania 125
Romney, M. 61
Russia 1–6, 11–14, 95–7, 100–6, 110n, 125–6, 137–51; Moscow 104, 144–5; Putin 11–14, 118, 137, 142–7; Soviet Union (USSR) 72, 82, 88, 93
Russian Orthodox Church 90

Salafist (Al-Nur party) (Egypt) 118
Samaras, A. 46
Saudi Arabia 13, 47, 65–71, 96–7, 105–6, 111n, 120, 140–1, 148
secularism 99; orthodox 99
securitization 10
security: actors 128; domestic 5; national 107, 114–16; physical 45
September 11 attacks (USA, 2001) 58, 72n
Serbia 125
Shaked, E. 127
Sharansky, N. 118
Shehata, D. 58
Shiite Muslims: Bahrain 5, 65
El-Shimy, Y. 49
Sinai Peninsula 71, 119–22, 125–8
el-Sisi, A.F. 2–5, 47, 106–7, 119–20, 141
Sochi Winter Olympics (Russia, 2014) 87
social constructivism 11, 146–8
social media 117
social mobility 49
societal actors 10
societal polarization 97
society: civil 10, 24, 27, 43–5, 58, 79, 87, 97, 105, 145
sovereign debt crisis: European 4
sovereign democracy 13, 90, 145
sovereign states 11–12, 83
sovereignty 12, 90; Israeli 122
Soviet Union (USSR) 72, 82, 88, 93
Spain 20
SPRING programme (Support for Partnership Reform and Inclusive Growth) 27, 43
Springborg, R. 64
stability 1–5, 14–15, 40–1, 78, 81, 135–40, 143; authoritarian 118; political 96, 107; regional 60

stable democracy 12
Stalin, J. 86
START Treaty (Strategic Arms Reduction) (1991–4) 82
Stevens, J.C. 44
strategic actors 19, 34
Sudan 119, 125
suicide bomb attacks 121
Sunni Muslims: Bahrain 5
Sunni-Shia power battle (Turkey) 108, 120
supremacy 138
Supreme Council of the Armed Forces (SCAF) 63
Surkov, V. 89–90
sustainability 124
Switzerland: Davos 96, 111n; Geneva 78
Syria 2–6, 66–70, 95–110, 113–18, 121–8, 136–51, **149**; al-Assad 2, 69, 99–102, 120–1, 126–7, 136, 151–2; Al-Nusra Front 126; Damascus 109, 123, 126; PKK 103, 107–8
Syrian Kurds 103
Syrian National Council 103

Tajikistan 81
Tartus (Syria) 84, 88
Tatar Muslims 90
Tehran (Iran) 117
terror attacks 119; September 11 (USA, 2001) 58, 72n
terrorism 38–41, 58, 61–2, 140; transnational 9, 50
terrorist organizations 122
TESEV (Turkish Think Tank) 110n
Teti, A.: Thompson, D. and Noble, C. 39
thinking: geostrategic 144; realist 143–4, 147; *Realpolitik* 143, 147
Thompson, D.: Noble, C. and Teti, A. 39
tourism 125
trade liberalization 29, 32–3, 42
traditional actors 21
transformative power 139
transnational terrorism 9, 50
Truman, H.S. 70
Tunisia 2–6, 41–4, 60–3, 78–80, 97–100, 108–10, 115–20, 135–7, 149–51, **149–50**; *En-Nahda Party* 41, 54n; *Et-Takatol* 41; *Nidaa Tounes* 54n; *Union Générale Tunisienne du Travail*

INDEX

(UGTT) 41; *Union Tunisienne de l'Industrie de Commerce et de l'Artisant* (UTICA) 41

Turkey 1–3, 9–14, 88–9, 95–112, 117–19, 122–9, 135–9, 142–7; Ankara 124, 144; Erdogan 3; foreign policy and Arab world 95–112; Gezi protests 108–10; Islamic Justice and Development Party (AKP) 3, 13, 73n, 95–102, 105–10, 119, 124, 136–7, 146; Istanbul 108; Izmir 101; Kurdish movement 102; Sunni-Shia power battle 108, 120; TESEV (Think Tank) 110n

Turkish-Syrian relations 103

twenty-first century 124

Ukraine 25, 77–9, 87, 93

Union Générale Tunisienne du Travail (UGTT) (Tunisia) 41

Union Tunisienne de l'Industrie de Commerce et de l'Artisant (UTICA) (Tunisia) 41

unitary actors 11, 22

United Arab Emirates (UAE) 47, 65, 96

United Kingdom (UK) 65, 82, 96, 143

United Nations (UN) 62, 66, 83–6, 97, 103, 147; Security Council (SC) 5–6, 72, 84–6, 101, 136, 144

United States of America (USA) 1–4, 7–14, 77–82, 95–100, 104–9, 121–9, 135–48; Georgia 84; Hurricane Katrina 111n; left-wing Democrats 147; Obama 87, 137, 147; Obama Administration 126, 140; Pentagon 71, 147; right-wing

Republicans 147; -Russian relations 78; September 11 attacks (2001) 58, 72n; START Treaty (1991–4) 82

universality 24

USSR (Union of Soviet Socialist Republics) 72, 88, 93; START Treaty (Strategic Arms Reduction, 1991–4) 82

value-based foreign policy 106–10, 141, 147

Visa Liberation Action Plans 25, 30

visa-free zones 98

Washington (USA) 63–5, 68–72

West 77–89, 93, 118, 124

West Bank 121–3

Western actors 2–3, 99

Western allies 100, 104

Western democracy 58, 80, 147

Western intervention 82–7

Western liberal democracy 77

Western media 116

Western powers 2–6, 138

Western-oriented NGOs 82

Westphalian state system 69

White House (USA) 70–1

World Trade Organization (WTO) 82

Ya'alon, M. 122

Yakhont P-800 126

Yeltsin, B. 82

Yemen 97, 100, 108–10, 115–16, 121

Zidan, A. 54n